Child of Mine

Marianne Edwins

Onwards and Upwards Publishers

3 Radfords Turf
Cranbrook
Exeter,
EX5 7DX
United Kingdom

www.onwardsandupwards.org

This first edition published in the United Kingdom by Onwards and Upwards Publishers (2017).

ISBN: 978-1-911086-57-4
Typeface: Sabon LT
Graphic design: LM Graphic Design

Printed in the United Kingdom.

About the Author

Marianne Edwins started out in life as an ordinary young girl, born into a typical lower middle class family, but during her teens she entered over a decade of living a turbulent lifestyle. Following a chain of unwise decisions and the ensuing trauma, which would impact her for the rest of her life, she became a volunteer for the Probation Department, which led to her being offered the position of Manager for a pilot project in North Devon working with 'Heavy End' offenders.

Some years later she established a charity offering frontline street access to those who were homeless, addicts, or suffering from mental health problems, in rural Wiltshire. From there her life journey took her to The West Bank, Palestine, then even farther afield to manage the Oasis coffee shop on the military base in The Falkland Islands. Returning to the UK she graduated from Bible College before becoming a pastor in a Methodist church in Essex and an Anglican church in West Sussex.

Marianne now lives on the Dorset coast with one of her sons, a daughter-in-law and four grandchildren. This three-generational household is no less manic and busy, just different, and although health conditions cause her limitations, she adores engaging with people she encounters, family gatherings and one-on-one deep and meaningful conversations.

To contact the author, please send an email to:

MarianneEdwins@gmail.com

Endorsements

Some of us may have to live a lifetime with the consequences of the mistakes we have made, temptations given into, the wrongs we have done to others, but Marianne's frank and honest account of her life gives us all hope for our release from the inhibiting sense of guilt.

Sitting on a rock overlooking the sea and the rolling waves, she had a spiritual wake-up call and began to find the answer to the question we all ask: "What is the meaning and purpose of my life?" For Marianne it was to show compassion in practical ways to those on the margin of society who have no voice to be heard.

It was through her vision and drive that 'Action on Homelessness' opened a drop-in centre in Trowbridge; and through her prayers and persuasion I was drawn into her plans to make it "the best in the west!" How rewarding it was to see hopelessness turned to hope and to have shared with Marianne in bringing the vision to reality. But that was only the beginning of her ministry of care and compassion, which would take her to other cultures and far-flung places.

Richard Clarke
Chair (1990-2006), Action on Homelessness Trowbridge

This is a story of love; of pain, heartbreak, struggles and hardship; of fun and excitement; of a life turned around in most unusual circumstances against all the odds.

A most compelling read, this truly remarkable story of an amazing life shows that we never know, when we meet people, what struggles they have come through; how our life experiences shape us for the next phase of our lives, if we are willing to learn from them.

Gina Watson MBE
Rustington, West Sussex

Child of Mine is a moving and inspirational read. The author's transition from vulnerability to strength is a reminder of the resilience of the human spirit and the capacity within all of us to rise above the challenging situations we may find ourselves in. The poignant descriptions of the loss of two babies through different circumstances stands out and offers an insight to professionals working with such situations as well as giving voice to the many mothers who bear their pain silently. This book is difficult to put down and offers a tough and honest account of loss and pain but ultimately restoration. I thoroughly recommend this book.

Judith Russ
Head of Service Children's Social Care

Acknowledgement

This book is written in thanks to my parents; for all I learnt with them and through them. They journeyed with me for over fifty years and helped me to become the person I am today.

Marianne Edwins

Dedicated to all my family.

My life is richly blessed by
my sons, daughters-in-law and grandchildren.

Contents

FOREWORD 11
AUTHOR'S NOTE.... 12
INTRODUCTION. My Child.... 13

1. Childhood Simplicity 19
2. The Unforgivable Sin? 37
3. Desperate for Acceptance and Love 43
4. Bright Lights, Big City 54
5. Time to Move On 60
6. Married Life 65
7. Love at Last 71
8. It's You I Want, Not Money 83
9. Carl 88
10. Does Life Go On? 93
11. No Peace of Mind 105
12. A Fresh Start 117
13. A Challenging Time 126
14. Confronted 135
15. Commitment 144
16. Action on Homelessness 150
17. Blessings 169
18. A New Season 177
19. Obedience 189
20. Grow in Me, My Child 199
21. Go into All the World 216
22. Study and Serve 224
23. Family 228
24. Manna and Quail 237
25. Restoration 242
26. Reconciled 253

Download Free Supplementary Material 254

In memory of

my unnamed baby,
who never took a breath;

my son Aidan,
whom I knew for just a few days;

and Carl,
taken so quickly from this world.

Foreword

Child of Mine is, quite simply, the amazing story of one woman's life experiences. It is compelling reading – a book you cannot put down.

Marianne and I met one Sunday morning, about thirty years ago, and quickly became very good friends. We were both single mums and we both liked to chat! Since then it has been my privilege to walk some of her journey alongside her. It was not long before I was encouraging her to write her story because I was certain it could be such a help and encouragement to many.

There are many elements contained within these pages:

rebellion, desperation, heartache, grief and loneliness
...and yet...
joy, peace, reconciliation and love.

Marianne's journey has not been easy, but throughout the years her grit, determination, sense of humour and, above all, faith have driven her on. In this book she sets out, very honestly, the decisions she made, the actions she took, and the consequences for herself and her children. Nothing is held back and at times it is a painful read. *But,* as you, the reader, share Marianne's sorrow and the pain, you will also share the ultimate joy and knowledge of forgiveness.

Even though I already knew most of the story, I found it a captivating read and I cannot recommend it highly enough. Be prepared to be saddened, maybe shocked, surprised – and then challenged...

Jean
Cirencester, Gloucestershire

Author's Note

This is a true story and has been told as accurately as I recall it. Only certain names have been changed, in order to protect the identities of those persons. However, as with all autobiographies, there may be some details that others will remember differently.

INTRODUCTION

My Child

Gradually I stirred. I was in that weightless floating state between sleeping and waking. I sensed that my husband Gary was awake and as he got out of bed he said, "I'll go down to the kitchen and warm a bottle of milk for Carl's breakfast and then bring him in here so that you can feed him." I drifted off again, enjoying the tranquillity. Adrian, my three-year-old son from my first marriage, and Carl, just three months old, born since my marriage to Gary, were still quiet in the bedroom across the landing.

My marriage to Adrian's father had been traumatic, with experiences of life that I could never have contemplated. Gary was different. From the day I met him he was caring and loving towards me. We had overcome immense problems but he adored Adrian, and now we had been blessed with our son Carl, a placid baby who slept well at night.

It was March 1st, 1977 at 8.00am. I was still dozing peacefully when Gary knelt beside the bed and said, "HE'S DEAD!"

I opened one eye and said, "Don't be so stupid!" But having been jolted out of my state of slumber I looked up at Gary and saw that his ashen face was serious. I ran to our son's bedroom and on seeing Carl in his cot screamed, "How did he get on his back?" In those days the maternity hospitals always taught us to sleep babies on their tummies or side.

"He was on his side," said Gary. "I picked him up to bring him in to you. I've just laid him down on his back."

I ran down the stairs to the phone. The sight of my baby's rigid body, his face deep blue on one side and pure white on the other, was piercing my mind.

Gary, realising I was phoning the ambulance, called down, "What are you doing that for? There's no point. He's dead!"

In a state of numbness, out of step with reality, I said to the operator, "My baby's dead!"

Calmly she replied, "Give me your phone number and address." Then after I gave her the details, she assured me, "An ambulance is on its way to you."

Gary was now at my shoulder. "What are you doing?"

"I've phoned for the ambulance,' I replied.

"There's no point," he repeated. "HE'S DEAD!"

I just slumped on the stairs. "But I don't know what else to do!"

The rest of the day was to be like watching a morbid theatre production unfold before my eyes. So much activity, so many dazed faces, yet I felt removed from the depth and enormity of this horrific event.

Still in my nightclothes, I stepped over the fence to knock on the front door of my neighbour's house. The people living in our close in Exeter were mainly in their twenties, around the same age as Gary and me. Like us, many of them had young families and had woken to the start of the day like any other. There was the usual general chaos over breakfast as husbands got ready for work and mothers prepared the children for school. Invariably, panic and mayhem, looking for a missing shoe or P.E bag, was the norm in most homes.

Pauline, my neighbour for six months, came to the door smiling.

"It's Carl... He's dead..." were the words I heard coming from my mouth and I then simply turned and stepped back over the fence.

Pauline's face drained as she asked, "What can I do?"

It was only at that moment that I thought of Adrian as I saw him walking down the stairs. "Please take Adrian," I said, as I scooped him up and handed him over the fence into her arms. Although I was already heavily anaesthetised by shock I knew that at this moment I could not cope with Adrian's questions and needs, and that with the ambulance on the way it would be better for this little three-year-old boy to be next door playing with Mark, Pauline's four-year-old son.

No sooner had Adrian happily gone to play with Mark than I could hear the siren of the ambulance trying to carve a way through the rush hour traffic; it was the new American-sounding siren that was piercing the airwaves, shrieking louder and louder, and my heart and head seemed to pound with greater and greater intensity. Gary ran past me, out to the end of the street, to signal to the ambulance crew and direct them to our home; they screamed to a halt outside the house and two men ran into the house, vaulting the stairs three at a time with Gary close on their heels. I followed, but could only manage to get halfway up the stairs, and then I froze... I physically could not go up to the bedroom, yet neither could I move myself back downstairs. As I stood motionless I heard one of the ambulance men announce to Gary, "I'm so sorry, there's nothing we can do."

Three months and three days previously I had given birth to a healthy son. Apart from one visit to the doctor because of a slight cold, he'd needed no medical attention; he'd fed well, slept well and been a happy, contented baby.

I heard Gary being asked if there was someone who could sit with me, as he would be needed to see the coroner and complete various papers. Janet, my other neighbour, came in, and she and Gary coaxed me into the lounge.

It was then, whilst I was in the lounge, that my baby son Carl was carried from our home. Never again would I cradle him in my arms, stroke his fine fair hair. Never again would I see his large blue eyes looking up into mine. Never again would I smell his skin after his bath. Never again would I feel his soft skin close to my face or see his smile. I didn't see them take him from our home. I didn't say goodbye.

Gary had been told whom he should go and see and what he had to do in order to register Carl's death. I worried about him driving whilst still in shock, having gone through the experience of holding Carl's small stiff body in his arms as he'd picked him up and turned him over, yet I knew that he had to be busy and feel that he was doing something.

Janet made tea. As she sat with me, not knowing what to say, I was aware that a crowd of people had gathered outside our home. Having heard the siren and seen the ambulance arrive, curiosity had brought them out on to the street, thinking that perhaps Adrian had had an accident. A stunned silence fell over the neighbourhood as news spread that we'd found Carl dead in his cot. It just didn't seem possible. Little was known about cot death and there had never been any media coverage or information given to parents.

I needed to keep talking, although I was aware I was quite incoherent. I picked up the phone and dialled the number for my mother in Plymouth. No answer; she wasn't at home. I phoned my father. I'd never phoned him at work before and as I was put through to his extension I simply said, "It's Carl; he's gone!" No hello or how we'd come to find him dead, just those four words.

I wasn't able to consider what the situation was for him in his office or how this very blunt, cold, out-of-the-blue information would affect him. He was in fact listening to me on an open intercom telephone. One of his directors was in the office and heard the news along with my father. Dad immediately said in his firm, unwavering voice, "Now, Marianne, you'll have to be strong." He then added, "Your mum is at the hairdressers. I'll phone her there." Although it was just 9.00am he would not be able to come up with her until the afternoon. My father's director had already indicated to him that he could not be released from a work engagement that morning. Still numb with shock, I accepted that it would be many hours before I would see them.

Looking back, it still saddens me that my father had to immediately continue his work and give a presentation to his sales team when he had just heard that his grandson was dead, but work was paramount. Dad phoned my mother at the hairdressers. She answered the phone with a towel around her shoulders and her hair dripping wet. She walked home on her own – dazed, shocked, her hair still dripping wet. At home in their bungalow, she sat and waited. She had no means of getting to me other than to wait for my father to pick her up and drive up to Exeter.

Janet was marvellous. She kept making tea and sat with me as I phoned everyone I knew and told them that Carl was dead and just as abruptly hung up the phone. Gary arrived home an hour or so later, shortly followed by our doctor. I'd been his patient for many years and he'd been very supportive and understanding, especially when I'd been suffering from severe depression whilst married to Phil, my first husband.

As the doctor sat holding my hand I looked up into his face. He cried with me. I could see the pain and questions in his eyes. Was there anything that he should have detected when Carl had had a cold and I'd taken him to the doctor for examination? He injected me with a sedative and said he'd call again the next day.

I drifted under the sedation, but this was not the comforting twilight zone I'd been experiencing just a few hours earlier. I was now in turmoil and distress, whimpering with emotional agony and groaning with anguish. How? Why? What had I done? What hadn't I done? Was I being punished? Was this because of what Gary had said? Was this because of my past? There had to be a reason! My child was dead!

Gary's parents arrived from their home on the other side of Exeter. His mum kept saying, "Nothing like this has happened in our family before," and I felt she was implying that it was therefore all my fault. Still moaning under the effects of the sedation, yet vaguely aware of what was going on around me, I heard her say, "Gary, can't you get her to be quiet?" The tensions and shock were affecting us all in different ways.

Mum and Dad arrived. What could they say? Nothing! No words were adequate; no utterance would suffice. Yet there was a strange comfort in them being there. We sat, still numbed, unbelieving; it was a ghastly nightmare, yet a living reality. Prior plans had to be changed, postponed or cancelled.

Gary phoned the company he worked for as a sales representative. He'd not been with them very long and they had already been very understanding, giving him his job back after he'd served a prison sentence. His area manager was full of compassion and said, "I'm placing you on immediate leave from work; take as much time as you need."

We also had an appointment with the minister from the church where Gary and I had married. At three o'clock he arrived. My father met him at the door and explained that we would not now be discussing the arrangements for Carl's christening but for his cremation. The minister, shocked and full of sympathy, sensitively led us through the arrangements.

I sat, dazed under the sedative. Was it all my fault? Was God punishing me? Already I had lived what might be called a 'colourful' lifestyle. This was my second marriage. I'd had four pregnancies and I was just twenty-four years of age. I had experienced and caused others so many problems and much physical, emotional and mental pain and anguish. Many would say I still had all my life ahead of me, but a son I cherished was now a statistic of cot death. I'd never even heard of Sudden Infant Death Syndrome. Very little research had taken place into S.I.D.S. at that time (the 1970s) and we were simply told that the findings of the autopsy were "unexplained infant death".

"What is life all about?" I asked myself. This vital question hit me as I still had vivid pictures in my mind of Carl lying blue, stiff and dead in his cot. There is nothing like unexpected and unexplained death to challenge a person to consider the reason and purpose of life.

Chapter One

Childhood Simplicity

I made my entrance into this world on a very foggy night in January.

It took my father several hours, following one cat's eye after another, to travel home from his work in Bath to Timsbury, a village in Somerset, where he, my mother and my older brother, were staying with his parents. Frequently throughout my childhood Dad recounted the story: "The fog was so thick you couldn't see your hand in front of your face."

After a very difficult drive home he was met at the cottage door by his mother only to be told, "Tonight's the night. Nita's in labour."

"Oh no, not tonight!" he exclaimed. It was a long slow journey back into the city to the hospital with Dad repeatedly saying, albeit in vain, "Not yet! Get back! Get back! Hold on! Don't come yet!" He was thankful that I waited until we got to the hospital to be born on January 14th, 1953.

My parents Nita and Claude had met and married in Bath at Walcot Street Methodist Church. Bath was Dad's home city and for much of his childhood he was known as 'the Bath boy soprano'. He regularly sang in the Abbey, The Pump Room and other venues in the city.

Mum was billeted to Bath with the Admiralty at the start of the war. They courted throughout the war but much of it was a long distance relationship. Mum wrote regularly and Dad replied whenever he could. He was in the R.A.F. and, due to the nature of his work in radio and radar, was posted to various places, including North Africa and the Middle East. Letters, for many years, were the only way for their relationship to deepen. My mum kept every letter he sent, in date order, in a box. Throughout their lives that box was kept under their bed. They married on November 9th, 1946.

Dad, a confident, extroverted young boy who had singing lessons, was the only surviving child of William and Gladys Hasell, who lived for much of his early years in Timsbury, Somerset. Both of Dad's parents sang. His father was a tenor and his mother an alto. Together they were members of the church choir, along with others of the extended family. His maternal grandfather had, with others, taken the Methodist church in the village out of the circuit and formed an independent Wesleyan chapel. As a local preacher he would walk miles each Sunday travelling on foot from one village to another to preach the Word of God. Dad's other grandfather was a chronic and violent alcoholic.

Dad's father, my grandpa, had worked as a young lad in the Somerset mines. He was small in stature and he could be used to work the very small seams to extract the coal. All his working days he ate and inhaled coal dust, grovelling on his stomach whilst chipping away at the coal face like a mole. His reprieve was the time spent playing cricket for the local villages and his county, and singing in church. Dad's mother was a physically and mentally strong woman. She'd been placed in service as a young girl and knew what it was to work from dawn till late into the evening. During the final fifteen years of her life her body was eaten away by cancer but she battled against all the odds and well outlived the "few months" the doctor had predicted in his prognosis.

When Dad's voice broke he was gifted with a tenor tone that took him into singing in concerts and churches, broadcasting on radio, entertaining the troops during the war years, organising shows and meeting with celebrities and dignitaries. At the end of the war he was offered a position with the D'Oyly Carte Opera Company.

My mother had a much quieter disposition. A genteel lady, meticulous and precise, the eldest of three girls, she wanted to be a homemaker, housewife and mother with a schoolmarm manner. She'd been brought up in south-east London. Her father was a Regimental Sergeant Major during the First World War. Gassed twice in the trenches, he received numerous medals including the Military Medal and Bar, now known as the George Medal. He was proud of his three daughters and when Dad started courting Mum, Dad was welcomed warmly into the family.

Following WW1, Mum's father worked as a messenger for a London bank and throughout the blitz of the Second World War he would travel up to the city to check on the security of the bank. His war record meant that he would live the later part of his life at the Royal Hospital Chelsea as one of the famous revered and respected Chelsea Pensioners who wear their red coats with pride around the streets of Chelsea, London.

Mum and Dad discussed their forthcoming marriage. They realised that my father taking up the position with D'Oyly Carte would not be conducive to family life, as he would be travelling all over England and would be abroad for fifty weeks of the year. Decisions were made, my father went into business and I arrived four years after my brother Mark. And so it was that I was born into a stoic, high moral, striving-to-better-themselves, religious family with a strong Protestant work ethic.

My childhood seemed to me to be normal, disciplined, quiet, methodical and controlled. As I became older Dad was away most of the week and I saw little of him. At that time, he was working for a television and radio company establishing shops throughout England. From the age of three I lived in Downend, Bristol and it was to this place that Dad returned each weekend. Mum had the onerous task of getting all the washing and ironing done in thirty-six hours before he took off for another week's work. She had a washing machine with a mangle and there was always damp laundry hanging over the wooden clotheshorse. Mum was the homemaker, always waiting for me when I came in from school; the kettle would be on and tea quickly made. After we'd sat and watched 'Crossroads', a popular television programme, we'd enjoy a proper gravy dinner: stews, cottage pie made from the leftover Sunday meat, liver and other delights served with vegetables, always followed by pudding and custard.

Mark and I played and squabbled like most brothers and sisters. Imagination was our greatest toy. A favourite game was 'ships'. We'd place a plank of wood on the seats between two chairs. I sat underneath the wood in the lower decks and Mark would always sit on the wood, the top deck, as he was the Captain. My imagination ran riot as I travelled the oceans, but I always had to go where the Captain told me.

I was never allowed to choose or take control. Mark, being older and bigger, was always quicker and better at things than me. I looked up to him. He was clever and was never thought to be in the wrong. Even when he did something naughty he never got caught. I was not that clever and always seemed to get caught!

I was more outspoken and had a strong will but our home was disciplined, there was an expected code of conduct. As I walked from the kitchen, often the backs of my legs would be stinging as Mum had slapped me because of my attitude or due to answering back. I don't remember much laughter, but we were expected to be well behaved at all times, tidy and conscientious.

Blackberry-picking was a popular and necessary pastime. I fondly remember lengthy, late summer walks with Mum, carrying a large plastic container full of berries. We walked for miles searching the hedgerows. Summer days always seemed to be long, warm and hazy. When we arrived home Mum would make pies or bottle the fruit. She was very thrifty, salting runner beans and making jam as well as many of my clothes. Mum was always busy – preparing meals, cleaning, mending, gardening – and she always walked me to and from my infant school.

We lived on a new housing estate and as yet the local school hadn't been built. It was a mile's walk to the village of Downend where I attended the old Church of England school. The classrooms there were cold and draughty, with high ceilings, and I felt very small within its vastness. The outside toilets were damp and miserable. In the winter the pipes were frozen and the constantly used toilets wouldn't flush. They were grossly disgusting; I didn't like using them and would try to 'hang on' all day. A constant smell of cooked cabbage from the kitchens providing school lunches wafted around the school. The bottle of milk provided for every child would be outside the school building in crates. At morning break we would be dismissed from class to collect our straw and get our milk; in the winter the milk bottle lid would be raised an inch or more above the bottle due to the milk having frozen.

Walking home I'd carry my satchel and Mum would have both arms full, having done the daily shopping. Each day she bought fresh bread, vegetables and produce. Money was not plentiful but our needs were always met. She'd go from one shop to another to try and find the best bargains, often walking more than a mile to save a few pennies.

Although basic, for me it was the era of innocence and childhood simplicities. I was occasionally given pocket money of an old three-penny piece which would buy four 'Black Jacks' or 'Fruit Salads'[1] for one old penny. Saturdays were spent playing on my tricycle or with my favourite Christmas present: a Hoopla ring. I was so excited when on Christmas morning I looked through my open bedroom door and saw a really peculiar-shaped parcel out on the landing. My hula-hoop was my pride and joy as I twirled it around my body for hours. I was always full of energy.

From the early hours of Christmas morning I would hold my bedclothes around me tightly trying to retain my bubbling excitement until I thought it was an 'OK time' to wake Mum and Dad and open my stocking. As I walked past Mark's bedroom I'd look in and say, "You coming to open your pressies?" but he'd answer, "There's no rush; I'll open them later." How could he wait? How could he contain his excitement? We were very different.

Out of the two weeks' annual holiday that most working people had at that time, we would have one week away and one week was for Dad to do any painting and decorating or gardening jobs at the house. One year we went to the Isle of Wight. Going over the water on a ferry was just like going abroad. The weather was not too good but, typically British, we made the best of it.

On the last day Dad asked, "What would you like to do before we catch the ferry?"

"Go on the paddle boat again," I replied without a second thought.

"OK, Mark," Dad said, "walk your sister down to the boats whilst your mother and I sit in the car and read the papers."

I had already been on the boats several times but was now skipping along very happily at yet another go on the boating lake. Mark handed over the money Dad had given him to the attendant and off I paddled. Round and round the lake I went! Then my number was called, my time was up, and I paddled my way back to the side.

The man in charge caught hold of the rope attached to my boat and I stepped out. The next thing I knew I was in the lake! He'd let go of the rope just as I was about to put my foot on the side. I tried to swim but my wellingtons filled up with water and my heavy gabardine mac

---

[1] varieties of sweet

dragged me down. I thrashed about trying to catch hold of the man's hand that was reaching out to me. Eventually I realised that the lake wasn't deep and put my feet on the bottom. The man caught hold of me and lifted me out. Mark was still strolling around from the other side of the lake, obviously quite unperturbed about my predicament. He looked at me despairingly as I sloshed my way back to the car, crying. It wasn't my fault; the man had let go of the rope. I'd tried my best to swim but the weight of the clothes had dragged me down.

I felt foolish and a failure. I always wanted to be good at things like Mark, but there was so much I got wrong and there was so much I couldn't do. I always wanted to be able to climb the ropes in the school gym but all I could ever do was jump up and hold on! I felt so stupid as everyone else pulled themselves up the ropes. Now the thought of not being able to climb the rope, not being able to swim when I had fallen into the lake and many other 'failings' passed through my mind. In my bedraggled state I was embarrassed and frightened as I waited patiently for Mum to unpack the case and get out some dry clothes for me to wear home. I stood on the side of the road and pulled on the dry clothes. Not outwardly cross, but rather quiet and exasperated, Mum was clearly concerned about Dad's reaction. He sternly asked me what had happened and was obviously not pleased to be packing up my wet clothes into the boot of his car. The journey home was in silence, no one wanting to do or say the wrong thing. This was not a perfect ending to our holiday.

As the decades have passed I've come to realise just how much lifestyle, attitudes, expectations and discipline have changed. In the 1950s and 1960s, children were not analysed or studied for their wellbeing; there were no such things as 'health and safety' or 'children's rights'. Children were generally taught discipline at home and school; corporal punishment was meted out as was considered appropriate. In our house a child's role was simply to be 'seen and not heard', to learn by rote, constant repetition of arithmetic times tables, poetry and grammar. We were to be early to bed, with plenty of quiet time to calm down, before 'going up the wooden hill'[2].

We were provided with home-cooked meals prepared from basic staple meat and veg. Chicken was a luxury, with beef or lamb the

[2] going to bed

preferred option for Sunday roast. Monday was always wash day for Mum and whenever I was around I helped to 'pull' the sheets. Mum would hold two ends of the sheet and I would hold the other two. We then walked away from each other until the sheet was taut, and pulled out the wrinkles – or at least that was the plan!

Clothes for Mark and I consisted of a best outfit, school uniform and an outfit to change into when we got home. Underclothes were changed once a week with fresh to start on a Sunday after we'd had our weekly bath on the Saturday evening. After Mum's busy day of doing the laundry on a Monday, a quick meal was rehashed from Sunday's leftovers. There was no choice in what we were to eat; rather we ate whatever was put in front of us and knew not to 'mess with food' but to clear the plate. When we were sat up at the table for meals there was to be no talking; we were to use our knife and fork properly, keep our elbows tucked in and never ever lean on the table.

We didn't have a television until the middle of the 1950s and then we had a choice of just two channels and a limited range of programmes. Viewing was restricted to just half an hour or so per day. 'Watch with Mother' was one of my favourites as a young child, 'The Woodentops' and 'The Flower Pot Men' also being among my top choices. As a family we always watched the 'Boat Race' and the 'Eurovision Song Contest' doing our own family voting and sometimes "nil points"!

We lived in a modern semi-detached house with large kitchen, separate dining room and lounge. Mum and Dad had aspired to being homeowners and held a rather snobbish view of those who lived on the council estates. Appearances were everything. Rarely did we enter the lounge, or 'front room' as it was often known; it was only for best or special occasions. The television was in the dining room, which had a drop-leaf table, four dining chairs and two fireside chairs. For our meals we always sat up at the kitchen table, except on high days and holidays when we laid up in the dining room. Cooked breakfast at weekends was always fried; sausages and bacon were never grilled and we always had fried bread. We never had coffee, that was too expensive; cups and saucers for tea were the order of the day. We didn't have sugar in our tea; it wasn't thought to be necessary. And no one had mugs – they were for navvies!

Mum and Dad never bought anything 'on the never-never'. The quote was often voiced, "Other than the mortgage, if we can't afford to pay for it outright, then we don't have it." As my brother and I got older we did tasks for our pocket money and, being in the Scouts and Brownies/Guides respectively, did 'Bob a Job Week'. My 'job for a bob[3]' was to polish the two copper plates Mum had inherited from her mother. It was a messy job and required a lot of rubbing with 'Brasso'. Mum always checked how shiny they were, and when they weren't up to her standard she would have me repeat the task several times until those two plates gleamed and shone reflecting the light; only then did I get my shilling piece to pass on to the Brown Owl. I always enjoyed Brownies and Guides, especially marching behind a band once a month around the streets before going to Church Parade.

Compared to today's ways, childhood back then seems harsh. An example is when I went into hospital to have my tonsils out at six years of age. It was my first experience of being away from my parents and having been admitted on a Sunday, the operation was to be on Monday morning. If all went well, the next time I would see Mum and Dad was Wednesday, at which point I would be discharged. When the day finally came my throat was still bleeding so they were allowed to see me for just an hour and then told to collect me the following Saturday. Alone in an unfamiliar place, feeling poorly and quite frightened, even as a child you 'toughed it out' because that was just the way things were.

I had always been prone to nose bleeds and to my distress I had a nose bleed during one night at the hospital. The matron in charge was very angry with me because of the mess on the bed. Finally, after I was discharged there were some more enjoyable moments: I had a few treats of ice cream and 'Jubblies'[4].

Notable dates in the calendar were always recognised. On the first day of each month my brother and I would see who could be first to do and say, "Pinch, punch, first day of the month." The other would then respond, "A punch and a kick for being so quick." For my birthday I was always taken to the Pantomime where we would sit in a 'Box'. Mothering Sunday was celebrated (but not Fathers' Day), although even on Mum's special day she still had to cook dinner. My dad didn't do

[3] one shilling in old money or the equivalent of five pence today

[4] frozen orange juice in an unusual triangular carton

any housework or cooking; he didn't even make himself a cup of tea until he retired from work. On hot days we would have the washing up bowl in the garden and paddle our feet. In autumn we celebrated Bonfire Night with a few fireworks in the garden. We were never allowed to go out with a guy to raise money; Mum and Dad had strong opinions about raising money for yourself, and making a Guy Fawkes and begging for money did not sit with their strong Protestant work ethic. Throughout the day, however, we frequently repeated, "Remember, remember the fifth of November, gunpowder, treason and plot. I see no reason why gunpowder treason should ever be forgot."

When I moved to the junior school, which was conveniently built opposite our house, my worries had lessened. I still couldn't climb the ropes, but my swimming was improving thanks to the swimming lessons Mum and Dad took me to each week. We had to drive into Bristol and the baths were very old-fashioned but the swimming teacher was kind and very patient. Whenever we went swimming we always had to wear a swimming hat with a strap under the chin, which seemed to pull half your hair out when you took it off.

During break time at school, cat's cradle, cartwheels, handstands against the wall, hula-hoops and skipping were the normal pastimes. There was a tuck shop, but my pocket money didn't stretch that far and I certainly wouldn't have been given money each day for such non-essentials. For the same reason we rarely had fish and chips, which was the only takeaway generally available at that time, nor would Mum dream of stopping for a 'cuppa' whilst out shopping. Many of my friends would receive a weekly comic, but in our house that was considered to be an unacceptable expense and not 'proper' reading.

As children we were to be grateful for the necessary school clothes and shoes, even when that meant cutting out the toes so that they lasted through the summer holidays until new ones could be bought for the start of school in September. I did have one treasured doll with a china face that became very cracked, but I was never allowed to have a teddy or soft cuddly toy, as it was thought by my parents to be far too 'namby pamby'!

Appearances and how one presented oneself were very important to Mum and Dad. Mum would always change out of her morning housework clothes just before she expected Dad to arrive home. My parents paid for me to have private elocution lessons in an attempt to rid me of my Bristol accent and teach me to speak properly. They believed it was 'common' and working class to have an accent other than, of course, one that sounded of the Queen's English! Such an attitude always seemed hypocritical to me as Dad had a very strong Somerset accent, but he only spoke that way when he was with his parents; the rest of the time he spoke 'posh'.

And so it was a lady came to the house each week and in the dining room she listened to me recite the poems that I'd had to learn since the last lesson, as well as various exercises. "Put the pots in the pantry," was a favourite, but I never mastered "t, d, r," which was supposed to help me roll my r's. I took part in many competitions and eisteddfods and generally did fairly well.

I was asked to recite two pieces at a school concert and at the appointed time stood up to give my recitation. My mind went blank; I couldn't remember a word! Not even the title of the poem! My headmaster stood up and said, "Never mind, Marianne, I'll go and get your books from over the road and you can read them later in the concert." By now I was in such a state of nerves that even when he handed me the books my hands were shaking and it was difficult to focus on the words; my voice was trembling so much that the gathered students and staff could barely hear me. I hung my head with such a sense of shame. I knew that Mum and Dad would not only be disappointed with me but also somewhat annoyed that I had failed to perform well in spite of all the money they were paying out for my private tuition.

Dad was always at work Monday to Saturday, earning the money, so he was rarely able to attend anything I did at school during the week. I was so pleased when I was due to sing a duet with a girl called Janet at another school concert and Dad was going to be able to come. I sang my heart out and thought I'd done quite well, but when we got home that night he said, "You were flat and Janet was sharp; it would have been better if the piano had stopped playing because that was in tune!" Again I had disappointed him and had failed to measure up to his standards.

Mum was always at home. Sunday was typically a day for going to Badminton Road Methodist Church to the family service in the morning, Sunday school in the afternoon and, as I got older, the evening service. Both my parents were Methodists; Mum had been instrumental in being part of a group that campaigned for there to be a church on the new housing estate; Dad, with his busy working week, the car to clean every weekend and other bits to catch up on, rarely made church in those early days.

Sunday was the one day in the week when we stayed indoors, apart from when we wore our best clothes to go to church. I would put on my hat and gloves and try to keep clean; that wasn't too difficult as Sunday was a day for quiet things like reading or jigsaws.

I really rather liked having one day in the week that was a bit different. But often I asked, "Why can't I talk to Ann over the fence?" Ann was my neighbour, a year older than me. We played together in the week but I wasn't allowed to play on Sundays; I wasn't even allowed to speak to her. She didn't go to church and I'd hear her outside playing on her bike. She could ride a two-wheeler but she did have stabilisers. Although I only had a tricycle I could come around the corner by the kitchen very fast – but never on a Sunday. As always I'd be told, "You're not going out to play on a Sunday. Sunday is for reading and quiet games and, anyway, we're going to see your grandparents this afternoon."

We went to see Gran and Grandpa every other Sunday. From the beginning of their marriage Dad had told Mum that every other Sunday afternoon he would be going to visit his parents and she could come if she liked but if she decided not then he would go anyway. Dad felt strongly that it was his duty to regularly spend time with his parents even though he worked a six-day week and had just two weeks' holiday a year. 'Me-time' and 'social', 'relax', 'downtime' or 'chill out time' were not in the vocabulary. 'The devil makes work for idle hands' was very much the order of every day.

I quite liked visiting Gran and Grandpa; they still lived in an old-fashioned cottage in the country. The toilet was up at the end of the garden and you had to take a bucket of water with you when you went. A large hook hung from the ceiling just outside the front door of the house and it was here that the village pig was left to hang. There was also a handle for the water pump although by this time they did have piped cold water coming into the house. Gran made delicious scones on a griddle and she'd always put sugar in my tea when Mum and Dad weren't looking. On the way home we'd have the radio on in the car and we'd all sing along to 'Sing Something Simple', a popular weekly programme. Driving home in the dark there was always a competition as to who would be the first to see the 'green light'. This was the illuminated beacon on Hanham Mount that signified where John Wesley and George Whitfield preached outdoors to the mining community in 1739.

Although sometimes upset at not being allowed out to play, I enjoyed going to church, dressing up and visiting my grandparents, but one Sunday was to be very different. I awoke to a loud crash and the sound of Dad saying, "Nita, are you alright?"

There was no answer.

Soon I was told that Mum had passed out in the bathroom. My father carried her back to the bedroom and noticed that the side of her face had dropped. Mum was thirty-eight years old.

Dad shouted to Mark, "Get dressed quickly and go and fetch the doctor."

Mark seemed to be gone a long time. When he finally returned with Doctor Hill, the doctor explained that he'd been on a maternity call but had come immediately, leaving the expectant mother with a midwife. He knew that Dad would not have called him if it wasn't urgent.

"Your wife will have to go to hospital," Doctor Hill stated. We didn't have a phone, so he went back to his house and phoned for an ambulance.

Dad went next door to Ann's house and asked her mother to look after us until other arrangements could be made. His parents arrived later that day from Timsbury which was a thirty-minute drive away but as they didn't have a car it took them two hours on the bus.

My mother, who had always been at home, was now being whisked away. I had no idea of the seriousness of the crisis or the possible implications, but I felt the worry and anxiety of all those around me. Mum was unconscious for three days and I was told that she'd had a stroke; it was a cerebral thrombosis. She regained consciousness to realise she had what was to be a permanent blind spot. This was to cause many problems for her in the coming months and, for me, the quietly confident, capable mother I'd always known was not the mother that came back home from the hospital. She'd told Dad that she wanted to stay in hospital. This shook him to the core; his wife, homemaker and our devoted mother felt safer and more secure in hospital.

When Mum left the hospital six weeks later, the specialist suggested that we go away for a few days' holiday. I enjoyed the time we spent in Cornwall, unaware that Mum was unable to make any decisions and lacked her normal quiet confidence. Whilst Mum had been in hospital, Dad, aside from visiting, had not been able to be of much help in aiding her recovery. He worked ceaselessly trying to keep his mind occupied, yet continually worried as to what was going to happen to his wife. Now he took time off and we went away to spend time as a family and give Mum chance to recuperate.

Mum had lost her calm, capable, self-confident personality. She was constantly anxious, hesitant and unable to make decisions. Dad was anxious for her but also very frustrated. To them, a wife's role was to be in the home, to look after her husband and children; a husband's role was to go out to work. Dad needed Mum to keep order in the home, provide meals and be the housewife.

It took Mum a long time to settle back into her role as homemaker, housewife and mother, and there were occasions when I fuelled her own frustrations. For example, my grandmother had given me, as a present, a glass deer ornament; it was to be the first of a collection. The clear glass animal with red ears stood proudly on the mantelpiece in the dining room. One day when Mum was dusting, she failed to see the ornament due to her blind spot. She knocked it off the mantelpiece and it fell to the floor shattering to smithereens. When I later returned from school and she told me of the accident, I felt angry towards her and frustrated at her situation. Even though I knew that she had been crying, I did not hold back my anger. Mum searched the shops for weeks to find another deer, but she could only find one with blue ears. Even as she gave it to me, I showed my displeasure that it was not the same. I wanted everything to be just as it had been but my capable, consistent mother was not coping and I felt insecure. Reacting to the foundations of home life being shaken, I acted selfishly and heartlessly.

As Mum adjusted and gradually became her old self, she started going out of the house more often. Occasionally I'd return home from school and be unable to find her. I'd search through the house looking in cupboards and under the beds in case she'd passed out again, somehow thinking she'd fallen into the cupboard or rolled under the bed. Within minutes she'd be in, just a little late getting back from the shops. My relief at seeing her was tempered with anger due to my worry.

Gradually life returned to some semblance of normality. My brother had passed his 11 plus exams and gone to the local grammar school. As an incentive he'd been told that if he passed he would get a new bike, and one was duly bought. He now had a greater freedom and, four years younger, I often wanted to be doing what Mark was allowed to do.

When I was in the fourth year of junior school I sat the 11 plus exam myself. Then the dreaded day came when the results were to be read out in front of the entire school during morning assembly. *I didn't quite make it.* I just wasn't quite good enough. As a 'borderline pass' I had to sit another examination, and was then accepted to go to the local technical high school. A *second hand* bike was bought for me. I had not quite made the grade and so didn't warrant a new bike.

Mum and Dad thought the school would suit me well. Rodway Technical High School in Mangotsfield was a new building three miles from our home. I found myself surrounded by people from a much larger geographical area – few of the children from my junior school were at Rodway – but I soon settled in and made friends.

Throughout the first year I worked really hard at my studies, conscientiously did homework and was a well-behaved student, but the end of year tests placed me third from last. All this effort and I felt I had nothing to show. If I'd gone to the comprehensive school, where students who'd failed their 11 plus went, I could well have been amongst the top ten students. Starting the second year I once again tried to improve my marks.

I was aware that Mum and Dad had always wanted what they believed was the best for me. Mark was a good student, well behaved and a credit to the family. Throughout my junior school years Mum and Dad had put me through the private elocution lessons, I'd been encouraged in Brownies and now Guides, given swimming and horse riding lessons. As a family we were starting to enjoy holidays abroad in Europe and Dad frequently took us out to restaurants to eat on a Saturday night. I knew in my head that I was loved but in my heart I always felt second best. Not quite accepted for myself, I felt I was always being compared to someone else and never quite coming up to the expected standards. Now here I was at school, striving away and getting nowhere. Eventually the day came when I said to myself, "Why bother? I may just as well enjoy myself; my marks can't get much worse."

My whole attitude to school and learning and life changed; I became insolent, objectionable and rude, battling against authority and being a bully to my peers. I was frequently in fights, reducing teachers to tears and causing general mayhem; it became my norm. Yet I was living a double life. As soon as I walked through the back door of my home I would be much quieter, almost locked in on myself. I knew the standards expected of me and tried to show them, that I was living up to them. But there were some occasions when I got caught out: when Mum found cigarettes in my school bag or asked why I had so many detentions on my report; when a policeman came to the front door and told Mum that I'd jumped off the school bus whilst it was moving or had been riding two on a bike.

My main interest was boys. Constantly out to impress, and breaking school rules, I'd wear make-up and hitch my skirt up so that it looked more like a belt than a school uniform skirt, which was supposed to be just two inches above the knee. In the days of strict uniform, if you were caught not wearing your regulation beret it was an immediate detention. I flaunted the rules any way I could and was on the slippery slope of rebellion. Most of the time I got caught and the number of detentions increased.

Guides and youth club were my main social life. Many times I'd want to give up Guiding; I found the written exercises boring and tedious, but Mum cajoled and encouraged me to keep going by getting out all the books and paperwork I'd need. She laid it all on the kitchen table and said, "Just do an hour and then we'll sit down and have tea." I'd been a Brownie, flown up to Guides and acquired numerous badges. Mum sewed them on to my uniform and was as proud of them as I was. I enjoyed Guiding evenings, particularly the wide-games with the Venture Scouts, canoeing on the River Avon and camping. Mark was in the venture scouts and for a while Dad was one of their leaders. I still had a highly competitive nature in sport and always aimed to win. The more adventurous the activities, the better I enjoyed them.

Before I could complete the tasks for my Queen's Guide I had to attend a camp and joined with another company in Bristol to go to the Gower Coast in Wales for a week. I sat amongst forty Guides on the floor in the back of a furniture lorry; the tailgate went up, we were in the dark and we took off. Arriving at our campsite I spotted another camp already pitched in the next field. I asked the Guide Captain who was in the next field. "Venture Scouts," she said, "and they're out of bounds." That, of course, didn't stop me. One night I crept out of camp with a few other girls and joined the boys around their campfire. We had a great time and it was all innocent fun and harmless, but on the way back to our tent I caught my leg on a barbed wire fence, badly cutting my leg. I couldn't go to the Captain for first aid; how would I explain a gash on my leg when I should have been asleep in my tent? So I bound it tightly and hoped for the best. It was a memorable week, made even more so by our return trip.

Halfway home we stopped at a transport café to find the members of a famous pop group – Dave Dee, Dozy Beaky, Mick and Titch – sitting at one of the tables. I sat and swooned along with the rest of the Guides but went totally unnoticed by this top-of-the-charts group.

I was proud to be presented with my Queen's Guide award, but whereas my brother had been presented with his Queen's Scout award at Buckingham Palace, the Guides were only given a local presentation. However, I was pleased that my mother wrote to the paper informing them that they'd left my name out in the write-up; I got a special mention the following week. I knew Mum really deserved the award as much as I did. It was only due to her encouragement, particularly in getting me to settle down to the written work, that I obtained this coveted award in Guiding circles.

My other main source of enjoyment came from the youth club run by our local Methodist church, which had obtained funding for a youth worker. During the week there was a coffee bar and we could play games like table tennis and snooker. My competitive nature still evident, I always played to win. At school I was in the teams for athletics, swimming, netball, tennis, rounders and hockey. I knew I was lethal on the hockey field and would vent my frustrations on the other players. I was amazed when, one Saturday, Dad came to see me play; he shouted encouragement at me from the side-line and with him watching I tried to play a fair game.

At youth club I played badminton and table tennis. But the best night of the week was Friday, the youth club dance! Live bands played and young people came from all over north Bristol. I loved to dance, especially the jive with Mark. Most people at the club didn't know he was my brother and I proudly danced with this good-looking guy who was four years older than me. I knew we looked good on the dance floor; we practised at home, playing records on our 'Dansette' record player, and I knew I was making an impression on those watching.

Mark and I were quite close and as soon as he learnt to drive and had a car he'd pick me up from school. I always felt very proud, particularly when he had an M.G.B. convertible and we'd drive home with the top down. Often he would put the record player out on the landing and with the 'stacking arm' back we just constantly listened to 'A Whiter Shade of Pale' by Procol Harum.

Most of the people who attended the youth club were not from the church, and although I still attended church with the family and was a Sunday school teacher, these other people, who brought a new life and wildness into my week, excited me. Mods and rockers met and clashed at the meetings. I met Steve, a local mod with a flashy scooter. His father and mine worked together and he came from a nice home so Mum and Dad accepted our friendship. But Mum wouldn't let me go on his scooter, so if I was with him we were supposed to walk. Well, I did walk *as soon as we were near the house,* having only got off Steve's scooter just around the corner!

I soon learnt from his behaviour that how you look is not necessarily how you are, and coming from a nice, privately owned house does not make you a nice or good person. It made a mockery of the emphasis on how one presents oneself externally and challenged the standards set by my parents. So I reasoned, "Why put on a show? I don't want to be conventional." I'd tried working at school and got nowhere. I'd always felt second best and was never good enough. The outer image was no indicator of the inner person, so why not hang out with those who didn't try to conform?

I chose to become involved with the rockers, or 'greasers' as they'd become known. The north Bristol Hells Angels had their headquarters a few miles away and they frequently came to hang around the church youth club. The mods were too clean, tidy and well presented. So I started hanging out with the rockers, and loved the bikes and their way-out lifestyle. My choice of wardrobe was jeans that looked like I'd peeled them on – I'd lie in the bath for ages shrinking them to fit like a second skin – black tops and make-up. I spent hours painting my eyes black like Dusty Springfield's. I acquired a leather jacket and really felt I was now 'living'. I had to put most of my attire on at a friend's house, knowing that Mum and Dad would be horrified at the way I chose to dress. Then at the end of my evening out I'd go into a public toilet to remove my make-up so as not to give the game away.

Mum and Dad were very strict about the time I had to come home so I was limited in how much I could join in the activities of the Hells Angels. What I could do and get away with I did. As I became more rebellious I knew some behaviour could be hidden and I determined to 'do my own thing' and simply become deceitful and hide my actions. However, it was not long before I realised that some actions and mistakes could not be hidden; I was soon going to find myself in a situation where that would become all too apparent.

Chapter Two

The Unforgivable Sin?

Robert was a member of the local Hells Angels Chapter and at seventeen to my fifteen years of age I thought he was mature, exciting and adorable. We started going out together, meeting at the youth club or going to each other's homes. I'd had several other boyfriends – in fact, most of the guys at school. I was always looking for the one who would think I was really special and like me for who I was rather than what they could turn me into. I then turned my attentions to guys outside of my school: Steve; then Theo, another lad who travelled with the fair. Theo was a dream – very polite, always respectful and treated me well – but his family were gypsies, he had long hair and Mum most certainly did not approve. She forbade me to see him, saying he wasn't "our type" of person. He didn't come from a good, respectable home. For many people back in the 1960s, gypsies were looked down on as a lesser form of humanity. In fact, despite his appearance and nomadic lifestyle, Theo always respected me and ensured that I was home safely at the time my parents had instructed.

At fifteen I left school and started an apprenticeship with a local hairdressing salon. School had been "a laugh"; not surprisingly my results in the mock exams hadn't been good. Rather bizarrely, my main interest was Religious Studies. I'd taken several exams in Bible Knowledge through being a Sunday school teacher, but there weren't enough students interested to take the G.C.E. course so the school wouldn't put me through to the exam. Dad complained to the governors, but they weren't to be swayed. It was decided in consultation with the school that it would be better if I left full-time education. Through my apprenticeship I'd attend college one day and evening a week. I realised there was a peculiar battle going on inside me. I searched in rebellion for wild fun, wanted to be loved and accepted, and had an amazing interest in the Bible.

College awakened my interest in learning. I could see that the information I was being given had relevance to my course, and the college treated me more like an adult with a right to my opinions and individuality, whereas school had been all about conformity. College was a good place to be and I enjoyed my work.

The salon was just a few minutes' walk from my home. Yvonne, the owner, was a fair boss and I accepted that initially I would simply be brushing up hair, answering the phone to take appointments, handing up rollers to the stylists and watching the senior staff. Yvonne then had me practising on wigs and as I learnt more at the college I was able to start doing more work in the salon. I found I had an artistic flare and was doing well in my exams, both practical and theory. My wages started at two pounds fifteen shillings a week. I was so proud at the end of the first week when I received my money and went straight out and bought Mum and Dad a set of green drinking glasses.

Previously I'd been doing some Saturday work in a record shop that Dad was managing but this was proper work and once I qualified three years later, I could expect to earn ten pounds a week. It was a long working week – forty-eight hours plus a late night every Thursday – but even though I had to work most Saturdays, I enjoyed it and knew I'd found something that I could do and was gifted at.

Robert and I continued to see each other. This relationship was different to the others. We were serious. Mum and Dad were still strict though, and always wanted to know where I was and whom I was with, and I had to be in by nine o'clock in the week and nine thirty at weekends. At fifteen years old, many of my friends were allowed to stay out a lot later and I began to feel resentful that I always had to leave the youth club before it ended. Robert always walked me home; we'd hold hands and kiss, but never near the house where Mum and Dad might see. But all in all life was going fairly well.

My day off from the salon was on a rota and when it fell on a Saturday I'd occasionally be allowed into Bristol during the daytime. I'd go with my friend Zoe. She had gone to the same school as me but had stayed on to take exams. Mum and Dad liked her; she came from a nice home on a private housing estate and was also in the Guides. We met up, went into the public toilets to put on make-up, and spent the day looking around the shops or going to the ice rink.

My parents disapproved of many of my friends. Christine, who lived in a council house, was a close friend at school. She was naturally very clever so didn't have to work hard for her exams. She and I were often in trouble for fighting other girls, playing pranks and causing mayhem in the school. Mum and Dad didn't approve of our friendship and would try and stop me seeing her. I learnt to be deceitful and lie. I'd say I was going to meet with someone they did approve of, but then go to the local park or hang around the streets with Christine.

Resentment fuelled my disobedience to my parents' restrictions. One night it came to a head. It was New Year's Eve and there was a dance in the community hall in Downend, a mile from where we lived. Robert and I wanted to go and he promised to walk me home. The dance started at nine thirty and went on till one in the morning.

I asked Mum if I could go, see the New Year in and then be home by twelve forty-five. She said, "Ask your dad."

So I asked my father he said, "Yes, you can go. *Be back by eleven.*"

I was so upset. I knew it was useless to argue with him or to try to get him to reconsider; once he'd spoken his decision was cast in stone. There was also no point in going to a New Year's Eve dance and leaving before midnight. I rushed to Robert's house crying and wanting to have a cigarette. Why were Mum and Dad so against me being out late? Didn't they know that you could get up to things just as easily at eight in the evening as at twelve, midnight? I'd left school, was working all week and going to college, yet they still treated me like a child. It wasn't fair. I hung on to the fact that I had Robert, enjoyed my job and college, and was at least able to go into Bristol on my day off.

A few months later I was aware that the atmosphere was more than a little tense at home. Then the explosion came. Dad sat me down and announced that since the company he'd been working for had been taken over, he now had a new job in Exeter and we would have to move. I knew that there had been problems with his work and that to stay in employment he'd taken a job in London but it hadn't worked out. Now he was telling me we all had to move to a place called Exmouth. *Where the heck was Exmouth?* I'd never heard of it and certainly didn't want to go there.

"What about Robert? What about my job? What about college? What about Bristol?" I protested.

But Dad said, "It can't be helped." He had to take this job and we would look for another salon to take on the indentures for my apprenticeship and transfer me to Exeter College.

Then I found out that Mark, now working in a bank, would be staying in Bristol. "Well, why can't I stay in Bristol as well?" I cried. "I know I can't afford to live on my own money but I could go into lodgings and you could pay the bill just as if I was living with you."

"No, it's out of the question," I was firmly told.

I went to Robert's house and broke the news to him. We sat in his lounge devastated. How could we still see each other? We'd be so many miles apart and he'd only be able to afford to come down every six or eight weeks. Mum and Dad had never liked him; now they were going to split us up. I sobbed in his arms not wanting to leave his side.

"How much do you love me?" Robert asked.

"Very much," I answered.

"I love you too. *Prove to me* you love me, Marianne," he said.

We made love for the first and only time that evening. There were no flashing lights, I couldn't say it was a riveting experience, but I felt loved, wanted, cosseted.

It seemed that in no time Mum, Dad and I were on the move. I found out that Exmouth was on the coast and ten miles from Exeter. The house we moved into was very nice, even more posh than our home in Downend. Although a mile and a half from the coast I could see the sea from my bedroom window.

Mum and Dad were trying very hard to help me adjust to the move and said, "You can have your bedroom decorated however you like."

I'd never been allowed to choose my own colours before. Without hesitation I said, "Orange and purple!" Psychedelic was 'in' and I wanted to be 'in'!

My college course, still with two years outstanding, was transferred to Exeter. A salon called Mauveens was prepared to accept me as an apprentice. The salon was dingy, drab and dreadfully old-fashioned. One of the stylists, Margaret, was very nice to me but I no longer enjoyed my work or the area I lived in. The neighbourhood was full of elderly people. The church was dead; there was no youth club, no Bristol and no Robert. I felt miserable.

Then... panic!

I hadn't had my period. Mum had always been aware when my periods were due and it wasn't many days before she confronted me. I hoped it may have been because of the upset with the move but in the end I had to accept I was pregnant – and just fifteen years old. It was 1968 and such things were totally unacceptable. Mum told Dad and I became the outcast.

I phoned Robert. How could this be? We'd only made love once and now I was pregnant. He came down to see me, but what could he say? Nothing...

The atmosphere in the house was icy cold. Dad phoned Robert's father and the next thing I knew was that I was seeing a doctor and an abortion was to be arranged because of my age. No one talked to me, only at me, through me, around me, or about me. As an individual I ceased to exist. The night before going into hospital I sobbed uncontrollably into my pillow. I had no idea what was going to happen to me in the hospital and I felt so frightened. Mark was staying over the weekend and when he heard about my pregnancy he wouldn't talk to me either. I couldn't talk to anyone about my fears or feelings. I felt scared, isolated and alone.

I was taken to the hospital the next day; tests were done in readiness for the termination the next morning. None of the nurses told me what was going to happen. I didn't know how they would do the operation or how much pain to expect. Nobody talked with me about the life that was inside me and would now be taken away.

I awoke from the anaesthetic in a daze. *What had I done?* And yet, although I'd been actively involved in getting pregnant, once it had been confirmed, all actions were taken out of my hands. Robert's father had told my dad that his son clearly wasn't right in the head getting me pregnant when I was underage and that it was better this way. The decision had been made; I wasn't involved in any of the discussions and it was made clear to me that my mistake and mess would now be put right and cleaned up by others.

Sex before marriage was absolutely taboo to my parents. Many people thought of girls who had sex outside of marriage as sluts or harlots, the unacceptable and unclean of society. In addition, I was legally underage so I was even more despicable.

I was discharged from the hospital. The cramp pains in my stomach were horrendous. I felt like I was going to die, and lay on the couch *wanting* to die. The atmosphere in the house made it impossible for Robert to come to see me. I was miserable and alone. Had I committed the unforgivable sin?

Gradually the contact between Robert and me broke down. It was so difficult to be together when the atmosphere was so strained at home. I went back to work but only Margaret, the senior hairstylist who had been so friendly, knew what had happened to me. She was the only one I could talk to. At home I couldn't speak about how I felt; it was as if the whole situation had never happened. My boss and the other staff thought I'd been off work because I'd had a stomach upset, so I tried to continue as if that were the case. But I knew what had been done. I would never forget. I *could* never forget. A life inside me had been killed – and I was responsible.

CHAPTER THREE

Desperate for Acceptance and Love

Over the following months the big black stain that was my life was gradually pushed into the deep, deep depths of my soul. One night when I got in from work Mum showed me an advertisement in the local paper for people aged sixteen to twenty-five who wanted to be involved in the very popular 'It's a Knockout' television programme. Exmouth were to host this game and they were looking for participants and cheerleaders.

"Auditions are being held," Mum told me. "They want people over the age of eighteen for the games but over sixteen for the cheerleaders. Why don't you try?"

There was little else going on in the town so I thought, why not? I telephoned the number printed in the paper and was given an appointment. The choreographer for the games was ill in bed at the time of the auditions and all those interested in being cheerleaders were summoned to her bedroom.

As I walked in, the whole situation felt very odd – her lying in bed and me having to shout and move according to her instructions. Whatever I did or didn't do must have been acceptable, though, because she called me later to say that even though I was only just sixteen I was to be part of a team of seven, one for each letter of Exmouth. I was 'H' and there were to be two reserves. When I arrived for the first practice I realised I was indeed the youngest member of the team. Over the weeks we rehearsed our steps and were measured up for our outfits. I thought I looked stunning in a short, tight-fitting blue dress trimmed with white, and white knee-high plastic boots – quite the rage at the time! – with white gloves, straw boater hat and a white cane to twirl.

Eventually we were ready for the competition against Weymouth. Great excitement and nerves were clearly evident as the television cameras started rolling and the games commenced. Competition was fierce and my competitive nature was evident; I'm sure no microphones were needed to hear my shrieks when it was clear that Exmouth was through to the next round. 'Jeux Sans Frontieres', the international 'It's a Knockout', was to be held in Lucerne, Switzerland. After details were discussed amongst the organisers we were informed that the main team for the games was to fly out on a four-day trip. The reserve team for the games and the cheerleaders were to travel by coach down through Europe, publicising Exmouth as a holiday resort, over a ten-day trip. This was going to be fun!

I met up with the rest of the team and boarded the coach. We stopped in London on the Embankment by the River Thames, got out of the coach, did our routines in front of television cameras, then continued on our way to Dover. I soon got to know the others on the trip and gradually people started forming friendships. John was an amateur water polo player and in the reserve team for the games. As we travelled down through France staying in hotels, I spent every night with him, but we didn't have sex; he was just kind, gentle and caring. I told him about the abortion and he would simply hold me in his arms and let me cry. Just to be held and comforted was the greatest act of compassion I could be shown. I knew he had a girlfriend back in Exmouth and that I wouldn't see him once we got back but I'd never forget his unselfish care and concern for me. We had a lot of fun during those few days and although our team didn't do so well in Lucerne I enjoyed the experience of the trip and the feeling of John's comforting arms that expected nothing from me.

I went back to work, still not liking the salon I was at in Exmouth, but I'd now settled down and was enjoying college. I was getting good passes in my tests but there was no way of putting what I was learning into practice at the salon, which was old-fashioned and unaccepting of new ideas, fashions and hairstyles.

Now sixteen, I started to explore the entertainments of Exmouth. The town had nothing to offer, but just a few miles away at Lympstone the Marine camp was based; it was a training centre for new Marines following their square bashing at Deal in Kent. Every week they held dances and laid on coaches from Exmouth for girls to be able to travel to the camp.

I asked Mum and Dad if I could go.

Dad said, "Yes, you can catch the coach to go to the camp, but I'll pick you up outside the gates of the camp at ten thirty."

The dance ended at eleven, but I agreed. I just couldn't understand why it was I always had to leave just that bit sooner than everyone else. I'd always feel embarrassed and somewhat humiliated at being the first to leave the dance or party and it just seemed to set off a trigger in me to do all the things and more that Mum and Dad were trying to prevent me from doing. Rebellion and disobedience were becoming a significant flaw in my character.

Saturday eventually arrived and I was on the coach. The dance was good, the music good and most of the Marines good-looking. One of them accompanied me as I walked to the gates and Dad was waiting. This became the pattern of my life over the next months; work which I didn't like, college that was good, and the Marines who were great and made life worth living! Weekends in the summer saw me on the beach and swimming with whomever my latest boyfriend was. I moved swiftly from one to the other as they were moved to different camps after completing their training.

I was constantly seeking fun, happiness and love. The age of fast food and buy-now-pay-later was growing. I wanted fast fun without thought of the cost now or later. It was as if a vacuum inside me needed filling, yet however hard I tried I couldn't fill it. An inner pain needed soothing, I yearned to be caressed and comforted. Mum and Dad provided for all my material needs. I lived in a clean, comfortable home; my parents cared for and about me. I knew I had more than most but I wanted something even more in my life. I was searching, striving, seeking something special that would take away the void and loss and replace the pain.

I met Scott in a pub in the town. Although I was underage I looked eighteen and was served alcohol by the publicans. Drinking and smoking was what I did when I went out, but at home it was not allowed. Truth be told, my attitude was now spiralling out of control and many would say it was reprehensible. Occasionally I arrived home the worse for wear from the drink but usually I was able to disguise my intake. Scott came over to me and we started chatting. He was older than the other Marines and as a Corporal was responsible for the fire arms part of their training. He was based long-term at Lympstone and was becoming more desirable as the conversation went on.

Because of his age – mid-twenties – I was prompted to ask him, "Are you married?"

"Don't worry," he said. "There's no one else in my life."

We started going out but there was little to do in Exmouth. He had a car and wanted to take me into Exeter but Mum and Dad wouldn't allow it. I understood that he didn't want to spend his time at the Marine dances so before long he was driving us up to Woodbury Common.

Scott was the second man I'd had sex with and now I was pregnant for the second time in two years. He already knew of my previous pregnancy and the abortion, but he assured me saying, "I'm happy that we are to have a baby." We started planning names, listing things to buy and generally, I thought, being a close, expectant couple.

A few weeks later Scott arrived to take me out. My parents still didn't know I was pregnant. Mum didn't keep a track of my periods anymore in the way she had when I was younger. We went down to the pub and Scott said, "My wife and child are coming to visit."

"Your wife!" I exclaimed. "You told me you weren't married."

"We're separated," he explained. "What I said to you was that there was no one else."

I was stunned.

Scott went on. "I want you to meet my daughter. She's three and when we're married I want us to have custody. Will you meet her?"

I said yes, thinking, "Oh, my golly! I'm not yet seventeen, pregnant, planning to marry and being asked to look after a little girl just three years old."

The next day we met up and went on to the beach with his daughter. She was lovely and we continued with our plans, Scott telling me he was going to get a divorce and the three of us plus our new baby would be together. We arranged a time for him to come and tell my parents about my pregnancy. I was worried about breaking the news to them but felt secure knowing that he was pleased about the baby and would be alongside me when telling Mum and Dad.

Waiting, I kept dashing from my bedroom into the front bedroom to see if I could see the headlamps from Scott's car. It was six thirty and he was due at seven. Seven came and went. I waited. Half past seven. I was still waiting. Eight o'clock. No sign. The sickening feeling in my stomach was unbearable as I was scanning the top of the road just waiting for him to turn in to the close. I waited. No headlamps, no Scott.

I couldn't use the phone at home without Mum or Dad overhearing my conversation so I went to the local phone box and called him at the camp. Scott came on the phone. "Where are you? Why haven't you come?" I asked.

"I've just heard from the hospital," he explained. "My wife and daughter have been involved in a car crash. They're both hurt. I'm going to them now and we're going to get back together."

"What about me and our baby?" I said.

His reply was curt and cold. "You've had one abortion; get another! I must go to my wife." He hung up the phone; the line was dead.

I walked back to the house. I was nearly four months pregnant; an abortion was out of the question. Now I would have to tell my parents on my own that I was pregnant – *again.*

I felt sick as I asked Mum and Dad to sit as I wanted to tell them something. "I'm pregnant. Scott was going to come to talk with you but he didn't come and now he's told me he's going back to his wife. I didn't know he was married." It all came blurting out.

Mum and Dad were horrified. The silence was audible. Eventually Dad spoke. "Well, you can't have another abortion; you will have to have the baby and have it adopted."

"How many months are you?" "What about your job and forthcoming exams?" "How could you do this again; didn't you learn your lesson the last time?" "What will the neighbours say?" Questions and recriminations were rife. "How could you do this to us?" "We brought you up properly. What's the matter with you?" The anger and hostility hung in the air.

Mark came home on a visit and wouldn't speak to me; I clearly wasn't going to receive any support from my brother. I was the black sheep, bringing shame on the family, and this time it would be clear for all to see. Last time my pregnancy had been 'dealt with' and no one else needed to know; this time there would be no hiding of my actions and the life inside of me.

It soon became obvious at work that I was pregnant. I was given the sack. My boss told me such behaviour was disgusting and I couldn't possibly stay working at the salon; what would the clients think? This was the age of unmarried mothers being sent away to another part of the country to mother and baby homes for fallen women. Often these austere, cold and inhospitable places were run by nuns who would treat the women harshly for their sins whilst they awaited the birth of the baby that would then be adopted.

I told Exeter College and they were willing for me to stay on and sit my exams. They suggested I wear a ring on my third finger, as if I was married; perhaps then I'd feel less embarrassed. I declined. I now had no work, no money and was told nothing about Social Security. I didn't want to give my baby up for adoption, but how could I keep my child with no income? How could I go out to work and at the same time look after the infant? Mum and Dad would not let me keep the baby and allow us to live at home so I had no choice; I would have to give birth then hand my child over to be adopted. My parents had long discussions about me going to a mother and baby home, but in the end it was decided – I think, largely due to my mother – that they wouldn't send me away. I was constantly told that I had to try and hide my growing stomach, particularly when I was out. When walking down to the shops with Mum during the summer I had to wear a coat to disguise my 'condition'.

I had no money but was told that when I handed my baby over for adoption it would be my responsibility to pay the foster parents' fees; my baby would stay with them for six weeks before going to the adoptive parents. Also I needed to provide a complete layette. Where was I to get the money for vests, nightdresses, baby-grows, socks, mitts, hats, matinee jackets, sheets and blankets and nappies? I telephoned through to the Marine base but Scott wouldn't even speak to me. A social worker tried to make contact with him to provide half of the money for the foster fees, but again he was "unavailable". The Marine camp closed ranks and he couldn't be contacted. I would have to find a job. Six months into my pregnancy, I was pounding the streets selling door-to-door. I was paid on commission only, ceaselessly plodding from house to house, but I raised enough money to pay for what was needed for my baby to be handed over to the foster parents.

Once a week I still attended college. Here I had some freedom; no one was judgmental and it was good to be amongst friends. Mum bravely sat as my model. Her lovely hair was easy to style but as my body expanded it became more and more difficult for my arms to reach her. Soon the college and I realised that the date for my final exams was around the same date as my baby was due. The tutors set up contingency plans. Would the nerves of sitting my exams start my labour? Would I be able to stand for over three hours to do my practical exam? I gave them the phone number for the hospital and they had copies of all my health details, and together we were prepared for the arrival. This was another time for me to be stoic and simply get on with whatever was required of me. After all, I had brought about this pregnancy and now I would need to accept the consequences of my actions.

My days were busy studying for my exams and knocking on doors to earn some money. There was little conversation at home and no reference to the life growing inside me. My baby was active in the comfort of my womb but there was no one for me to share this life with; no one to tell when I felt the kicks; no one to talk to about my fears of giving birth; no one to tell how my heart was breaking that Scott had left me.

I continued to try to speak with Scott on the phone but he wouldn't accept my calls and I had to accept that I'd lost him and I was literally left holding the baby. I hoped he would be happy with his wife and daughter, that my loss could be their gain, but I was scared of going through the labour on my own and how I would feel at handing over my baby to the foster parents and then to be adopted.

Unwed teenage pregnancy was very different then to now. Over four decades ago as a single pregnant girl you were shunned by society. I was given no information on any statutory or voluntary agencies to give me advice or support. I wasn't made aware of any benefits and certainly no one was concerned about my mental or emotional wellbeing. I was alone in a family that was unable, or unwilling, to talk to me about my condition.

A phone call told my family that Dad's parents were to come down to Exmouth to stay for a week. They didn't know about my pregnancy so suddenly there were discussions about what could be done with me. It was decided that I would go and stay with friends of Mum and Dad who lived 'up the road' and my grandparents would be told that I was away on holiday at Butlins with friends. I packed up my few bits and pieces, plus what I needed to take to the hospital just in case I were to go into labour. I moved to "Nan and Harold's", just a few minutes' walk away.

Exam time came and I went off to college to sit my finals, after three years of study. Everything went well and there was much relief that I wasn't rushed away in an ambulance in the middle of cutting, colouring and setting Mum's hair. I returned to Nan and Harold's exhausted, pleased that one trial was out of the way, but anxious at what was to come.

My grandparents knew Nan and Harold and naturally wanted to visit them whilst in Exmouth. Every time they said to Mum, "We're just popping up to Nan's," Mum would phone through to her and say, "They're on their way up." Nan and Harold lived in a small, two-bedroom bungalow, and the bedroom I was in was at the front of the property. The bedroom window was just to the side of the front door so I would have to rush into the bedroom and quickly get down on the floor and lie there out of sight, staying hidden, until they left. The black sheep was a disgrace to the family and was not to be acknowledged or seen.

One night, as it was dark, still and quiet, I lay in bed feeling ill at ease – not ill in myself but just not feeling right. I tossed and turned as much as my bulging body would allow. I'd put on nearly four stone in weight and was very uncomfortable in the heat of the summer. Things were happening to my body – and then the pains started. I'd attended the antenatal classes and knew that I had to start timing the contractions. I paced the room. What if my waters broke and I made a mess all over Nan's carpet? When should I wake them up to say I'd started? How would I cope with the pain? My isolation was immense.

The contractions were coming every three minutes. I tapped gently on Nan and Harold's bedroom door and when they answered I said, "I think I've started; the pains are coming every three minutes."

Their sympathy showed as they kindly said, "You could have woken us earlier. You didn't have to spend all this time on your own."

I appreciated the kind comment but no one had told me what I should or could do when the inevitable started happening to my body so, like with everything else, I'd assumed I should go through it alone. They got dressed and drove me to the cottage hospital in Exeter, waited until I was settled in the labour ward, then left.

Now, to all intents and purposes, I was alone again. The nurses were cool in their attitude towards me; it was on my records that I wasn't married and that my baby would be adopted. I'd been admitted at five in the morning. Soon it was eight o'clock and, as I lay on the bed with the pains becoming unbearable, Dad walked in. He stood, apparently emotionally detached, at the end of the bed.

I felt so pleased to see him – I was frightened and there was no human warmth around me – but in a brusque voice he asked me how I was doing.

"OK," I replied. What else was there to say? I had gotten myself into this, it was my own fault and I deserved to be treated with contempt.

"Nan called us to say they'd brought you in. I've just called in on my way to work. I'll call again on my way back home tonight," Dad said. I watched him turn at the end of the bed and walk out of the door as I held my breath with the pain of another contraction.

The nurse gave me painkillers and throughout the day my labour continued. I was still in the same state when Dad called at five-thirty. Standing in the doorway, not even entering the room this time, he said in the same tone of voice as before, "I'll let your mum know how you're getting on," and he left.

There was no one to hold my hand or say soothing words. I pushed and pushed and felt I couldn't possibly go on any more; I was exhausted. But then I knew I couldn't just stop and give up. I had to go through with this, I had to finish what my body had started.

Aidan was born that night. Scott had served in Aden and even though my baby's father had walked away from us, this precious gift of life had been brought about by the two of us and I felt all I could pass on was his name. My beautiful, healthy boy was taken away to the nursery.

"You'll be in the hospital a week. Whilst you're here, it's better if you don't see him very much. Just change him, bath him, feed him with a bottle, then put him back in the nursery," the nurse curtly said.

"OK," I said. Alone, grieving and scarred, I just lay in bed and did what I was told; there was no one to support me. I'd done wrong, acted against the morals of society, against the teachings and upbringing of my parents. Now decisions were being made for me; I was being told what to do. Counselling, considering a person's emotions and feelings, was an unknown concept. I was left alone with my physical, emotional and mental agonies.

Dad came by the next day as I was giving Aidan his bottle. This time he sat for a while talking about general things and asking me how I was. He didn't touch me and I felt he didn't really want to hear the true answer so I just said, "I'm OK." He left. All the time he'd been sat with me, he had looked me straight in the eyes, never once looking down to see my precious babe, his grandson. Mum came by a few days later. I took her down to the nursery to see Aidan and she held him for a while, then left. There were tears in her eyes.

No one really spoke to me in the hospital. Nan and Harold visited once, as did a friend from the hairdressing salon, but there were no cards of congratulations or happy voices around my bed at visiting time. It was difficult for Mum to come again because of my grandparents staying at the house. Evidently my grandmother kept asking her, "Why haven't we had a postcard from our Marianne on her holidays?" The other mums had lots of people visiting, bringing flowers and cards, celebrating with great delight the new arrival. There was no one to celebrate with me the birth of Aidan. In the evenings only husbands could visit and I didn't have one. I tried to hide myself behind a magazine and pretend I wasn't there. I just wanted to be invisible.

Once after I returned Aidan to the nursery, I heard the radio as I walked back into the ward. Louis Armstrong was singing 'What a Wonderful World'. Tears cascaded down my face and with uncontrollable sobbing I sat alone on my bed grieving at the loss I was about to go through. This was *not* a wonderful world. As I listened to the last verse of the song, I heard, "I hear babies cry; I watch them grow; they'll learn much more than I'll ever know; and I think to myself, what a wonderful world." I was about to give up my baby. I would *not* be able to watch him grow. I could only hope that in doing what I believed to be right for him, that he would indeed grow up with better knowledge and learn of a better life than I'd known and that one day he would feel he lived in a wonderful world. This song, written by

Bob Thiele and George Weiss, was very popular and new mums in the ward were singing or humming along. My tears went unnoticed – or at least no one made any comment. I wasn't singing or humming, just crying on the outside and sobbing uncontrollably on the inside.

The social worker said it couldn't be guaranteed that they could find a couple who fitted any specific points that I might have, but they'd try. "I'd like him to go to a Christian couple please," was my quiet reply. Something in the depth of my being hoped he could be placed into the values in which I'd been raised, even though I'd chosen to rebel against them. I could only hope that because a couple were *choosing* to adopt him that they would treasure and nurture him with love.

And so it was that the social worker arrived and drove Aidan and me to the foster parents. Aidan was to stay with them for six weeks prior to him being passed to his adoptive parents. As I held him in the car the tears fell down my face like a waterfall; he was so beautiful but I would never again see his round face and chubby hands; I would never again smell the scent of his washed and talcum powdered body; I would never again feel the warmth of him cradled in my arms. I handed over the layette of clothes and then the foster mother took him out of my arms and I walked away...

My grandparents had gone back to Timsbury. I returned home but what could anyone say to me? There was nothing to be said. The papers for Aidan's adoption would have to be signed in a few months' time. I had no proper job in Exmouth and, although I'd passed my exams with good grades, there was nothing to keep me there, surrounded by so many painful memories. I needed to distance myself from the agony and anguish. Aidan was to go to his adoptive parents, people whom I hoped and believed would be able to give him so much more than I could, which was nothing. I decided to take off for London. I was damaged stock, tainted, defiled, marred. I had no more dignity or self-worth to lose. I was unlovable and a disgrace. My arms were empty, my heart broken and my mind in turmoil.

Chapter Four

Bright Lights, Big City

I thought, "London, here I come!" as Mum and Dad drove me up to my aunt's home. It had been agreed that I would stay with her at Penge in south-east London until I could find somewhere of my own to live. I sat in the car with my hair in curlers. I'd brush it out just before we arrived ensuring that I'd arrive with it looking just right... London was the place to be in the 1970s.

I was nearly eighteen years old and ready to join in the fun. A 1960s song by The Animals called 'Bright Lights Big City'[5] tells of someone enticed by the excitement of the city, ignoring the warnings of dangers ahead. It was a bit like that for me. I just wanted a new start. I'd had more experiences in the past three years than many would go through in their lifetime. I was hurting in a way I could never express. I'd sought love from two men and the results of those relationships had meant that two babies had been taken from me. Now on the pill, I would use men in the way I felt I had been used, but no longer would I be left 'holding the baby'. I was a wounded animal, desperately wanting someone to care for me yet, because I was so damaged, all I could do was lash out at anyone who got close. I had been hurt and had hurt others. I was damaged and had damaged others. I felt destroyed and had certainly destroyed another. I was messed-up, emotionally scarred, and was now going to work that out by becoming an even more rebellious teenager.

---

[5] You can read the full lyrics at www.metrolyrics.com/bright-lights-big-city-lyrics-the-animals.html

At the time I had no concept of how my parents felt about or struggled with me, their wayward daughter. I only knew their coldness and distance. Much later I came to some understanding of their great disappointment, enormous frustration, rising anger, emotional pain and abhorrent disbelief of my behaviour.

We arrived at the home of Sheila, my aunt. My hair was looking good although my body was scarred from the birth of Aidan; the midwife had commented how very bad my stretch marks were. "I've never seen such bad marks." I had not wanted to hear that my body was permanently scarred when I wouldn't even be able to keep my baby and raise him. Though invisible to the eye, my mind was even more badly scarred from having to hand him over to the foster parents and then give him up for adoption. Sheila knew about Aidan and welcomed me into her home. It was good to be accepted when I couldn't accept myself, let alone forgive myself for what I'd done. After I'd settled myself in with my aunt, uncle and three cousins, Mum and Dad left to go back to Exmouth.

I set about finding a job. With the good grades I'd obtained at college I got a job in Beckingham at a hairdressing salon by the end of the week. A couple of weeks later I saw a card in a local shop saying, "Fifth girl wanted to share large four-bedroom flat." I called round to the address on the card that night and a few days later moved in. The four other girls were great. Three of them were students and the other in work. The flat was just a five-minute walk across a park from my aunt's so I was able to still keep in touch with her and the family.

I soon grew bored with my job and decided to find work up in London. I wanted to be where the action was. Work was plentiful and by the end of the day I'd been given another job just off Tottenham Court Road in a wig boutique. Walking through the streets of London every day and travelling on the tube gave me a real buzz. I loved all the people, the noise, the hustle and the bustle. My working day was long – getting the main line train to Victoria, then tube, then a walk – but I was meeting up with new people and loved being part of the bright lights and big city. During my lunch breaks I walked down through Oxford Street and Carnaby Street; after the swinging 60s and now into the 70s this was still the place to be.

I was now in the position of totally fending for myself financially. Having been brought up with a strong Protestant work ethic had and always would stand me in good stead. One of Mum's sayings was, "Whatever you earn, you'll find that at least two thirds of your money will be gone on basic bills, before you can even think of what else you'd like to buy or save for." So from the day I'd started work earning £2.75 she took £2 for my keep and that continued to rise as my wages increased. Some may think that was harsh yet it was a lesson that I learnt from and has enabled me to manage throughout my life as I've frequently found myself in rapidly downward spiralling financial circumstances. How strange that I learnt and valued some lessons and standards but not others! As human beings we are often unfathomable, complex and unpredictable even though we are "fearfully and wonderfully made"[6].

Sheila dished up a Sunday lunch for me each week. It was great to have some proper food. My uncle was a butcher and the joints of roast beef with all the trimmings were delicious. In the week I lived on baked beans, tinned meatballs and packet 'Smash' and fried eggs. It was nice to be part of a family once a week yet have freedom to do what I wanted the rest of the time.

When I arrived at work one morning, the owner said, "Take this box down to the Post Office." (We exported a lot of wigs.)

"I'm not carrying that," I protested, "it's large, awkward and very heavy."

"Well, if you don't, you can look for another job," he replied.

"Fine, I'll do that," was my answer, and I walked out. I was bolshie and stroppy.

I wandered the streets looking for advertisements offering work and by the end of the day had been taken on at Samuel's, the jewellers, right on Piccadilly Circus. Now I could look out of the window whilst I worked and see all the action. The 'dilly' was known all over the world, with Eros at its centre being the god of love. I knew little of the meaning and actions of real true love, but at least I was now at the heartbeat of London and felt that I'd really 'arrived'.

I thought the manager of the shop was a small, insignificant-looking man, but the assistant manager, Mike, had a real way about him that attracted me. He lived in the East End and soon we were seeing a lot of one another.

---

[6] Psalm 139:14 (KJV)

I'd been out with many men since I'd arrived in London. One in particular I met at the pub I went to most nights. He was a rugby player and lived a ten-minute walk in the other direction from Sheila's.

Sheila would often pass me in the morning as I walked from his place to the station. She'd ask, "Everything OK?"

"Fine," I'd say.

"Be careful! See you Sunday!" she'd reply.

But now Mike had my attention. He'd take me to the clubs in the East End and either I'd sleep over with him or he'd come back to the flat. The other girls often had boyfriends stay over so sometimes it was bursting at the seams. I enjoyed walking around Berwick street market and Soho during my lunch breaks and meeting up with Mike in the evenings at Liverpool Street Station to do the pubs and clubs.

It was the days of purple hearts and the drugs were coming on to the streets. I fell over people in the underground who were too drugged to move. I was already drinking a fair amount each night; I wanted to feel happily numbed, to have the agonising, debilitating pain that was deep inside taken away. If I kept on partying and drinking it was as if the pain was pushed deeper down inside me; if I didn't let it come to the surface it seemed more bearable. Yet somehow, bizarrely, I knew that if I started on drugs I would never be able to stop. As I stepped over yet another body I vowed to myself that I would never smoke a joint, take a tablet or stick a needle in my arm.

Being a part of the swinging sixties with 'freedom' of sex became my habit of choice. I'd keep detached from the truth and emotions of the murder of my baby and rejection of another by finding momentary skin surface pleasure. I was locked into the perpetual decline of depravity.

In just a few weeks it was New Year's Eve. I was free to do whatever I wanted. The place to be was Trafalgar Square, in hearing distance of Big Ben striking twelve and with the revellers around the fountain. One of the girls from the flat went shopping with me for just the right clothes to wear; then we dressed ourselves up and caught the train to London. We joined with the masses passing from one pub to another throughout the evening, working our way down toward Trafalgar Square just before midnight. As the clock struck twelve we joined the crowd in singing, "Should auld acquaintance be forgot?" As some jumped in the fountain we joined in with the hugging and kissing of everyone in sight, and as we finally began walking toward Victoria Station I said, "This has been a night to remember."

We slept on the benches at Victoria along with the other revellers and the homeless. They looked such a mess, living on the streets. Why didn't they get a job, clean themselves up, get their lives sorted out? After all, I'd had a hard time and had painful memories, but now here I was working and having fun. As long as I didn't dig too deep, my life was 'sorted'! I was enjoying the hectic, colourful days and nights. Life in London was great.

Mike and I were still seeing one another. One day I waited for him to meet me as arranged at Liverpool Street Station. As I stood there, men kept coming up and asking me, "How much?" I'd glare at them, spit out a few choice words and they'd move on.

Eventually Mike pulled up in his car and I jumped in. "We're off to meet some guys in a club," he said.

As he manoeuvred through the traffic I looked at him. I really liked this guy but something in the tone of his voice rang some alarm bells.

We got to the club and Mike ordered the drinks; soon the other guys came in and joined us. The next thing I knew, Mike was showing them a load of jewellery. I stared at the rings then looked at him. His eyes warned me: "Don't open your mouth. Don't say anything." He knew I'd recognised the jewellery as new stock that had just arrived in the shop.

The deal was made and conversation continued around the table. I sat quietly listening. It was all too clear that the talk was of organised crime on a large scale that included a lot of violence. Fighting at school was one thing – I'd been on the edges of, though never actively involved in, many of the gang fights between the mods and Hells Angels – but this now was something in a completely different league and on a totally different scale. I had done things in my time that had been immoral, but nothing illegal. But what could I say to Mike? I'd heard and seen things which were not to be repeated and I didn't want my face 'rearranged', so I took a different approach; over the next few weeks I started telling him how much I was missing living by the coast.

"I used to work in a Country Club in Paignton," Mike said. "Why don't you give them a call? It's March now and the seasonal jobs start at Easter."

We parted company. In many ways I was sad to be leaving London, but I looked forward to being by the sea. I was nineteen and I'd had dozens of relationships, but none had lasted. What was wrong with me? I was irreconcilably tainted and marred.

CHAPTER FIVE

Time to Move On

I caught the train down to Exeter and went to spend a few days with Mum and Dad before moving on to Paignton. Whilst in London I'd travelled home approximately every six weeks. Arriving at Exeter station, Dad would be waiting to drive me on to Exmouth. I often used to laugh when I saw his face. I'd be wearing the latest way-out outfits, the like of which had never been seen in Devon. I was used to living life in the fast lane and being independent.

As you may recall, my mother's father was a Chelsea Pensioner now living in the Chelsea hospital in London. When he used to come for a stay in Exmouth I'd often travel back up to London with him. He had many a story to tell and had met many famous people. I liked spending time with him and he accepted my outward appearance; after all, he saw many such sights in Chelsea and along the Embankment.

I now moved on to the Devon Coast Country Club and it was as if I was now stepping into the words of the song by Tom Petty which starts with the lyrics, "It's time to move on." I had no idea what lay ahead but life *was* moving on and I needed to leave behind the bright lights and many relationships. I was still looking for something or someone to take away the pain of my past. I felt an agony buried deep that was beyond words. I so much wanted to love and be loved. I wanted to be accepted for who I was and loved with a passion that was unconditional.

I arrived at the Country Club to be shown to the staff quarters that I was to share with another girl. With inadequate heating and a toilet/shower block a short walk away it was very basic, but was to be my home for the next six months. There I was to be employed as a waitress.

I made contact with my supervisor who said, "You'll be given one clean sheet and towel a fortnight. Your meals are at set times, before the guests eat; don't be late or you go without. You'll work six days a week and your day off is on a rota. If you stay till the end of the season, you'll get a bonus." Showing me a uniform she explained, "You are to wear this uniform to serve breakfast and lunch, then you change into this other uniform to serve dinner. It is your responsibility to launder and iron your own uniforms. We expect you to be well turned out at all times and your behaviour on the site to be impeccable. Now, come with me and I'll show you the dining room." As she showed me around the dining room and kitchens she continued, "We serve two sittings at each meal. You will be responsible for thirty to forty people at each sitting. Each waitress has her own tables."

It didn't take me long to realise this was going to be a tough job. I'd enjoyed being part of a sales team in Samuel's; the working conditions and the money had been good. I'd not bothered to look for a job as a hairstylist in London because the pay was poor and I needed to pay rent, fares and have money left over to go to the pub. At one time I'd been interested in and made enquiries about working as a stylist on a liner. Dad had encouraged me, but to do that I would have needed more experience and I wouldn't be accepted until I was twenty-one years old. I had pushed away that idea. Life was for living now, not in three years' time.

Now here I was with all expenses found, eight pounds a week in my pocket plus tips. Little did I realise that on my one day off I would spend a fortune just to get away from the place. The work was physically hard. Carrying eight plates at a time on racks in my left hand and a tray with vegetable dishes in my right was very heavy. I'd fallen, from standing on a chair some years before and the heavy china plates now started aggravating my back. It wasn't until many years later that I discovered my pelvic bone had been put out of line when I had given birth to Aidan; back pain would plague my life, but painkillers got me through the summer season.

I started work at seven fifteen, having already had my own breakfast. The supervisor had been right; if you didn't go for your meals at set times, then you went without. I laid up the breakfast tables with marmalade, butter, toast, tea and coffee. The cutlery had all been laid out the night before. The guests came in at seven forty-five and sat at their tables. Some would speak and a few were friendly, but most treated you as if you weren't a person, just a body who was to serve and respond to every click of their fingers. I took the orders for cereal, porridge or fruit juice, to be followed by fried breakfast, kippers or eggs. Then it was a mad dash to the kitchen to stand in line and collect the food. Guests didn't like to be kept waiting, but they didn't seem to appreciate the mayhem in the kitchens. First sitting over, there was a mad rush to clean down the tables, brush the floor and reset the tables for the second sitting at nine fifteen. If all went well the dining room was clean and tidy by ten forty-five – just enough time to go to the toilet and walk up the hill to the staff canteen.

Lunch for the waiting staff was early, at eleven fifteen, because the first sitting guests came in at twelve o'clock for their three-course lunch, plus tea or coffee. Second sitting finished and I'd cleared away generally by three o'clock. There was now a chance for a break – time to do the laundry, wash my hair or have a sleep – before my dinner at four forty-five. The five-course dinner, plus coffee for the guests, started at five thirty. Most of the people on the first sitting had young children and it suited them to eat early. It didn't suit me that they were the ones with the children who made all the mess, grinding food into the table and floor, and then I had to get it spotlessly clean for the next sitting.

Each morning, six days per week, my alarm went off at 6am. Apart from an hour and three quarters to do my laundry or have a quick nap, the day was busy with work and passed very rapidly until I finished between eight thirty and nine o'clock in the evening. Then, exhausted, the only thing to do was go to the pub for a quick drink and collapse into bed.

"So this is what I've moved on to..." I said to myself. I felt trapped. I was working a sixty-hour week through split shifts six days a week and I wasn't even earning enough to save. My wages went on toiletries, drinks and going out on my day off.

One night I went out with Phil; he worked as a chef in the kitchens. He seemed 'OK' and over the next few weeks we'd often go to the pub together. Life was quite difficult at the Country Club and the night came when we went out with the sole intention of getting drunk. I'd been used to downing eight pints of draught Guinness a night in

London and soon drank him under the table. The seemingly inevitable happened and we ended up sleeping together.

The next morning, I woke up and said, "Now you'll have to marry me."

"Yes," he agreed, "I don't want you being pregnant and us not being married."

"It's OK," I said, "I'm on the pill."

But he still insisted, "Let's get married anyway."

It seemed as if this could be my answer. Of all the men I'd been with before, none of them had ever lasted long or wanted to marry me. Perhaps Phil actually would. I was still only nineteen but with the horrors of my past I felt I was on the shelf and nobody else would ever want to be my husband. Perhaps this was an offer I couldn't refuse, a way out of all that my life had been and become, a way into creating a happy family.

We started making plans. We arranged for our day off to coincide and I took Phil home to meet my mum and dad. They took one look at him and were clearly appalled. We'd come into the house through the side door and they wouldn't invite him in beyond the kitchen.

I explained to them that we were going to get married.

Dad said, "Hold on a minute. Come into the lounge." He left Phil sitting in the kitchen and took me through into the living room. "Stop and think about this. Don't rush into anything. Give it a year, then see how you feel."

I didn't say anything. I was used to one-way conversations with Dad and that meant I didn't pass comment. However, in my mind I reasoned, "That's a long time. He wants to marry me now. I'm frightened I'll end up on the shelf. I'm not going to let this chance slip by." As Phil and I caught the bus back to Paignton I said, "I don't want to wait. Let's get a special licence, then we can get married in three days' time."

We arranged the details. I phoned Mum and Dad and said, "We're going to be married this Saturday at the registry office. Come or not, just as you like." Clearly my attitude and respect towards my parents had not improved!

I really didn't expect them to come but, amazingly, there they were, waiting at the registry office. Phil's mother, brother and little sister were also there. His mum and brother were drunk and even as I repeated the words after the registrar, I thought, "What on earth am I doing? This isn't right!" But I didn't have the nerve to stop the ceremony. I'd gone against Mum and Dad's advice; now I would just have to get on with it. Perhaps it would all work out for the best. We all went on to a local hotel and had tea. It was a sombre although, for some, not sober affair.

Then Phil and I, having been allowed to have a few days away from the Country Club, went up to London. We stayed with Sheila, went to see 'Jesus Christ Superstar' and then returned to work. We were given a double room to live in and our working day continued much the same as before.

The work was hard and fairly joyless. The guests had entertainment every evening but if we joined in we had to be on our best behaviour so we tended to frequent the local pub, drinking 'scrumpy' cider and playing bar billiards. Michael, Phil's friend, hadn't come to the wedding but he spent a lot of time with us. He was older than Phil and also worked in the kitchen. Often in the evenings the two of them would go out and I'd sit in the chalet on my own. I was anxious to leave Paignton, but Phil said we should wait until the end of the season and get our bonuses. It made sense; at least then we'd have a little money to use as a deposit when we rented a flat somewhere. The days went by slowly but eventually at the end of the summer we collected our bonuses.

I said a cheerful goodbye to the Devon Coast Country Club and stood on the roadside with my husband to hitch a lift. We travelled in the direction of Gloucester, Phil's hometown, and found a flat in Cheltenham. "Now we can start being a proper couple," I thought.

CHAPTER SIX

Married Life

Phil soon got a job as chef in a steak house and I found work in a delicatessen. We also found a flat that we could afford to rent. Although it was small, the rooms had very high ceilings. The coal fire gave out little heat and most of the time we couldn't even afford the coal.

Phil's brother and older sister were frequent visitors. They always seemed to be drunk and then I realised they were bringing drugs into the flat. I said to Phil, "This has got to stop." He'd row with them but they took little notice. Although Phil wasn't taking drugs, he and they always seemed to be together and I was left out, on my own. His sister was separated from her husband; she had two young children whom she either left in the car outside the flat or back at their home on their own.

This was not the type of family set-up that I was familiar with. Although I was all too well aware that I had rebelled against discipline, conformity and all things respectable, I now valued all that those things stood for. Mum kept a tidy home and as a homemaker she was always there, caring, cooking and cleaning. Dad was a hard-working provider. I never heard them rowing or shouting at one another. They had a stable, loving marriage.

Phil and I used to visit his mother who lived just outside of Gloucester. I soon realised that if we delayed our visit till the afternoon, she would be drunk. She started drinking late in the morning and continued throughout the day and evening, at which time she would collapse in a drunken stupor. His younger sister would be left to her own devices throughout the day. She often wouldn't get to school or be given regular meals. She constantly wet herself and the house stank of urine and alcohol.

My life was really going from bad to worse. I was aware I was the female version of the Prodigal Son but I just didn't know how to turn around my life, so all I could do was to try and survive each day.

I started planning for our first Christmas together. The weather was bitterly cold but I bought some coal, a small turkey and put up a few decorations. Phil was home for Christmas day. His family arrived and the day turned into a nightmare: rows, fights and drunkenness. Then he told me he had to work on Boxing Day.

I woke up to find that the flat was freezing cold and in a mess from the previous day's events. We'd used all the coal the day before and all the food had gone. I sat in the lounge feeling desperate. I had a few coins so went down to the phone box and phoned Mum and Dad. Mum answered the phone but I couldn't speak; I just cried bitterly down the line. In no time my money was running out, so quickly Mum got me to tell her the number; then the line went dead. I stood in the phone box feeling alone and miserable; the sobbing had stopped, but my head and heart ached. Mum rang back. "We're on our way up," she said. "We'll see you in a few hours." They arrived with wood for the fire, food for lunch and tea, and faces that expressed concern for me. It was good to see them, but when they left, the loneliness returned tenfold. Phil arrived home after I'd cried myself to sleep.

I did not think married life would turn out like this. Phil's friend Michael started visiting at weekends and then Phil said, "I've heard of a good job going in Exeter. Let's get away from all this and move down there. There's a three-bedroom flat with the job, so we won't have to worry about finding somewhere to live."

We had little to pack; the flat in Cheltenham was furnished, so we just collected together our personal bits and clothes. Phil's sister Jacky insisted on driving us down to Exeter.

"I'd rather catch the train," I said to Phil, but he insisted, "It'll be a lot easier in the car."

The flat was lovely, in the centre of Exeter, and although we had to share the entrance with the head chef, who lived on the ground floor, once up in our own flat we were self-contained. Jacky helped us unload, had a coffee and then said, "Right, I'll be off. At least I know where you are now. It'll be nice to come down and stay for a few days when I get the chance." I thanked her for the lift but hoped she wouldn't visit. I thought if we could have some distance from Phil's family then maybe we could have a reasonable marriage.

Phil settled into his job and I picked up some shop work in the city. Michael was still visiting regularly, but generally life was beginning to level off a little.

Phil and I started talking about having a baby. I came off the pill and waited to get pregnant. Months went by and I started to worry that I hadn't conceived; I'd always become pregnant so easily before. I even went to the doctor. I felt quite stupid when it became obvious that since Phil and I were having sex so infrequently it was lowering my chances of getting pregnant. We had never had an active sex life. We started working at it, but there was little passion and even less love in these sessions to try and produce a baby. Eventually my pregnancy was confirmed.

For long periods of time I was confined to bed. Due to what I now know to be the problem with my displaced pelvis, I was in excruciating pain, unable to walk and the doctors feared I could become permanently paralysed in my legs if I were to put any additional strain on them by walking about. For weeks at a time I would lie in bed in addition to being sick the whole nine months.

Finally, the day arrived, the pressure was taken off of my pelvis and I held Adrian in my arms. He was small and fair, and I adored him.

Phil was like a child with a new toy – initially ecstatic but then quickly bored. Adrian soon started picking up on the tensions. Phil constantly berated me, told me in a menacing manner that I was no good, that no one else would ever look twice at me. He'd shout at me that I was just a blob of flesh, a nobody. I moved into the bedroom that had been made a nursery for Adrian. I felt tired, useless and lonely. Phil made it clear that he wanted nothing to do with me.

Still under the doctor for my postnatal check-ups, he picked up on the problems and diagnosed that I was suffering from depression. He suggested, "Why don't you get out of the house for a few hours each day, perhaps get yourself a little job and earn some pin money?" So I found a cleaning job from eight until ten in the morning, five days a week. If I gave Adrian his early bottle, then Phil could give him breakfast, wash and change him before bringing him up to meet me on his way into work. He didn't start work until half past ten and had to walk past the offices I was cleaning. I could then take Adrian around the shops, buy the bits we needed and be back home ready to do Adrian's lunch. I was to be paid three pounds a week, which I thought I could spend on buying the things needed for Adrian and myself. The money Phil gave me for housekeeping was barely enough to feed us and he wouldn't give me any extra for Adrian's clothes or enough to buy myself a pair of tights, even though he thought nothing of putting four pounds a week into the slot machines at work. I scrimped a few pennies each week to go to the jumble sales, but this money from my cleaning job would help a lot.

The first few days went well. I actually quite enjoyed going off early in the morning and having a few hours to myself albeit to wash floors and polish desks. Phil would bring Adrian up, I'd push the pram around the shops and we'd continue with our day. Then things started changing. After a few weeks Phil reduced my housekeeping by three pounds a week, the equivalent amount to my wages. When I complained, he hit me – never on the face, always on the body.

No one could see the abuse and I was too ashamed to tell anyone. After all, he'd made it perfectly clear that I was just a lump of useless flesh. He'd pick me up and literally throw me across the floor, then say, "You stupid woman! What are you doing over there?"

If I dared to reply, "You threw me here," he'd do it again.

What could I do? Nothing.

Life was becoming unbearable. Pushing Adrian in his pram I walked to the end of the road. I put the brake on, went into the telephone box and dialled.

"Hello?" I heard Mum's voice answer.

I started describing to Mum what was happening, about how, on a regular basis, Phil was treating me.

She said, "You've made your bed; now you must lie in it." In the rejection I understood that she could not cope with any more of my problems.

As the weeks went on things got worse. When Phil brought Adrian up to meet me on his way to work, it was obvious that Phil had not changed him out of his nightclothes or even his night-time nappy. Adrian was clearly very uncomfortable and hungry; Phil hadn't given him any breakfast. This continued for a few days and then I knew the time had come for me to give up the job. I couldn't let Phil mistreat Adrian like this. I'd stay at home with him and do all I could to put as much distance between his father and me as possible. I found myself in a totally helpless state, but this was no longer just about me; Adrian was my responsibility and I needed to provide for his protection. The glimmer of hope that I'd had to establish a happy, respectful and loving home was being snatched from my grasp – but above all I had to do what was right for Adrian.

If only I could leave Phil... but where could I go? I knew from years before that there was no way I could look after a baby and earn the money needed to provide for both of us. My low self-esteem had now bottomed out in the abyss. Phil told me so consistently that I was of no use that I believed it to be true. I walked around as if I was a zombie, a useless lump of lard. I looked a mess but I didn't care.

One time, as I came down the stairs, I saw the bottle of sherry on the lounge table. Not one drink or two, but maybe three or four would separate me from the pain, rejection and desperateness of my life. Thankfully something held me back and stopped me; somehow I knew that if I took a drink that morning I would never stop. Comfort in a bottle was not going to help me.

I carried on caring for Adrian as best I could. Since I'd left my job, Phil had given me back the three pounds a week in the housekeeping money. We'd go to the park and sometimes I'd catch the bus and go over and visit Mum for the day in Exmouth. Sometimes Mum and Dad would come and visit, but when they left I'd feel lonelier than ever. We frequently had visits by his brother, sister and mother. They were always drunk, fighting and causing trouble. His father visited separately, being divorced, and arrived on the door with a very small suitcase and a very large crate of beer. I tried to keep Adrian protected from these outbursts and sat for hours with him in the bedroom whenever there was trouble.

Even more frequent were the visits by Michael. I'd been feeling unwell and so as not to disturb Adrian, who was always a light sleeper, I was sleeping in the third bedroom. When Michael arrived I said I'd move back into Adrian's room so that he could have the other bedroom.

"No, that's OK," Michael said. "Don't worry, Marianne. I'll sleep in with Phil. I don't mind."

The next morning, I made tea and took up mugs for Phil and Michael. I knocked on the door, heard whispering and thought, "They're awake." Then I turned the handle to open the door – but it was locked...

For a moment I was stunned. I paused, then tried again. I couldn't enter. I didn't think my life could get any worse.

One day I was sat on the floor in the lounge playing with Adrian when Phil came in from work. He ignored us and went to put the television on. Adrian was nine months old and crawled across the room after a toy. As he came between Phil and the television, Phil yelled, "GET THAT **** CHILD OUT OF THE WAY!" and made a move towards him.

I reached Adrian first, afraid that Phil might hurt him, and I scooped him up in my arms and took him to the bedroom. I'd already found a nasty burn on his back; it was clearly made by a cigarette and although I wanted to think it must have been an accident, the clear round burn made me doubtful. But how could a father hurt his own son?

Life became more unbearable as I was constantly on edge looking out for Adrian's welfare and safety as well as my own. The doctor prescribed medication with the aim of easing my depression but pills would not change the desperate state Adrian and I were living in. Life, or rather existence, had become so horrendous that I would sit on my bed rocking backwards and forwards, banging my head against the wall for hour upon hour. Applying physical pain helped me to blot out the emotional and mental agony of my life. This went on not for days, not for weeks, but for months; when I'd done the chores and settled Adrian I would simply go to my room, and rock and bang my head repeatedly... I had no self-worth and was unable to communicate beyond mono syllables.

Chapter Seven

Love at Last

I spent hours walking around Exeter pushing Adrian in his pushchair. Then, as I walked out of a supermarket, I accidentally let the door slam behind me.

I turned around to apologise to the person whom I was vaguely aware of behind me. "Sorry," I said, not bothering to look up.

"That's OK. I can see you've got your hands full with the baby and your shopping."

I looked up. It was Gary, a person whom Phil worked with. I'd seen him a couple of times before when he'd been walking back with Phil after work and then, I assumed, continued on his way home.

I lowered my eyes to the floor again. Why should this young guy be speaking to me and showing even the slightest sympathy? I was a nobody and therefore not worth speaking to.

"Would you like to come for a coffee?" Gary asked.

"I can't," I said. "I've got Adrian and it's difficult with the pushchair."

"We'll manage," he said. "It looks like you could do with a sit down and a drink."

As we walked into the café I started to panic; there was no room for the pushchair. "You hold Adrian and I'll collapse the pushchair," Gary said simply. I felt awkward as he talked to me of ordinary things and played with Adrian across the table. How could someone be so nice to me? I wasn't worth human dialogue.

Over the next few weeks I seemed to keep bumping into Gary when I was walking through the high street. He always stopped and chatted; I liked his easy manner and his pleasant free-flowing conversation. The flat was a place of tension and stress. Browsing around the shops I could lose myself and feel a little less lonely. Adrian was a happy child during the day but as soon as I put him in his cot for the night he would scream. Nothing I did seemed to placate him. I got more and more stressed and he screamed louder and louder. But during the daytime he was calm and content. He loved the baby swings and I sat for ages with him on the roundabout.

One day we walked back from the park and I opened the door, picked Adrian up out of the pushchair and carried him up the stairs. As I went into the flat I heard voices. I knew Phil would be in from work. "I do hope one of his family aren't here," I thought. I took Adrian through into the lounge and saw Gary sitting talking with Phil. He stayed for tea and then watched a film with Phil as I took Adrian upstairs and changed him for bed.

As soon as I put Adrian in the cot he started crying. I tried to settle him but he wouldn't stop. I went down to make a pot of tea, then I took it into the lounge and poured out three mugs. Phil carried on watching the film.

"I'm just going up to see if I can settle Adrian," I said to no one in particular.

"Can I go?" asked Gary.

"He always cries like this at night. It's always difficult to settle him down," I replied.

"You sit down, drink your tea. I'll go up to him," Gary said as he went up the stairs. Ten minutes later he came down. Adrian was quiet.

"What did you do?" I asked as he sat down.

"Just played with him," Gary answered.

Much as I appreciated Gary settling Adrian, it left me with a sense of increased inadequacy. Here was someone who was almost a stranger who could calm Adrian when I couldn't. I went upstairs. Adrian was sleeping peacefully.

Gary's visits became more frequent. He often arrived at Adrian's teatime and would put him to bed. Every time, Adrian settled happily. I began to look forward to his arrival. Phil would be sat in front of the television and seemed to have no concerns that another man was putting his son to bed. I enjoyed Gary's visits; he talked to me, was attentive, caring and I found myself becoming more and more attracted to him. The words of The Beatles' song rang through my mind as I thought, "Surely all I need in my life is love, love; love is all I need."

One evening, the three of us sat in the lounge. Adrian had already gone to bed and Phil was intently watching a film on television. Gary said, "I thought I'd go down to the club this evening; would you mind if I took Marianne for a night out, Phil?"

I sat in the chair stunned.

"No, I don't care. Take her if you want," Phil replied.

I started to object, thinking, "I can't go out," yet feeling it would be so nice to go and dance and have a few hours away from the house. I hadn't been out for an evening since Adrian had been born.

"That's settled then," said Gary. "Go and get changed and we'll go out for a few hours."

I wondered about leaving Adrian, but he was sleeping peacefully and would not be likely to wake until the morning. "OK," I assented, "just for a little while."

I changed quickly, and Gary and I walked into the town. We had a lovely evening; I enjoyed dancing with him and being out amongst young people again.

A few days later Phil came in from work and said, "I've told Gary he can move into the spare bedroom. You generally sleep with Adrian so it won't make any difference to you. He's just gone to collect his things from his parents' house; he'll be here in half an hour or so." My heart skipped a beat. I enjoyed this guy's company and he was so good with Adrian, it would be a pleasure to have him living in the flat.

Gary had left the restaurant where he'd worked with Phil and now had a daytime job in the town. In the early evening we played with Adrian together, then he would take him upstairs to bed while I went into the kitchen and prepared something for us to eat. When we finished our meal Gary always thanked me and said how much he'd enjoyed it. I liked this feeling – of being appreciated and being shown attention. Phil rarely hit me now, but he did not demonstrate any care for Adrian or me either. Gary and I sat together in the evenings whilst Phil was at work; we talked, played cards or listened to music. Often tired from looking after Adrian all day and the effects of the medication which the doctor was still prescribing, I'd go to bed early.

At night my nightmares became vivid. I was deeply depressed and the pills were doing little to numb my agony. Curled into the foetal position I'd rock and bang my head against the wall. My marriage was a sham; Michael still visited every weekend. I felt trapped like a wounded animal; there was nowhere to go and even if there was I had no energy. Physically, emotionally and mentally I was drained to the point of desperation. How much more could I take? I knew I had to keep going for Adrian, but I had little left to give. Once, as I was sobbing inwardly – my breathing rapid and irregular, feeling that I was in the middle of a deep, dark vacuum – Gary gently touched my shoulder. Closed down inside of myself I was unaware that he'd come into the room. Embarrassed, I curled up even more tightly into the foetal position, but he put his arms around me, held me gently and rocked me comfortingly. My tears overflowed; so much pain released. After a while I heard his reassuring voice: "It's OK. You'll be OK."

Gary always seemed to be there at the times I needed him, just as he was always there for Adrian. More and more I wanted to be closer to him. One evening we were sitting watching television and I felt his arm loosely come around my shoulder. I looked at him and said, "I can't do this. It's wrong. I'm a married woman." My whole being felt as though it was on a rack, being torn between keeping the vows I had made and seeking the love I felt for this man, doing wrong morally but soothing the pain of my past.

As the days passed, it began to feel increasingly as though Gary and I were Adrian's parents, with Phil as a lodger who had no care for anything going on around him. Eventually Gary and I decided to pack up a few bits, buy a car with the little money we had between us and take Adrian up to London to start a life as a family on our own. When Phil left for work in the morning, Gary and I went to the bank and pooled our meagre savings.

"I'll take this and find the best car I can for the money. I'll be back as soon as I can, probably just after Phil's gone to work for the evening shift. If you and Adrian are ready then, we'll leave straight away," Gary said as he smiled at me and walked away.

I spent the rest of the day with a friend who lived just a few doors away. I didn't want to be in the flat when Phil came back for the few hours' break between his lunchtime and evening shifts. As soon as I was aware he'd left for work, I took Adrian into the flat and quickly packed his clothes, dismantled the cot and collected together his toys. I put my clothes into a case and carefully wrapped my few glass ornaments, including my deer with the blue ears. I placed them carefully into a box.

I was ready. Nothing else in the flat held any importance to me. The home I'd tried to create was worth nothing when there was not only no love between Phil and me, but also staying in this flat put both Adrian and me at risk of more violence.

I waited. Adrian was asleep in my arms.

Still I waited. *Where could Gary be?*

I'd expected him to be driving up the road in the car he'd bought at about six o'clock. It was now seven.

I stood staring out of the window waiting for the headlights of a car. Each minute seemed like an eternity as I thought back to the night I'd waited for Scott. My heart cried out, "Please, Gary, drive up the road. Don't leave me in this deep, dark vacuum." Over the months I'd come to love Gary in a way I'd never loved anyone before. I loved to cook for him and iron his shirts. We'd laugh together and talk endlessly about so many different subjects. He clearly loved Adrian and we'd spent hours playing with him and encouraging him to take his first steps.

Eight o'clock and still no car had pulled up outside the flat. I began to feel sick inside. *Not again!*

Just after nine, I saw the beam of headlights as they came around the corner of the road and an estate car pulled up outside of the flat. Gary got out. I rushed downstairs and opened the door to let him in. "Sorry I've been so long," he apologized. "I had to go to Plymouth to pick up the car."

We loaded the vehicle; just two suitcases, a box, the pushchair and the cot. Then I sat in the back with Adrian in my arms as Gary drove towards London.

We arrived just after midnight and booked into a cheap, fairly seedy hotel. We had little money and knew we would have to find something more appropriate in the morning. Adrian slept peacefully and Gary and I lay wondering what the next day would bring. Next morning, we were up early and started walking the streets. It was clear we couldn't afford to stay in the hotel for more than a few nights. By now Phil would have realised that Adrian and I had left and would probably have phoned Mum and Dad. I knew they would be worried but wanted to sort myself out before I contacted them.

For a few days we wandered around the city. It was comforting to be with Gary but very different to when I'd lived in London before. Back then I'd been independent, with a job and money in my pocket, and was able to go out in the evenings. Now I had Adrian and no money, but Gary was with me and I felt happy and secure.

"I think we ought to go and see Sheila, my aunt," I said to Gary. "She may have some suggestions as to where we can find somewhere to live. Outside of the city it will be less expensive."

We drove over to Penge and knocked on her door. Sheila opened the door, smiled and said, "Come in! I've been expecting you. Your mum and dad called and thought you might be making your way to London." Just like before, she welcomed me in. As we sat drinking tea, she played with Adrian and talked easily with Gary. They'd not met before but got on well together despite the circumstances in which we'd arrived.

I filled her in concerning the situation with Phil and explained how Gary and I now came to be calling on her. "I know we've jumped into this with apparently little thought," I said, "but we've just called in to let you know we're OK and see if you have any suggestions about where we could rent a flat."

She got out the local paper and we looked through the accommodation section, but everywhere was so expensive. Then I saw an advert for a live-in housekeeper-cum-childminder, single mother accepted. Gary and I talked it over and decided it was worth phoning; then, when I went to see the person, I could ask if Gary could live there as well and find independent work.

I made the phone call and we drove out to Cheam. We drew up outside of a nice modern house and were met on the door by the man I'd spoken to on the phone. He said he was divorced, in full time work and had custody of his nine-year-old son. He accepted our proposal and we moved in. The work I had to do in the house was simple enough: get breakfast for the young boy and be there when he came home from school. The man I was working for only gave us board and lodge, so Gary took off early next morning to look for a job.

Within weeks we were catapulted from one disaster to another. Late one afternoon Gary walked into the house, his face ashen. "The car's been stolen," he said.

I sat down heavily in the chair. "What happened?"

"I parked it up while I was walking around the streets looking for work and when I came back it had gone."

"Have you told the police?" I asked.

"No," he said. "There's no insurance. I can't afford to go to the police; they could prosecute me."

I knew he'd been in trouble with the law in the past so didn't press the issue. "Well, we'll just have to manage although it's going to be more difficult for you to find work."

In between looking for work Gary did several odd jobs around the garden and house, and in the evenings we spent most of our time in the bedroom we shared with Adrian. The man whose house we were in wasn't a particularly pleasant person and it was more comfortable to stay out of his way. But we were grateful that we had a roof over our heads and whilst Gary continued to look for work he was able to claim unemployment benefit.

One night the man came in from work and out of the blue said, "Gary, I don't want you here anymore. Leave now."

"Why? What's the problem? You can't just throw me out for no reason."

"Yes, I can. It's my house and I've decided I don't want you here. Get out now."

We had no contract, no signed agreement and there was obviously no point in arguing. Gary left, but not before we'd had a chance to agree that later that night he'd come to the bedroom window – fortunately, we were in a ground floor flat – and I'd let him in so that he could sleep overnight.

Each night for the rest of the week Gary continued climbing in through the window. During the day we'd carry on as before since there was no one else in the house and in the evenings he'd have to walk the streets until the man had gone to bed.

One night I prepared the evening meal, put mine and Adrian's on a tray, and walked out of the kitchen towards our bedroom. "Where are you going?" the man said. "Stay here and eat with me. I'd like to get to know you better."

"I want to give Adrian his tea and put him to bed," I said, and walked out.

An hour or so later I was sat on the bed watching Adrian sleep when the door opened. The man walked in and came and sat beside me. "Why don't we spend the night together?" he proposed.

"Get out! Get out!" I hissed back at him.

Thankfully he left and I sat sobbing on the bed waiting for Gary to tap at the window.

As soon as he climbed through the window he could see I was upset and asked me what was wrong. In a whispered voice, so as not to let the man know he was in the room, I told him what had happened. I had to stop him from going into the next room to sort the man out there and then.

"That won't help," I said. "If you do that, none of us will have anywhere to sleep."

"Then I'll hitch a ride down to Exeter, borrow some money from my father and come back up and collect you and Adrian, and we'll return to Exeter. You can't stay here any longer."

Gary left early in the morning and I stayed out of the man's way as much as possible and waited for him to return. When he did, we loaded our few pieces into a taxi, then caught the train for Exeter. We talked on the journey back and decided that we would have to go back to the flat I'd shared with Phil and see if he would let Adrian and me stay there until something else could be arranged. I still had a key for the flat and we let ourselves in whilst Phil was at work, and put Adrian to bed. I dreaded Phil's return but Gary waited with me and said he'd speak with him when he got in.

Phil arrived home from work and, when he saw us, was first surprised and then angry. Gary and I had already found a hatchet under his bed and removed it, so at least we weren't going to be the victims of a bloody attack. Eventually Phil calmed down and said Adrian and I could stay for a few days. I knew I was expecting a lot after I'd walked out on him. He'd come up to London looking for us but accepted that our marriage was over.

We talked about a divorce. Phil said, "I want to have access to Adrian." I agreed, although it seemed strange when he'd shown such little interest in Adrian when we'd lived together. Anything was OK as long as the divorce went through smoothly.

It wasn't long before the atmosphere in the flat became unbearable. I had no money for food and went to Social Security to tell them the position I was in.

"Asda is just up the road," the woman behind the counter informed me.

"I've told you, I don't have any money. What do you want me to do, steal?" I said.

She looked at me blankly. "We can't give you any money while you are living with your husband. It's up to you."

I walked out of the office and went to Social Services. They gave me a list of phone numbers for Bed and Breakfasts that might take Adrian and me, and also the address of a hostel.

Adrian sat fretfully in his pushchair as we walked to the hostel. It was a clean, austere building; I was shown in to a large room with perhaps two dozen high, metal-framed former hospital beds. The woman showing me around said, "You and Adrian will have to share a bed. At the moment we are fairly quiet but I must tell you that if someone comes in who's drunk or under the influence of drugs they will also share this room with you."

I thanked her but as I walked out thought, "I can't have Adrian staying in a place like that." He was nearly twelve months old now and aware of his environment.

Desperation was now setting in. I didn't even have enough money to make phone calls to enquire about the Bed and Breakfast places the Social Services had given me, so I waited to meet up with Gary as we'd arranged. He'd gone back to stay with his parents and although we were facing a lot of practical problems, our relationship was strong. His love for Adrian was clearly evident and he was doing everything possible to try and find us somewhere to live.

We met in Exeter high street and I told him about my visit to Social Security, Social Services and the hostel. "It won't come to that," he assured me. "Adrian is not going to go into care. There are problems with my benefits, they haven't transferred the papers from London to the Exeter office, but Dad's given me some money. We'll go and get something to eat, then we'll ring those numbers you've been given."

I sat in the café looking around at the other people. Everyone seemed to have not a care in the world and here were we with nowhere to live, and yet we were a family. I loved Gary so much and just wanted us to find a place where the three of us could be together. We left the café and walked down to the phone box.

"Yes, we have a room for you and the baby. You must be in by ten o'clock and there are no visitors allowed in the house after that time. You can use the kitchen to make drinks and a snack meal and do your laundry. There's only one single bed in the room so you'll have to share that with the baby," the woman said. I took the room; there was nowhere else. Social Security would pay for the rent and give me some money for food so at least Adrian and I would have somewhere safe to sleep and be able to eat.

Gary spent the days looking for work, but there was little about. The days of being able to walk out of one job in the morning and have another by the afternoon, as I had done when I first went to London, were over. In the evenings Gary would come down and sit with me until ten o'clock, then go back to his parents. A couple of times Phil came to see Adrian, but the woman wasn't happy about me having two men in the room. I explained the position to her but she still said, "I want no more of it or you'll have to leave."

We found a nice, small holiday flat that was now available out of season. We made all the enquiries. It was perfect, but the rent was more than Social Security would pay. By now I'd met Gary's parents several times and although it was initially awkward, they had been kind to Adrian and me. My relationship with my mum and dad was even more strained though. After all that had happened in my teenage years, I, their daughter, had now walked out on her husband and gone off with another man. They clearly despaired and had apparently given up hope of me ever sorting out my life.

Gary's father offered to help with the rent on condition that Gary stayed living at home. We really wanted to be in a place together, but his dad was being very generous and supportive so we accepted very gratefully.

I now started seeing the solicitor about divorcing Phil. The paperwork seemed endless. There were problems over him paying maintenance for Adrian and his access rights. We always seemed to be arguing. He'd say he wanted to see Adrian and then wouldn't turn up. When he did take him out Adrian always seemed to return with an injury. Eventually the divorce went through, and due to the concerns about the injuries Adrian had received whilst on access with his father,

Phil was only granted conditional access and we were given a social worker to monitor the arrangements.

Now Gary and I could plan our wedding. We found another flat. It needed a lot of work doing to it but Gary happily set about painting, decorating and putting up partitions. Mum was now visiting regularly; she obviously didn't approve of Gary and I living together, but she got on well with him and it was good to have her visit us.

One afternoon she and I were sat down playing with Adrian, who was now nearly two years old and a delightful toddler. As we were going through some old photos Adrian exclaimed, "There's a picture of Nanny," and then added, "Who's that man next to her?"

I explained it was his grandad.

"I don't know him," Adrian answered simply.

It was true. It had been so long since he'd seen him. When Mum came to visit, Dad always dropped her off at the top of the road on his way to work. At the end of the day she'd then meet him there, at the appointed time, for him to drive her back to Exmouth. Dad was so disappointed in me and now his disapproval of me "living in sin" had created an ever-widening chasm.

"This can't go on," I said to Gary that night. "I'm going to write to Dad and tell him what Adrian said and that if he doesn't come and visit now then he'll never see Adrian or me again." I put the letter in the post the next morning.

The following afternoon Dad and Mum pulled up outside the flat. Gary and I welcomed them in. It would obviously take a bit of time, but at least we were meeting up again and were able to start bridging the chasm as we tried to rebuild our relationship.

Gary and I had a simple, small wedding at the local church. I chose my dress carefully. I didn't want anything too tight; I was three months pregnant. Gary and I were ecstatic. Although Gary treated Adrian as his own son and clearly adored him, this new child would be *our* baby. I felt unbelievably happy as Dad drove me to the church and Gary and I made our vows. We had a small reception back at the flat, before Mum and Dad took Adrian for a few days' holiday with them whilst Gary and I went to London for our honeymoon.

We sat on the train dazed from the day's emotions. We'd both been through so much. In the past Gary had been in trouble with the police. Several times he'd been to court and his father had paid fines, and once he'd served a sentence in Borstal. But all that was behind him now. The pain of my past failed relationships dimmed into the memory, though the shame, guilt, regret, horror and pain of the loss of both my aborted and adopted baby were buried deep inside. Gary and I were in love and Adrian would soon have a brother or sister. We were a family that may have had a traumatic past but now could look forward to a fantastic future.

Chapter Eight

It's You I Want, Not Money

Gary and Adrian came with me to the antenatal check-ups. They'd listen as the doctor held the instrument for them to hear the baby's heartbeat and feel the kicks and movement of the life inside me. When we got home Gary washed out a yogurt container and tried using it as an alternative instrument to hear the baby's heartbeat; he and Adrian would place it on my tummy and listen intently, then Adrian would chase Claude our cat around the room to try and listen to his tummy and see if he was going to have a baby! Claude was a lovely pet and had settled in well to the new house we had been given by the local authority. It was a maisonette on two floors and although it meant climbing a flight of steps to the front door, as it was above a small ground floor flat, it was a lovely home for us. We were now in a different part of Exeter, over the river and alongside the canal in Exwick. It was nice to walk with Adrian, now three, along the canal to his playschool. He enjoyed being with the other children and now had a new friend at home. Claude had lovely markings and soon grew into a large, loveable cat.

Gary was working and our life was becoming more comfortable. I slept for several hours during the afternoons in the later part of my pregnancy but always got up in time to get a meal ready for Gary when he came in from work. Our marriage and family life was so different to that which I'd had with Phil. I eagerly waited for Gary to come in, always pleased to see him and knowing that we would enjoy the evening together.

One day I heard the van pull up outside the maisonette and went down the steps to greet Gary. He handed me some money and said, "Buy something for Adrian, the baby and yourself."

I looked down at the notes he'd put in my hand. "This is a lot of money," I said. "Where did you get this? It's far more than your normal wages."

He looked into my eyes and smiled. "I've been given a bonus. Honestly, on the baby's life, it's OK."

I went to the sales the next day and bought some clothes for all of us and some items for our new baby. Gary was working hard, travelling all over Devon and Cornwall selling dairy produce to small shops. I was pleased his employers valued his work and had given him some extra money.

I was ten days overdue from the expected date of arrival for our baby, and Gary and Adrian came with me to the hospital. The medical staff decided to induce the labour and Gary made arrangements for someone to have Adrian, then came back to stay with me in the hospital. He sat in a chair beside the bed but my labour was not advancing, so he popped out to the local Chinese takeaway and brought us in some supper. Eventually he fell asleep beside me. No sooner had I heard his rhythmic breathing than the pains started. I woke him up and he immediately went to inform the nurse.

Gary held my hand, helped me with my breathing and panting, and several hours later we proudly looked down at Carl, our beautiful son, who lay sleeping in my arms. Gary was almost speechless at the wonder of the arrival of our baby. Five days later he drove me back home; we were now four, and with Claude, our pet cat, we had a perfect family.

Just six weeks later Gary came in and told me, "I've just come back from the police station. They arrested me for fraud. I have to go to court!"

"What? Why?" I said, and sat devastated in disbelief as he told me the details.

"I wanted to get some extra money for you and the children," he explained.

I looked at him, astonished at what he was saying. My heart sank as I said, 'But the money's not important; all I want is to be with you and the children. We can always make do, however little money we have." I wanted to scream the lyrics of 'Can't Buy Me Love'[7] by The Beatles at him.

Typically, he replied, "Don't worry, it'll be OK."

But I *was* worried. I'd never been involved with the police and courts. What would happen?

Having arranged for my neighbour to have Carl and take Adrian to playschool, I went to the hearing with Gary and sat stunned in the courts as I heard the judge say he was to be sentenced to three years in prison. I watched as a prison officer either side of him led him down to the police cells. I couldn't move; he'd told me not to worry but what was going to happen now?

Gary's probation officer came up to me, introduced himself and said, "You can see Gary for just a few minutes in the cell before he's taken to prison." He put his arm around me and led me down to the cells.

"I'm going to appeal," Gary said. "Don't cry. I love you. Tell Adrian I love him and give Carl a cuddle for me." I was being ushered away; unbelief that Gary was not coming home with me numbed my senses. What was I going to say to Adrian? He'd said goodbye to Gary that morning before being taken to playschool and Gary had replied, "See you tonight," as he'd given him a hug and kiss goodbye. I was completely naïve when it came to crime and punishment. I had no experience of criminal courts or sentencing. The stigma of being married to a criminal would exacerbate the practical realities. The shock caused me to reel from the blight of yet another very obvious shame.

I sat down with Adrian and tried to explain to him that his daddy wouldn't be coming home for a while, but I was so distraught I knew my words were only adding to Adrian's distress.

His nightmares went on night after night. "When's Daddy coming home?" he'd sob.

"I don't know, darling," I said as I cuddled him close.

Life over the following weeks was a surviving hell. Still in a very obvious post-birth time, I was now also constantly sick to my stomach, highly stressed and sleep-deprived. I struggled with the systems of Social

---

[7] You can read the full lyrics at www.metrolyrics.com/cant-buy-me-love-lyrics-beatles.html

Security, waiting for payments, frequently going without food myself to simply provide the absolutely essential basics for the children.

Six weeks later I sat in the crown court waiting for Gary to be brought up from the cells. I had my best coat on and my gloves stuck to my hands as I grew increasingly anxious. I was to be asked to take the stand at his appeal; the barrister thought my circumstances might get his sentence reduced. Gary came up the stairs and stood in the dock. I couldn't look at him, I was so nervous.

The judge was given a letter from Gary's new employers. Just a few weeks before being sent to prison he'd started work with a company selling a stylus for hi-fi equipment. They'd provided him with a company car, good salary, plus commission. I'd phoned them to explain what had happened and although they came and took the stock and car away, the director said, "I'll write to the courts and say that Gary will be given his job back if he's released." These employers were being far more than fair; would the courts be the same? The judge read the letter, then I was asked to take the stand.

I stood shaking as I was handed the bible to swear the oath. "Please remove your gloves, then say the words on the card." My heart was in my mouth and my hands were sweating as slowly I managed to peel off my gloves and then start reading. "Speak up, please," the same voice said. My voice quavered as I answered the questions and told the judge how Adrian was having nightmares and Carl was just six weeks old. "Thank you. You may stand down," the voice said again.

I sat in the court still unable to look at Gary. I was so tense I knew that if I looked at him I'd be liable to start crying hysterically. Sheer nerves and panic engulfed me.

After waiting for the judge to come back in, the voice eventually said, "Please stand for his honour." Everyone stood. After we were told to sit, Gary continued to stand, as the judge addressed him. "The crime you have committed deserves the custodial sentence you have been given, but your wife is suffering more than you are, as are your children. Because of them you will be released from custody and given three hundred hours' community service instead."

I walked out of the court and waited for Gary to be released from the cells. As he walked towards me I longed to run towards him, hug and kiss him, but as he came up to me I abruptly said, "Don't you ever do that to us again." We walked home through the streets of Exeter happy that he was free and eager to be home with the children – and yet the trust and hope that I'd had in our marriage left me. I was ill at ease and unsettled. I had lost all sense of peace and joy. Although I could feel happy on the surface, I was aware of having been betrayed; the foundations of my marriage were not only battered but crumbling.

Adrian was delighted at his daddy being back and later that night went to sleep happily. I started to tell Gary all that had been going on in the six weeks he'd been in prison. "We've been offered a new house," I said. "Because of Carl, the housing association has said that from next week we can rent a two-bedroom house over the road. It's got a little garden at the back and it'll mean I don't have to carry the pram and Carl up the steps."

"That's fantastic," said Gary. "We'd better start packing, but first I must phone the company and tell them I've been released, and hope I can still get my job back."

A few days later Gary collected the company car and stock and then we moved into our new home. Both our parents had been shocked to hear of Gary's crime but had been supportive to the children and me while he'd been in prison.

An additional upset occurred when Claude disappeared. He'd always been a home cat and never strayed far, but after two days of absence I became concerned. I put cards in the local shops asking if anyone had seen him.

Adrian stood on a chair looking out of the kitchen window for hours, but there was no sign of Claude. "Someone's taken my cat. Nobody take my baby," he cried.

"No, darling," I said, "of course not. No one is going to take your baby."

I lifted him down from the chair and took him into the lounge with Carl. Then I watched as he sat with him on his lap. He looked down at him, the proud older brother with his baby; they made a lovely picture.

CHAPTER NINE

Carl

Numbed by the sedative injection the doctor had given me, after we'd found Carl dead in his cot, my mind started to recall things said over the previous weeks.

"Nobody take my baby," Adrian had said and I'd assured him no one would. How could I have known that so soon after Claude his cat had gone missing, Carl too would be gone?

The judge had let Gary out of prison because of the difficulties for me managing with Adrian and Carl. "I swear on the baby's life that this money is legal; it's my bonus," Gary had vowed – but he had blatantly lied. He was guilty of fraud in many different ways.

Then I recalled another conversation I'd had with Gary just a few weeks after he'd come out of prison. I told him that I was thinking of taking out an insurance for the children and as we discussed it he said, "If anything were to happen to either of the boys, it would be better if it were Carl."

"How can you say such a thing?" I said. "I know you think of Adrian as your own, but Carl is your son."

"Yes," said Gary, "but he just wakes for his feed and then gets washed and changed and put back to bed."

I smiled back and said, "But not for long. Before you know it, he'll be crawling around and into everything."

But now I wasn't smiling; I was groaning deep inside. Carl would never crawl and be "into everything". I'd never watch him take his first steps or hold his hand as we walked to playschool.

I became aware of the hushed whisperings around me. Mum was asking Gary to help her take down Carl's cot. "I think it might be too upsetting for her when she goes into the bedroom to say goodnight to Adrian if she sees the empty cot," she said. They went upstairs and I heard them collapsing the cot.

"Where is Carl?" I asked when they came back down.

They looked at me blankly.

"I know he's dead," I said, "but where have they taken him? I didn't see them carry him out and I don't know where he is."

Gary held my hand. His voice was gentle yet choked as he said, "Carl's at the hospital. They have to do a post-mortem." My beautiful baby was going to be cut up. "They need to find out what happened, why he died," he said with tears in his eyes.

That night Gary handed me the sleeping pills that the doctor had left for me to take. The enforced sleep wasn't restful.

I woke up and went downstairs. Mum was in the kitchen with Gary, and Adrian was having his breakfast. Mum passed me a cup of tea. I was thankful that although Dad had had to go back to Plymouth for work, Mum had been able to stay up with us. We sat waiting for the undertaker to come. When our minister had called and, instead of discussing the arrangements for Carl's christening, had talked to us about his cremation, he'd said that he would contact the undertaker for us. We knew it would be ten days before Carl could be laid to rest because of the post-mortem, but we felt the need to get on and make the necessary arrangements.

The undertaker came in. He quietly gave his condolences and said, "It's always so difficult when there is the death of such a young child. I'm so sorry but I'll take you through these arrangements as sensitively as I can. Please ask me any questions you have and I'll try and answer them." We talked about the flowers, service and formalities and then he left.

The results came through from the post-mortem. *No known reason.* "How can this be?" I asked Gary, but what could he answer?

The doctor arrived and said, "Sometimes we just don't know why young babies die in their cots. We do know that it happens to young infants under the age of twelve months old and there is research to try and find out the cause. Some friends of mine, also doctors, had a baby die of 'cot death' as we call it. Would you like me to contact them? You might find it helpful to speak with other parents who have lost their baby in this way."

Gary and I met with the friends of our doctor a few days later. I could see the understanding in their eyes when I spoke of my fears that it was my fault, that God was punishing me, that Gary felt guilty having been let off a prison sentence because of Carl and that now he was dead. Some of our fears, anger and questions were laid to rest as we talked through our mutual experiences and emotions at having lost a baby, but a sense of why remained and where was God in all of this?

There were a lot of arrangements to make and people to contact. I phoned Mark, my brother. He'd made it quite clear he didn't approve of my divorce from Phil although he'd also made it quite clear that he had never approved of him either. We'd not been in contact for quite some time. He knew through Mum and Dad that I had married Gary and that Carl had been born, but now I thought I should tell him about Carl's death and invite him to the cremation; after all, he was Carl's uncle.

"Hi, Mark. I'm just calling to let you know that Carl, your nephew, has died. We found him dead in his cot and his cremation will be in a week's time."

There was silence on the end of the phone. He said nothing.

"Would you be able to come to the service?" I asked.

"I don't have any transport. My car's in the garage at the moment," he said.

Gary was sitting next to me and realised what Mark was saying. "Tell him I'll drive down and pick him up and take him back at the end of the day," he offered.

I passed his suggestion on but Mark said, "No, I don't think this is the right time for us to meet up."

I couldn't believe what I was hearing. "Well, if this isn't the right time, when is?" I said feeling exasperated.

"I don't know. Maybe later," Mark answered.

I put the phone down. I knew I'd done a lot of things in my life that he didn't approve of, but Carl's death was not my fault. Was I always going to be punished and be the black sheep of the family because of my past?

That weekend there was a disco being held in the local community hall. Janet's husband, Robert, was the D.J., and Gary and I decided to go. I knew some of the neighbours wouldn't understand our going to a dance, but I didn't care. Carl was my son and I cried into my pillow night after night as I felt the softness of the brushed nylon pillowcase next to my face. I lay for hours, gently rubbing the material against my skin, just as I'd held him cradled in my arms and felt the softly downed hair on his head next to my face. I knew of my own grief and didn't feel it necessary to conform to what others may expect. Adrian was staying at Mum and Dad's for a few days so Gary and I would be able to simply concentrate on our own feelings and needs.

In the depth of grief there was something strange yet reassuring that for others life was going on as usual. We arrived at the community hall and saw that we knew most of the people there. Most of them didn't know what to say, but our close neighbours rallied round and were very supportive. Gary and I danced and talked with others through the evening, then just before midnight Robert played the last record: 'You'll Never Walk Alone'. My heart echoed the lyrics[8] and I saw Gary's eyes fill with tears. We walked back home, our arms around one another.

Carl's death was moving me to question what life was all about. In my heart I needed to hold on to hope. As J.R.R. Tolkien says in 'The Return of the King', "Oft hope is born when all is forlorn." The build-up of undealt-with grief, of death and loss was overwhelming. The depth of undealt-with guilt and desire for forgiveness was crushing. Emotionally I knew I was damaged; spiritually I knew I was in a dire place; mentally I knew I was fragile; but I needed to believe there was some hope, otherwise what was the point in living? But living *for what?* What was the purpose?

Gary and I woke up; Adrian had come into the bedroom and was chatting away about his time at his grandparents'. They'd brought him back a few days ago and he was still recalling all that he'd done. I started preparing the breakfast and food that would be needed for later. Today was Carl's cremation and after the service we'd invited people to come back to the house for lunch.

Mum and Dad arrived in time to help me lay out the food so that it would be ready for when we returned from the crematorium.

---

[8] You can read the full lyrics at www.metrolyrics.com/youll-never-walk-alone-lyrics-gerry-and-the-pacemakers.html

"Is there anything specific I can do?" Dad asked.

"Yes," I said. "When we walk into the crematorium, I'd like Gary on one side of me and you on the other." I needed to feel the strength and love of these two men.

"I'll be there," he said.

Pauline my neighbour had offered to have Adrian whilst we were at the service so once again I passed him over the fence into her arms.

"I'll see you later, darling," I said to Adrian as he happily went to play with her son Mark. Although he asked questions and became upset if he saw me crying, at three years old he seemed to spend most of his time much the same as usual. We were all doing our best to keep our grief away from him, yet answer his questions in a way he could try to understand.

There were a lot of people at the service: friends, neighbours and our parents. As the small coffin was carried in, I thought my legs would buckle under me. I held on tightly to the arms of Gary and Dad. We sat with Mum and Gary's parents in the front row of the church. Our minister spoke words of comfort and hope. I tried to sing the hymns we'd chosen, but little sound came from my mouth. As we filed out at the end of the service I saw our friends weeping uncontrollably. Passing them, I wondered if there was something wrong with me – no tears were flowing from my eyes – but then I remembered the many nights when my pillow had been wet from my overwhelming grief.

As we ate lunch we were subdued, struggling to get a hold on life. I heard Gary's mum say to him, "Will you get me the teddy I gave Carl when he was born? I'd like to have it."

Gary went upstairs and fetched the teddy. Passing it to her he said, "Take it and leave."

We were all strained. His mum and dad left.

My parents had offered to take Adrian again for a few days. Gary had decided to get back to work and needed to visit the shops in Cornwall and I was to go with him. A few days away, quiet on our own, might help the healing process and start to ease the pain. The beautiful countryside, pleasant weather and time with Gary started the long, difficult journey of putting one foot in front of the other, helping me step towards the future with hope.

Chapter Ten

Does Life Go On?

The doctor had advised Gary and me to try straightaway for another baby and weeks later my pregnancy was confirmed. We also had another addition to the family. Gary had come in from work and said, "I've seen an advert for a five-month-old Alsatian puppy; I think we should go and look at it."

"That's the last thing I need right now!" I exclaimed.

"Just come with me and have a look. I think it will be good for you to have something to look after and keep you busy," he said.

We went to the house, the woman opened the front door and we looked down to see a puppy staring up with hope in its eyes. The woman who had placed the advert had rescued the puppy from a farm where it had been abused; she was now looking for a good home for this bitch Alsatian. When she heard why we were interested she said, "Take her. I know she'll have a good home with you."

We took Cindy home with us. I'd never had a dog before and was anxious as to how best to look after her. She was very nervous after the abuse she had received. Whenever someone came to the front door Cindy would run to the back door shaking from head to tail. She'd cry to be let out and would then go the bottom of the garden and tremble until the visitors had left. We started training her, knowing that soon there would be a baby in the house in addition to Adrian. With consistent care and love she became protective of us, but gentle and very good-natured. Adrian adored Cindy and they became the closest of friends. He often used to cover for her when she made a mess or ate things off the table. I soon had to learn not to leave half a pound of cheese or a packet of butter on the table. She was just big enough to stretch out her neck and it would disappear down her throat in one swallow!

A few weeks after Cindy came into our home, Gary said, "Let's take Adrian and Cindy down to the beach at Exmouth." Exeter was a lovely city to live in, close to the sea with Exmouth one side of the estuary and Dawlish the other, Exmoor and Dartmoor within easy reach and the rugged North Devon coast just a little farther away.

We got out of the car and as Adrian ran on to the beach, Gary put Cindy on her lead. We sat on the sand, Cindy beside us, watching Adrian play down by the water's edge.

Suddenly Cindy started to whine and anxiously I said to Gary, "What's the matter with her?"

"I don't know," Gary said. "Maybe she wants to be off her lead."

I sat worried as he let her go, afraid that she might run off and we wouldn't get her back. After all she'd only been with us a few weeks, we were a long way from home on a beach over a mile long and she'd not been off the lead before.

Adrian had wandered a little way up the beach, but he was quite safe; there were few people around on this spring evening and we could see him clearly. We watched as Cindy ran straight up to Adrian, placed herself on the other side of him and sat down. She'd decided that she didn't want him to go any farther and that she was his minder. A relationship between him and her was established, one that would be cherished and bring fulfilment. Cindy was always loving, trusting and loyal.

Gary was back into his work and sometimes, due to covering a large geographical area, had to stop away overnight. One night Adrian was asleep and Cindy had settled quietly in the lounge when the phone rang out in the hall. I sat on the stairs and picked up the receiver.

"Hello."

Silence.

"Hello? Who is it?"

Silence.

I was just about to hang up when I heard Gary's voice. He sounded strange and distant. "The clouds are lovely," he said.

Panic gripped me. What was going on? Gary was speaking, but not coherently. He was vague and in an almost dreamlike state. He'd never cried over Carl's death, had kept busy and strong, refusing to show his emotions. Now, months later, was it all coming to the surface? Was he cracking up?

"Where are you?" I asked.

"In a phone box. The clouds are lovely," he answered.

I kept on talking, trying to establish where he was in the south of England. Eventually I identified his location and said, "OK, get into the car and drive to the next town. When you get there, ring again."

I rushed to the phone each time he stopped to ring me at various places on his way home. Eventually, as I heard the car pull up outside the house, I put the kettle on and made some tea. I needed to remain calm and reassuring.

Gary walked in, ill at ease in himself, and as we sat and drank the tea I said, "Do you think it might be a good idea to see the doctor tomorrow?"

"Yes, I'll go to the surgery first thing," he agreed.

Gary wasn't registered with my doctor but I sighed with relief thinking he would get some help now to get him through this.

Much of my grief had been outward, but Gary had kept his feelings bottled up over the months and his reaction to Carl's death was now coming to the surface. Gary slept fitfully that night and reluctantly went to the doctor the next morning. When he walked back into the house a few hours later he appeared removed from reality. "The doctor has told me it will take time; there's nothing I or he can do." He was offered no other support. Still trying to come to terms myself with losing Carl, I was at a loss to know how to help.

Gary started spending long times away from the house, but it was obvious he wasn't going to work. His employer kept phoning up to see why he wasn't sending in his orders. All I could answer was that he was having difficulties after Carl's death and hoped that they could give him a little time. They had always been very fair to him but I realised this could only go on for so long. I kept trying to talk with Gary about how he was feeling and what he was doing when he was away for hours at a time, but he was unable to give me a coherent answer. All I could do was to try and carry on with the daily mundane tasks and care of Adrian and my unborn child. My pregnancy was progressing and Adrian had now started at day school.

Once again my hormones were doing somersaults as the new life grew inside of me, but it was still only months since Carl's death. I woke to the start of each new day not knowing what would happen to upset me. Walking up the street I'd see a friend walking towards me, then watch as they'd cross over the road and pretend they hadn't seen me. I knew they'd heard about Carl and didn't know what to say, but to be ignored was hurtful.

I knew the time had come to sort out Carl's clothes. As I walked back from the shops with Pauline my neighbour I told her of my plans for the day. "Would you like some company and help?" she asked. I gratefully accepted and as we went through each item of clothing we talked together about Carl and what a beautiful baby he'd been. I needed to talk about him and bring his name into conversations. I couldn't just push his memory into that dark cavern that held so many other painful memories.

One day Gary left the house and said, "I must get off to work. I'll see you later this afternoon." He gave Adrian and me a kiss goodbye and I stood in the porch as he drove away.

Adrian was now ready for school so I put Cindy on the lead and walked him up to the local school. "See you later," I said. "I'll be waiting here at the school gates when you come out."

It was a typical day. I walked Cindy down on to the canal path for half an hour and then we went home. I got on with the housework, washing and cooking, and then sat down with a coffee before going to collect Adrian. When we got back I gave him a drink and biscuit to keep him going until we'd all have dinner together when Gary came in.

Five o'clock...

Six o'clock and still no Gary...

I began to worry. There was no way I could contact him.

As I put Adrian to bed he asked, "Where's Daddy?"

"I guess he's had to work late. He'll be home in a while," I replied.

Eleven o'clock and still Gary wasn't home...

I went to bed but couldn't sleep. The hours of darkness crept by slowly. Every time I heard the sound of a car I jumped out of bed and looked out of the window. My head ached and I felt sick. *Where was he?*

At seven thirty Adrian came running across the landing. He climbed on to the bed asking, "Where's Daddy?"

What could I answer? "I'm sure he'll be back soon," I said, hoping my anxiety didn't sound in my voice. I busied about getting breakfast, feeding Cindy and preparing the items Adrian would need for school. We walked up the road and I waved Adrian off as he walked into the playground.

The day stretched out before me, but perhaps even now Gary would be at home waiting for me to get back. I walked around the corner into our close. There was no car; he wasn't there. I made myself a mug of tea and simply sat waiting. I was unable to do anything constructive; all I could do was sit and wait. I felt physically sick with worry and I just couldn't motivate myself to do anything. I sat mindlessly in front of the television – not watching, just staring at the screen. Eventually it was three o'clock and I walked up to the school to get Adrian.

Pauline next door was picking up Mark, her son, and we walked back down the hill together. As the boys walked on in front of us she said, "What's up? You don't look too good."

I told her that Gary hadn't come home and I was worried.

"Come in and have a mug of tea," she offered. "The boys can play together upstairs."

It was nice to have someone to talk to and company for an hour. But she had no ideas as to why Gary hadn't been home and there was no way to stop the tearing pain inside my stomach.

I took Adrian indoors and we sat together eating our dinner as I asked him about what he'd done at school. Then, after I put him to bed, I once again sat down waiting for the hours to pass until I'd hear the sound of Gary's key in the door. Eventually I was lying in bed waiting to hear the car pull up, the door slam or the sound of our front door opening – but it didn't come.

The night seemed endless, but as the sun rose I had to pull myself together for Adrian's sake. We went through our normal routine and again I sat into the evening, numbed in front of the television. Cindy lay with her head on my lap. She could sense that I was upset and offered me comfort the best way she could. As I stroked her soft fur, tears fell down my face. I was so at a loss as to what to do.

Maybe Gary had had an accident. I ran to the phone and started to call the local hospitals. "No one by that name has been admitted," the voice at the other end said, "and if your husband was in a car accident your address would have been traced and you would have been notified. Have you phoned the police?"

"No," I answered, not wanting to think that maybe he was in trouble again.

My hands were shaking as I dialled the number for the local police station. "No your husband has not been arrested. If he's not been admitted to hospital, then I'm sure he'll be back home soon."

Another trauma and endless, endless waiting; there was a pattern of this in my life. I watched as the hands moved all too slowly around the clock face.

The next day, early morning, I carefully got out of bed. Everything was quiet as I eased my way downstairs to the phone. I dialled the number and heard a pleasant voice say, "Heavitree maternity hospital, how can I help?"

"I'm six months pregnant and I think my waters have just broken." I looked up. The front door had just opened and I watched as Gary walked into the hall.

"Can you come straight to the hospital?" the pleasant voice said.

"I'm on my way," I answered.

"What's the matter?" Gary said, looking down at me sitting on the stairs.

"My waters have broken. I need to go to the hospital now."

Gary calmly called up the stairs, "Adrian, we're taking Mummy up to the hospital for a check-up. Get dressed and put your shoes on; we need to hurry."

I got my things together, knowing the doctors were likely to keep me in on the ward for at least a few days. This was not the time to be asking Gary where he'd been. I was just so thankful to see him, although worried that his face was so ashen. Now he was swiftly manoeuvring the car through the traffic.

The doctor examined me while Gary stayed with Adrian. "I want you to come on to the ward for a few days. There is a risk you could lose the baby, but with bedrest you should go full term," he said.

I looked up at him and explained how we'd already lost Carl and that with Gary being as he was now, I didn't want him told that there was a chance that I could lose this baby.

"OK," he said, "but I guess he'll know that it's not a good thing for your waters to break at six months pregnant."

Soon Gary was sitting by the bed in the ward holding my hand. "This is all my fault," he admitted. "I just wasn't handling things. It was all getting too much; I needed to get away. I've been down on the coast walking for miles. I'm so sorry. Then when I get back you're phoning the hospital..."

"It's OK," I said, "I'll be alright and so will the baby. I just need to keep my feet up for a few days." I tried to sound more confident than I felt.

Gary looked down at Adrian who was sitting quietly at the bedside. "I'll take Adrian up to my mum and dad's. I'll let them and your parents know what's happening and then I'll take Adrian to the park. We'll come in and see you this afternoon. Don't worry, everything will be fine now."

I watched him as he held Adrian's hand and walked out of the ward. He was being strong, having to deal with yet another crisis. He was able to suppress his own feelings and concentrate on getting on with the task in hand. My heart went out to him and all of us as I closed my eyes and tried to rest. *Dear God, please don't let me lose this baby.* The words cried out inside my head. Over and over they tumbled as I drifted into a shallow sleep.

Three days later I was discharged from the hospital. The doctor had said, "As long as you rest and take things easy and don't worry, your pregnancy should go full term." Gary returned to work and we resumed our normal routine with me resting in the afternoons. Gary did as much as he could to help me with the housework; he seemed to be much better and we waited as the months passed for me to give birth.

Tom was born ten days before Christmas, another brother for Adrian, and the doctor kept a very close eye on him, anxious to do all he could to prevent another tragedy.

One morning I opened the door to the smiling face of the midwife. She would visit once a day. I'd just made tea and handed her a mug as she went in to the lounge. Tom was in his carrycot. Wherever we went in the house we took him with us, worried to leave him alone for a minute. At night I was frightened to close my eyes for fear of what I might see when I looked in to his cot; the picture of finding Carl dead was still vivid in my mind. The midwife did her usual checks then announced that she'd like the doctor to see him.

I sat staring at her, almost afraid to ask why he needed to see the doctor.

"I'm sure everything's alright," she said as she looked back at me. "I just want to make sure."

Before I had a chance to get dressed and change Tom, the doctor arrived. I watched as he checked Tom's breathing and listened to his chest. As he sat beside me on the settee he said in a calm voice, "Just to make sure, we'll have the hospital run some tests."

I nodded, feeling his reassurance and thinking we'd take Tom up to the hospital when an appointment had been made.

"I'll ring an ambulance now. It should be here in a few minutes," the doctor continued.

Panic rose inside me. Once again I heard the sound of the piercing siren as the ambulance made its way to our house. I sat inside the vehicle cradling Tom in my arms. Gary sat next to me, his face expressing disbelief that we could be on our way to the hospital.

I assumed we would return to the maternity hospital I'd left just a few days before, but we drove right past the entrance. "Why aren't we going in to the maternity hospital?" I asked.

"We're taking you to the main Royal Devon and Exeter Hospital. Once a baby has left the maternity hospital it has been subjected to germs outside and is classed as 'dirty' so we're going to the general hospital," the ambulance driver explained.

I looked down into Tom's face, numbed with shock, and thinking, "They're saying my baby's dirty." Cradling him protectively in my arms I carried him into the hospital and we were taken straight in to see a specialist.

"We're going to admit your baby for a few days to have him under observation and monitor him. We'll also run some tests. He'll be in a room on his own right behind the nurses' station and we can put a bed in there for you if you'd like to stay with him."

I looked at Gary as I felt overwhelming despair. He said, "Pauline's taken Adrian to school but you go back and collect him when school comes out this afternoon. I'll stay with Tom tonight, then we can make arrangements for you to come up tomorrow. Perhaps your mum can come up to stay with Adrian."

We spent the day watching the nurses move around the ward. A sign was put on the door saying "staff and family only"; the nurses said that a new baby on the ward always caused a lot of interest and they didn't want any extra people going into his room. As I left to fetch Adrian from school, I looked back through the glass and saw Gary sat beside Tom's cot looking down on his sleeping son. I could only imagine what was going through his mind.

The following day Mum arrived from Plymouth and we went up to the hospital. They were waiting on the results of tests but Gary said he had slept well and that the nurses were very friendly and helpful. The next forty-eight hours I stayed by Tom's cot. Life was obviously going on as normal outside of this building but there was nothing normal for me here as I watched my son being taken away for one test after another. I waited anxiously to hear what the specialist would say. Gary was with me when we finally heard, "We can find nothing wrong with your baby. You can take him home."

The courts were still allowing Phil access to Adrian, even though by now there was a list of incidents and accidents that had occurred when he was with him. Eventually my solicitor acquired court agreement that access should not only be defined, but that a social worker should be present. I felt happier with this arrangement until, a few months later, I was told that the social worker had decided that Phil could take Adrian to his mother's for the weekend. I expressed to the social worker my fears and the issues regarding Phil's mother's drinking. "Please, go and see her first and go in the afternoon because she always starts drinking at lunchtime. That way you'll see just what sort of environment you're saying is OK for Phil to take this five-year-old child into." I detailed all my concerns and they told me they'd look into them.

Just days later I couldn't believe the letter I was reading: "It has been agreed for Phil to have Adrian for the weekend. He will take him to his mother's and we have discussed the food he will be given and where he will be sleeping. We are quite happy with this arrangement and the court has sanctioned that this access is to take place."

I phoned the social worker. "When did you go to visit Phil's mother?"

"Well, I didn't personally go. A colleague from the Gloucester department made the visit."

"At what time of day?"

"Let me just look at the file... She went in the morning."

I slammed the phone down. These people were a waste of time. I knew all too well that in the morning Phil's mother would be sober and would have put on a good show for the social worker, but this was not an accurate picture.

Phil took Adrian off as if he'd won a prize at the fair. I worried and fretted all weekend as Gary failed to keep me calm. Sunday afternoon Phil brought Adrian to the door and left quickly.

Even though he had just driven for two hours, I was used to him taking straight off. Often it was because Adrian was bruised or had obviously been crying. Many times Gary had gone chasing after Phil, and if he had found him, I think would have ended up doing time for manslaughter. He was always so angry whenever Phil had either failed to look after Adrian or had clearly harmed him in some way.

I took Adrian by the hand and led him into the lounge. As I pulled him up on my knee I said, "Have you had a good time? Tell me, what have you done over the weekend?"

Adrian started to tremble as he said, "I have to lie to you."

Alarm bells started ringing inside my head as I cuddled him closer and gently said, "No, darling, you never lie to Mummy. Just tell me what has happened over the weekend."

In between the sobs Adrian described the events of the past forty-eight hours. None of what he was telling me was in line with the agreement between Phil and the social workers.

I looked across at Gary who was looking on anxiously. Emphatically I said, "Ring the social worker at home and demand that she comes here now to see the state Adrian is in."

He picked up the phone and I could hear her saying that she would call by in the morning.

I took the phone from Gary. "I want you here NOW. There is no way I'm going to try to settle Adrian down for the night only to have to rake all this up again in the morning when it's more convenient for you to come. I am fed up with you people telling me what is best for Adrian and insisting that his father sees him, and always he comes back in a state. Something really serious has happened this weekend, even when I tried to tell you people that it wasn't safe for Adrian to go away. Now I'm telling you, you're to come here NOW. I don't care if it is a Sunday afternoon and you've got guests. If you don't come here, I've got your address; I'll come and stand on your doorstep until you see me."

She arrived about twenty minutes later. Adrian was still sobbing as again he went through the events of the weekend.

I was stunned as the social worker looked at me and said, "We don't believe that fathers abuse their children. Even if you take this back to the court, I can tell you that they'll still say that Phil has the right, as Adrian's father, to have access to him."

I couldn't believe what I was hearing. This social worker had just listened to Adrian recount the weekend with Phil. He had clearly violated the ruling of the court and Adrian had been at serious risk.

Angrily I replied, "Well then, they'll have to find us first, because he and I will disappear. I will do everything in my power to stop Phil from seeing Adrian until he is old enough to keep himself safe and then he can make his own decision."

She seemed amazed that I should dare to stand against the court's ruling, but she could see I was serious. Some weeks later Phil's solicitor contacted me about access. I wrote back telling them that I would disclose information about Phil and if Phil wanted to fight then he'd have a costly legal battle – and first they would have to find us. I was ready to do whatever it took to keep my son safe.

A few days before Christmas, Gary said, "What would you like for Christmas, Marianne?"

"Peace of mind," I answered with no hesitation.

His reply reassured me. "You have that now, but what would you like as a present?"

I knew there were second-hand items for sale in the paper and said, "A second-hand tea maker would be quite cheap and it would be nice to be able to have a cup of tea in bed when I'm feeding Tom in the early mornings."

Christmas arrived and we sat around the Christmas tree watching Adrian open his presents. Although Gary was working we didn't have a lot of money to spare and I'd carefully shopped for toys and clothes for Adrian. It was a pleasure to watch the smile on his face as he opened the parcels from his grandparents and us. He played happily with his new toys as Gary passed me a large box. I guessed it was a tea maker.

I unwrapped the parcel and stared in surprise. This was not second-hand but brand new. Immediately I thought of what it had cost. Gary must have been saving up for some months to afford my present. "I would have been just as happy with a second-hand tea maker, but thank you so much," I said as I gave him a kiss.

The turkey cooked well and we enjoyed being together as a family with our parents visiting and spending time with us all. Tom was feeding well and slept through the night. Gary and I were anxious about him and constantly kept checking to see that he was breathing, but as I watched my family and held Tom in my arms, I looked forward to the New Year. From now on life could only get better and better.

CHAPTER ELEVEN

No Peace of Mind

Gary and I were just a few days into the New Year when he said, "I have to go to court tomorrow."

"What!" I exclaimed.

"I've been charged with fraud. I didn't want to tell you over the Christmas." He told me the details and added, "I just wanted to bring in some extra money."

"How many times have I told you, we'll manage on whatever money we've got? I don't want you breaking the law. I'd rather have you here with the boys and me, and have peace of mind. What's going to happen now? You must tell Adrian; it's not fair on him to think that he'll see you in the evening when you might be in prison."

"I'm sure it'll be OK. The court will probably just fine me," he answered unconvincingly.

That night I slept fitfully although Gary seemed to be sleeping peacefully next to me.

The next morning, I walked up the road with Adrian to the school wondering whether he would see Gary that evening. Then I made my way up to the town with Gary and Tom in his pram. I sat silently in the court as I heard a string of offences being read out that Gary was accused of. The magistrates listened, talked between themselves, then asked Gary to stand for their decision. "You are to receive a custodial sentence of twelve months."

I watched for the second time as the officers escorted Gary down to the cells. Yet again I found myself with just a few minutes to say good-bye to him. "When you get home, Marianne, you'd better look in the sideboard drawer." I looked blankly at Gary as he spoke. "You'll find an envelope with an H.P. agreement for the tea maker; you'll need to pay three pounds each month up to September."

I looked at him despairingly. He hadn't saved the money; he'd paid just three pounds as a down payment, with the rest to be paid on monthly instalments even when he knew there was a possibility he'd go to prison.

He went on, "Also you'll have to phone the company; they'll need to collect the car."

Gary was to be denied his liberty for the crimes he'd committed, but I hadn't done anything wrong. Now I was the one who would have to find the money for the new gift he'd bought me for Christmas when I'd have been happy with a second-hand one and I would have to phone his employer who'd always been so good to him and say that Gary was in prison. I was also the one who would have to explain to Adrian, now five years old, why the person he thought of as his father would not be living with us for the rest of the year. I would have to go to Social Security and sign for benefits, which would be far less money than Gary had earned. I was also going to be totally responsible for the raising of our sons, looking after Cindy and keeping our home. The next twelve months were clearly going to be a far worse sentence for the boys and me than for Gary.

"I'll send a visiting order tomorrow. Come down and see me at the weekend," Gary said as I left him.

I walked back through the town towards our home, my conflicting emotions fighting with each other. Anger, numbness, worry and thoughts of the many things I needed to organise, do and arrange all scrambled my brain. As soon as I got indoors I phoned Gary's employer. He'd been so understanding when Gary had been sent to prison last time and I knew there were very few employers who would have given him his job back; then when Carl had died, the company had given Gary time off work, sent flowers and a lovely card. I felt so embarrassed as I told him that Gary had just been sent to prison for twelve months.

I realised from the silence at the end of the phone that he was stunned. Eventually he said, "I'm sorry, Marianne, I'll have to close Gary's contract with us."

Tears rolled down my face as I replaced the telephone receiver. Why, why? I couldn't begin to understand why Gary had ever felt the need to steal, commit fraud or anything else that was illegal. I'd never asked him for extras and was happy just to have him earn whatever money he could. I knew he'd really enjoyed this job as a sales rep and I also knew he was good at the job and in so many ways his employers had shown how they valued him. Now the job had gone, but I couldn't dwell on that anymore. I had to go and pick Adrian up from school and I'd have to tell him what had happened during the day.

Adrian came through the school gates and I took him by the hand to the shop to buy a few sweets. I knew I couldn't hide the truth from him. If we were to go to visit Gary then he needed to know, and even if I didn't take him on the visits then I'd need to explain why Gary wasn't going to be at home for a year. I took Tom out of his pram, made a cup of tea and pulled Adrian up beside me on the settee. As gently as I could I explained to him what had happened. I knew that Gary's court appearance was likely to be reported in the papers and parents may well mention something to their children. Adrian could be in for a very difficult time at the school, knowing how unkind children can be. I would also need to contact his headmaster. Adrian and I cuddled closely as in our different ways we started realising how Gary's crime and sentence were going to affect us.

That evening after I settled the children, I phoned both sets of parents. Gary's mum and dad were immediately worried about him and, I felt, blamed me, as if I'd encouraged him to commit the crime. My mum and dad said they'd come up to visit us as soon as they could. They'd had all the problems with me in the past and now they were being affected by Gary's involvement with crime. I'd never been to a prison or even a court before I'd met him and now I dreaded the thought of going to see him at Channings Wood prison at the weekend – and yet my whole body ached to see him and talk with him.

That evening I looked at the H.P. agreement and made a list of the people I needed to see and things I would need to do. First thing next morning I went to the Social Security department and they told me how much money I would get each week. I knew I couldn't afford to keep the television we had been renting so I called into the shop and made arrangements with them to come and collect it. The children and I would manage with a very old black-and-white set that was in the back of the cupboard. The sound was distorted and it was hard to listen to it for more than half an hour – also the picture kept rolling – but my philosophy was, if you can't afford it you can't have it!

I arrived home to find Gary's probation officer with another lady outside the house. "Hello, Marianne, this is Jane. We just called by for a visit and to see if there's anything we can do to help." We went into the house and after I made tea we all sat down and talked through some of the practical problems that I would face.

Jane offered to drive the children and me down to the prison for the first visit. Grateful that I would have someone to show me the ropes, I accepted the offer. Then she added, "Perhaps you'd like to think about coming to a prisoners' wives group we run twice a week."

I looked at this kind, gentle lady and said, "I don't think so. I don't think I'm like them."

She smiled back, seeming to understand me.

I didn't feel I was one of 'those types'. I didn't want to be associated with criminals. The stigma, shame and embarrassment I felt of being the wife of a prisoner would only be heightened by spending time with other prisoners' wives.

Jane called to collect the children and me the following Saturday. The drive to the prison would take under an hour but I'd already found out that when we went on our own the journey would take nearly three hours each way. When Gary had sent the visiting order I knew I would need to pack a lunch for the children and me, toys to keep them occupied, nappies and changes of clothes. Once a month Social Services would pay for the train ticket, but Gary had already made the point that at the prison he was in we could visit every two weeks and he wanted me to make the journey fortnightly.

We pulled up at the prison and said goodbye to Jane who'd said she'd go and visit friends whilst we were with Gary. I took Adrian's hand, as much for my comfort as to guide or comfort him, and together we pushed Tom in his pram through the large gate that had been unlocked by a prison warden. One door after another was unlocked and locked as we were herded through along with other women and children. Then we were shown into a large room with tables and chairs and told to sit where we liked. Adrian and I sat down looking around; it was strange and uncomfortable as we waited. Eventually, through the window I saw a line of men obviously coming into the building. I looked away feeling awkward, then I saw Gary in front of me. He looked different – not just because of the prison clothes he'd been issued, but almost as though he'd lost his identity.

We hugged briefly.

"Don't cry. I'm alright," he said as he took Adrian on his lap.

We sat and talked about the children. On the one hand I didn't want to burden Gary with my problems but on the other hand I felt he should know what was happening to us at home. The atmosphere was strained as we tried to adjust to the way we would be living our lives for the next twelve months.

I needed to be careful just how much I said in front of Adrian who sat nervously at the table. He was always a good little boy who tried to please. His need for love and stability was clearly obvious and already in his young life the mistakes and wrongdoings of older people had affected him. I was well aware that I had not given him the best start in life. My choice of husbands was having such a detrimental effect on the boy's early years.

Before long the prison wardens were telling us that it was time to break for lunch. Gary was escorted away and I followed the other women to a hut where we could eat our lunch. The ninety minutes dragged slowly as I sat with Adrian close to my side and Tom on my lap. All around children were screaming and causing chaos. Mothers shouted and swore and talked to each other about the crimes their husbands had committed. They seemed to be comfortable and used to the lifestyle, but this was not something that I wanted to be a part of and I certainly didn't want my children becoming familiar with or used to this environment.

Once more we were led back through the gates. I was now expecting the security check that I'd gone through in the morning. The warden looked through my bags and cleared the boys and me to go into the visiting room. Tom was fretful as we waited for Gary to be allowed to join us. I tried to keep him and Adrian amused with the toys and books we'd brought with us.

When Gary came back in I was giving Tom his bottle. Gary took him into his arms and carried on feeding him. I asked him about the prison routine. "I'm sharing a cell with another guy but he's only here for a few months so it won't be long before I have another cell mate. They haven't allocated me any work yet so I spend most of the time in my cell. I think about you and the boys all the time and wonder how you are managing."

"What's the food like?" I asked.

"It's OK but it's not as good as your cooking," he humoured me.

I sat looking at him. How much should I tell him about the hardships we were going through? Should I tell him how angry I was at him for putting us in this position? The humiliation I felt at entering a prison where my husband was being held? The difficulties we were facing with paying off the debts he'd left us with? That he was getting more and better food than I could afford for the boys and me? That he didn't have to worry about paying the electricity and gas? That he had recreation time and was able to watch programmes on a decent television? Should I tell him that the boys and I often cuddled up under a blanket in the evenings to save the cost of putting on the fire and that I'd had several days when I hadn't eaten?

I decided that there was time later to let him know of my feelings and how we were living; now was not the time with the children around. So we sat and played with the boys and I just told him the detailed information about having phoned his employer, Social Security, about returning the television and that I had found the papers for the tea maker and was dealing with the payments. I didn't tell him that every time I looked at the tea maker I felt sick with anger; that I didn't think it was fair that he should have a choice of which programme to watch on a colour television when the boys and I could hardly follow a half-hour programme on a distorted black-and-white set. I didn't shout and scream that it wasn't justice that he should be provided with three cooked meals a day, when I was struggling to make the housekeeping money stretch until the end of the week. As we were told that time was up, I simply said, "I love you," and watched as he was led away.

I settled Tom into his pram and once more took Adrian by the hand. "Why can't Daddy come home with us?" he asked. "I don't want him to stay here." His big blue eyes looked up at me as he spoke. Mine filled with tears as I turned around and, looking through the wire fence, could see Gary walking through the prison grounds back to his cell.

Jane was waiting just outside and as I took Tom out of his pram she put our luggage into the back of the car. I could see sympathy and understanding in her eyes. Jane had told me of how she'd been working as a volunteer for many years supporting prisoners' wives. Now once again she asked, "Would you like to come along to the support meeting we have each week? I can pick you and Tom up and we'll be back in time for Adrian coming out of school."

I thought back to the hut where we'd just had our lunch, to the swearing women and screaming children. My feelings, just hidden under the surface, of anger, humiliation and loneliness wanted to cry out from my mouth. "No, thank you," I said quietly. "I really don't want to be a part of all this any more than I have to." As Adrian and Tom slept, I talked with her about the time I'd just spent with Gary, of all the things I'd wanted to say but couldn't. "I'll write to him, put it on paper; that's what I'll do," I said aloud just as we drew up outside our house.

As soon as the boys were settled in bed I found my writing pad and a pen. "Dear Gary..." As I wrote the words all I could think of was my love for him and how much I missed him being here at home with the boys and me. He'd done wrong and life was now going to be very difficult, but somehow we'd come through it. "It's only just a few hours since I saw you and I miss you so much. I know you're worried about the boys and me but we'll cope. Already I'm waiting for the next two weeks to pass to see you again." Unbelievably the letter omitted to mention anything about my other thoughts and emotions.

On the next visit the boys and I needed to go by train. We'd received a visiting order in one of the letters from Gary. I always rushed to the post to see if he'd written and yet at the same time I felt so embarrassed. The envelope was clearly prison issue; what did the postman think as he put it through the letterbox of our house? There were always funny pictures on the back of the envelope and Adrian looked forward to seeing them and hearing what Gary had to say.

It was Friday night and I busied myself in the kitchen preparing food for the following day, as we'd need to be away early in the morning. Adrian dressed himself as I fed Tom and prepared his bottles for the day. The bag was overflowing with bottles, baby food, a change of clothes for Tom, nappies and packed lunch. Adrian carried his school bag with toys and books inside. We walked for just over a mile to the railway station, handed over the travel warrant I'd collected from Social Security during the week and waited on the platform for the train. Ten minutes later the guard announced the arrival of our train and we stood back as it pulled into the station. I hooked Tom under one arm and collapsed the pram. Adrian and I struggled on to the train with all our belongings, knowing that it wouldn't be long before we'd have to struggle to get everything off the train. We'd then have to wait on another station platform for a connecting train, struggle to get on that train and then when we reached Newton Abbot railway station struggle yet again. Eventually we walked out of the railway station on to Newton Abbot high street.

I asked directions to the bus station. It was a mile walk; Adrian held on to the pram as we trudged through the streets, then stood waiting for the bus. Embarrassed, I showed the bus driver the travel warrant, then Adrian and I struggled once more to get the pram, bags and Tom on to the bus. I felt even more embarrassed as the driver called out to inform me we'd reached our stop. My face flushed, as I knew that all the local people sat on the bus would be aware of the reason I was getting off at this stop. I stood and paused for breath as I watched the bus pull away, then turned and looked at the long, narrow road that led down to the prison. Ten minutes later we were waiting with all the other women and children at the prison gates. The journey had taken three hours.

Channings Wood was a semi-open prison; the high wire fence meant that you could see in to the grounds and we strained to see if we could spot Gary walking towards the visiting room. One of the women started shouting at the guy on gate duty, "Come on, let us in," but we soon came to realise that whatever the weather conditions they would not open the gates until the appointed time and there was nowhere to wait in the dry. The hut we were allowed to use for lunch was only opened for that period of time.

We sat and waited for Gary to arrive. I'd already put cigarettes on the table for him and bought some coffees at the W.R.V.S. canteen that provided drinks and snacks. Paying for all these extras and the train and bus fares once a month was going to be really difficult. But I'd already adjusted to having only one small meal a day, Adrian had a cooked lunch at school and I made all Tom's baby food; Adrian had a few sweets just once a week; I bought all clothes at jumble sales; we saved on fuel by sitting with the blankets around us at night and going to bed early. I made biscuits without sugar so that it was enough to nibble one at a time. I knew that if they were really tasty the temptation would be to eat more and I couldn't afford for that to happen. The boys were restricted to one glass of squash a day and I never bought things like cola.

The time with Gary passed much as before, as did the hour and a half when the boys and I were in the hut eating our sandwiches, whilst Gary was provided with his cooked lunch. Yet despite my resentful feelings it was with reluctance that I pulled away from him ten minutes before the end of visiting time to ensure that Adrian and I had time to walk up the road and catch the only bus back in to Newton Abbot.

As we saw the bus coming I was aware that Adrian was now tired, Tom fretful, and that my head was banging, dreading the return journey. We'd left home at seven in the morning and it would be after six and dark when we walked back into the house. On and off the bus, a mile walk, on and off two trains, and then before the mile walk back to our home I'd have to negotiate the steps over the railway line. We arrived home exhausted, too tired to eat, limbs aching; this was going to be part of our life every two weeks for the next year.

Weekends and evenings were times of deep, dark loneliness and isolation. During the daytime there was always something to do with the children, or one of the other mums to meet with and have coffee. But once tea time came they were busy getting dinner for their husbands who'd soon be returning from work. I had no husband coming back to me at the end of his working day; no one was going to walk through the door and say, "Hi, sweetheart, how's your day been? How are the boys?" I wasn't going to put a nice dinner, which I'd lovingly prepared, in front of my husband and say, "Well, some of the day's been good and some not so good, but you look tired; have you been busy? Are there problems at work?"

Once the children were in bed, the hours seemed endless. One evening I picked up the phone and dialled the number printed in the telephone directory.

"Samaritans, can I help you?"

"Talk to me. Please, talk to me." I was desperate to hear a voice that was kind and concerned for me. To know that there was someone who cared. To know that I could say whatever I liked to them and not have to worry that they would be hurt or upset at what I was saying. I couldn't take on someone else's pain as well as my own. Even though I loved, and knew I had to take responsibility for, Adrian and Tom, I often thought of committing suicide. I would take large numbers of pills and want to sleep, to stay in the nothingness, where there was no pain, anguish, tiredness or exhaustion of life. As I frequently listened to the non-judgemental, calm, encouraging, anonymous voice on the end of the phone I was helped through many a bleak evening.

As time went on I grew stronger emotionally, and ached for the time Gary would be back with us and we'd be a family again. Jane continued to visit and eventually I gave in to her repeated invitations asking me to attend the prisoners' wives group. I soon realised the other wives were just like me: frustrated, angry and struggling to survive.

Groups were held twice a week in different parts of Exeter and soon I was helping Jane organise the group activities. We talked about our problems, our children and how other people in the community treated us because of our husbands' crimes. Many of us felt like lepers because of the way neighbours snubbed us. We were outcasts and we talked of our emotional need for acceptance, as we too were victims. We shared about feeling bereft and physically needing the comfort of a cuddle, especially at the end of the day before going to sleep. Just down the road from where we met was the orthopaedic hospital. "Perhaps we could get them to make us a pair of arms that each of us could attach to the bottom of the stairs in our homes and then whenever we need a hug the arms could give us a cuddle!" I said. As we shared our different stories and strife it was clear that wives and families suffered far more than the men who had committed the crimes.

As I got to know Jane better I discovered she was a Christian who put her faith into action. Her practical, consistent and patient support of so many women and their children was widely appreciated and valued. I grew to admire and respect this older woman who came from a very different background to us prisoners' wives yet never judged, only gave ceaselessly of her time and often opened up her home to offer hospitality. Her empathy was endless, a quality I came to greatly respect. She didn't offer platitudes or shallow sympathy, rather she had the ability to truly stand alongside each one of us and have a relationship with us that wasn't patronising.

Mum and Dad continued to visit and support, often bringing up food supplies and sometimes helping with other costs. I could have a cup of tea in bed made by the new tea maker but I did not have peace of mind. I knew it was going to be difficult for Gary and me to adjust when he came out of prison. I'd had to become much more independent and Gary had not yet experienced the regular trips to hospital that I now had to make with Tom.

Tom had been just a few months old when he started holding his breath and turning blue before he would eventually exhale. I talked with the doctor who said, "He's picking up on your anxieties, particularly over Carl's death, and he's reacting to your nervousness and stress. You need to ignore him and it'll pass." I walked out of the surgery. How do you ignore the fact that your baby is not breathing? Carl had died because something had happened and he'd stopped breathing. My anxieties grew. I worried that there was more to it; perhaps he was having some sort of fit. Whatever it was, it got worse. Tom seemed to stop breathing six or more times a day. I took him to the hospital and they ran various tests but found no physical explanation.

At one time, Mum was staying for a few days. It was good to have the help and company, and we chatted as we got Tom ready for bed. He'd been unsettled most of the afternoon and was now crying as I laid him down on the bed to change him. Suddenly he stopped crying and held his breath.

I picked him up and held him upright. "Come on, sweetheart," I said, gently patting his back. He wasn't inhaling or exhaling.

Mum followed me into the bathroom as I splashed cold water on his face. Still no sound.

"Oh, God," I cried, "I can't lose another baby."

Tom was becoming more and more rigid when I suddenly thought, "He's swallowed his tongue!" Instinctively I prized open his mouth. He was so rigid it took all my strength yet at the same time I was afraid of hurting him. I pulled on his tongue, and as his airway opened he started to breathe and then sob. Mum and I cried over him, aware of just how close we'd come to losing him.

Tom continued to stop breathing many times a day. I learnt to react but not overreact, but I wondered how Gary would cope when he was released, even though I told him about the incidents.

That Christmas Mum and Dad visited. They brought clothes and a toy for each of the boys. Tom was now walking; he was steady and sturdy on his feet and would often move purposefully across the room towards Cindy our beloved pet and disturb her sleep. She would patiently rise up on her paws and saunter to another part of the room, lay herself back down and resume her sleep. The boys and I had adjusted to our family life without Gary in the home. They had changed so much in the last year. I knew I had as well and I was sure the experiences Gary had gone through in prison would have changed him; we would need to readjust to living together again.

Gary was released from prison early the following year. It was good to have him back, but we often felt strange in each other's company. By now I was used to making decisions and taking responsibility for the children and running the house. The first time Tom had one of his turns and stopped breathing, Gary went into a panic and, as they continued several times a day, he became very anxious.

Gary couldn't adjust to the simple way we were living. "I don't know how you can watch this distorted black-and-white set," he said.

"Because it's all we can afford," I answered. "I don't want us living beyond our means."

The next day he went up to the town and rented a colour television.

It was difficult for Gary to get work and we adjusted our claim for state benefits. We were only given a few extra pounds to live on and more than that went on his cigarettes. I fell again into a deep, dark pit. Tiredness overwhelmed me; physically and mentally I felt exhausted. If only I could just sleep a long sleep and not wake up... Several times I made half-hearted attempts at suicide but life held on to me. It wasn't long before Gary was in trouble with the police again and sent back to prison. How could I go on with him constantly breaking the law?

Chapter Twelve

A Fresh Start

Once again Mum and Dad gave the boys and me a lot of support. They started talking to me about having a few days' break at the Butlin's holiday camp just an hour-and-a-half drive from our home. Mum offered to come with me to help with the children. Dad would drive us up, pay the cost of our self-catering chalet and come back five days later to collect us.

We loaded the car and set off looking forward to a lovely break. The camp was fantastic and once inside all the entertainment was free. I didn't even have to wash Tom's nappies as there was a service provided by the camp. This was such a treat. Each morning Tom went into a nursery where he played with other children his age; there were lots of colourful toys and trained staff to look after him. Adrian went to football coaching. Football was his passion and 'ball' had been the first word he'd said. Now he was able to spend a week with a professional division one football player. Mum and I walked around the camp and enjoyed the opportunity to sit and have a cup of coffee in peace and quiet without having to keep an eye on the kids. We collected them at lunchtime and took them back to the chalet to eat. In the afternoon we'd take them to the fair, swimming or for a walk into Minehead.

One afternoon we headed off in the direction of the local town. All of a sudden, pennies and other small coins were raining down upon us. Literally thousands of coins were all over the road and pavement. I realised that a man had just been to empty the machines at the nearby amusement arcade, had put the bags of money on the roof of the car and then driven off. He soon realised his costly error and stopped the car to retrieve the money but accepted that most of it was lost. Children were swarming all over the roads collecting the coins and filling their pockets. "Pennies from heaven," came to mind. I stopped the boys from going out into the road but as I saw the man drive off I let them pick up the money close by.

Adrian and Tom immediately started talking about all the sweets they could buy.

I knelt down beside them. "Is this your money?" I asked.

"No, but the man's gone so we can't give it back to him," they said.

"No, you can't, but it's still not yours. I think you should put it into the charity boxes as we walk up through the town."

They accepted the idea and happily put the pennies into the different boxes, often watching the lifeboat move over the waves or the dog wag its tail as the coin was accepted. I didn't want them to grow up thinking they could have, or had the right to have, something that didn't belong to them.

We arrived back in Exeter refreshed from our few days away at the coast. Whilst Gary was still in prison I started making enquiries about moving to a new house. We could exchange our house with another person who wanted to move into our home and soon all the plans were underway. Tom was now attending a day nursery and the new house was almost next to the nursery. Adrian would still be going to his primary school and I would need to walk him the mile to get to school but I felt that a new location would be good for all of us. And it wouldn't be long before Adrian would be changing schools and the next one he was to attend was also near the new house. Gary was only serving a short six-month sentence and plans were made to move when he returned.

A few days after he was released, Gary hired a van and, together with the help of friends, we loaded our furniture into the van and drove the mile to our new home. It was lovely; the boys had their own bedrooms and the garden was big enough for Tom to play in; there was even an outside loo to stop them coming in with their muddy boots. The garden backed on to a park and Adrian happily rode his bike and played football with the local children.

I'd started doing some cleaning work in the home of a local social worker and that enabled me to earn the few extra pounds the government allowed me to work for, in addition to the benefits we were receiving. Knowing Gary was coming out of prison, she said, "I guess it's difficult for Gary to find work with a prison record but there's some painting and decorating work I'd like done on the house, if he's able to do that." I told her he was very good at doing all sorts of jobs around the house and I'd have a word with him and mention the offer. At long last it seemed that life was taking a turn for the better.

One evening Mum and Dad were visiting. Dad had to do some work in Exeter during the evening and Mum was to stay with me until he picked her up. We'd just finished eating tea with the boys when Gary came in from doing his painting and decorating.

"I'll get your dinner," I said to Gary.

"Don't worry about that now," he said. "I've been offered an interview at the local motel for a sales rep job. Could you get a shirt ready for me to wear?"

As I quickly ironed his best shirt, Dad offered to drive Gary to the motel.

"It's OK," Gary said, "I can hitch a lift out there."

"Don't be silly," Dad insisted. "It won't take me long to run you out there and I've time before I go to my meeting."

They left together as Mum and I got on with the washing-up. A short while later Dad returned to find me feeling very uneasy.

"It doesn't make sense," I said to him. "How did Gary suddenly hear about this job? I can't explain it but I just feel something is wrong."

Dad could see I was worried and immediately left to go back to the motel. A little while later his car pulled up outside of the house, Gary got out and Dad drove off to his meeting.

As Gary walked in the door I said, "I'll get your dinner ready."

"Alright," he said, "but I just have to go to the phone box and call the guy who was going to interview me. He didn't turn up and I want to know what's happened."

As I prepared his dinner he walked up the road. Ten minutes later he wasn't back so I went to the front door and looked up towards the phone box. He was nowhere in sight. I ran up the road and asked some boys playing football if they'd seen him.

"Yes, he was in the phone box and then a taxi came. He got in it and drove off."

I walked back to the house feeling sick. This wasn't the first time Gary had taken off. In the past he'd said he was going to buy cigarettes and we wouldn't see him for two, three of four days. It was just too much. I had to either keep making excuses or give explanations to the boys. I never knew where I was with Gary and I certainly didn't have peace of mind. I walked back into the house and just reached the bathroom in time before vomiting up the tea I'd eaten earlier.

I told Mum he'd gone.

"It doesn't make any sense," she said. "It's not as though you two had a row or anything."

She was right; we never rowed and apart from the few days it would take for us to readjust to one another when he came out of prison we always got on well. I loved him dearly and when he was at home he had a good relationship with both the boys. I knew we were struggling to manage financially but as long as we were a family I thought we could live within our means until such time as he could find a better paid job.

"He hasn't got any money, Mum, and yet he's got in a taxi and obviously cleared off. He probably won't be back for several days so somehow he's acquired some money."

Mum looked at me blankly.

"I must phone Sue, the lady I clean for and where Gary has been doing the decorating," I said. I rang the number and told Sue what had happened. "Please look to see if anything is missing," I said and waited whilst she looked around the house.

"My credit cards have gone," she said in disbelief. Once again I made a dash for the bathroom. This was a lady who had become a friend and had been kind enough to give Gary some work. How could he do this? But then I thought back to the times he'd taken the rent money just minutes before the rent man had called to collect the fortnightly payment, how he'd stolen money out of the children's money box, and money that I'd painstakingly saved for Christmas had disappeared from my purse; how he'd even taken the money people had given us to pass on to the charity working to establish the cause of cot death at the time of Carl's death! It had taken me many months to replace that money and send it to the charity. If he could do this to his wife and children, then why shouldn't he do it to someone who had given him a job? My husband, the man I loved, was a heartless, selfish con artist and crook.

Dad returned several hours later to hear the events of the evening. "There never were any interviews being held at the motel," he said. I asked the receptionist when I went back to get Gary. "He was sat in the bar, so I just went up to him and said, 'I don't know what's going on but get in the car; I'm taking you back home.' He wouldn't speak to me in the car and because I needed to get to my meeting I just dropped him at the door and then had to drive off."

It was as I thought; Gary had stolen from my employer and planned his getaway. It just happened that Dad had caused him something of a hiccup when he offered to drive him to the motel.

Mum helped me settle the children and then she and Dad left to drive back to Plymouth. I went to bed but couldn't sleep; I dozed fitfully. I put the lock on the front door. I'd had enough; even if Gary did come back I couldn't take any more.

At 3.00am there was knocking at the door. I looked out of the window and saw Gary looking up at me whispering loudly, "I'm sorry, please let me in."

I said nothing, just looked down at him.

"Can I just come in and we can talk?" he implored. This too had happened many times before and once he started talking I always gave in. I knew about his affairs and had even consoled one of his girlfriends when he'd stolen her car, television and stereo. But I loved him and he knew it, and once he started chatting me up he could twist me around his finger. This sales rep had a good line in buttering people up and either making a sale or getting what he wanted.

"No, you're not coming in," I said calmly and quietly.

"But where will I go?" Gary pleaded with me.

"Wherever you've been for the last seven hours," I said and shut the window.

He kept knocking but thankfully not loud enough to wake the children. I ignored him and eventually fell asleep exhausted and sickened.

The next day I saw to the children and then Jane called by. I told her what had happened and then I made the decision to build a life for the boys and myself. I would not let Gary reduce me to a psychological wreck. I'd already started doing some voluntary work for the Probation Department and I now contacted the manager and arranged to help at the day centre five days a week. I would start after the school summer holidays. Adrian would then be moving to the middle school just down the road so each day I would take Tom into nursery at 8.30am, walk Adrian down to his school and then wait for a bus to take me to the other side of Exeter. It was strange; I really enjoyed working at this centre for offenders and was being told that I had a lot to offer, yet my husband was a criminal and I could do nothing to stop his behaviour.

Several weeks passed and I did not see Gary. Since locking him out, I'd no idea where he'd been staying but there was one certainty: he would always find someone to take him in. I was aware that he'd had numerous affairs, that he knew people all over the city and had a way of ensuring that his needs were always met. Now I needed to focus on the needs of the boys and myself. I needed to be solely the one to look after us because at long last I accepted that he would always put himself first.

Some weeks later I bumped into him in Exeter. I'd been managing OK – after all, the boys and I were used to managing when he was in prison – but now as I saw him I felt sick. Even after all that had happened I still loved this man. Almost inevitably he came back to the house with me. We talked, but this time I laid it on the line that I was not going to sit around waiting for him whilst he went off with other women and committed crimes so that he could spend the money in clubs and travelling around the country in flashy hired cars. I'd give him another chance.

To my surprise, my employer decided not to inform the police of the theft and within a few days Gary had a job. Although he wasn't happy with me doing voluntary work at the Probation Department, he accepted that I enjoyed the work and often told me that he thought I would be very good. When we talked about his behaviour he always said it wasn't my fault and that he was selfish and if he saw something he liked he just wanted to have it. Knowing it wasn't my fault didn't make me feel much better. I just wanted us to be a family but it wasn't to be…

Before long Gary had committed further crimes. This time he wasn't sent to prison but to a hostel in Bristol. This was now the fourth time he'd been sentenced during our six years of marriage. But I saw hope in this hostel; perhaps they could help where custodial sentences had failed. I was afraid it might affect my working at the day centre but I was assured that it wouldn't. The manager said, "You are not responsible for your husband's behaviour or offending."

Gary was allowed to come home at weekends and for several months all went well. I told him that this was his very last chance and to make the point clear I had seen a solicitor and started divorce proceedings, however, I'd made arrangements not to action the final papers and as long as Gary didn't get into any further trouble they would stay on file. I made it quite clear that should there ever be any problems, with other women or crime, then the divorce would be finalised within minutes of me entering the solicitor's office.

The next six months were good, but then Gary told me he'd been charged with drink-driving whilst in Bristol. Immediately I thought, "That's it. He's been out to the nightclubs and drinking when he's supposed to be working at saving our marriage." I looked at the man I loved and said, "That's it, Gary. I can't and won't take any more. Four custodial sentences – this is not the right way to bring up the boys. What sort of role model are you for them? Our marriage is over; we will not be affected by your behaviour anymore."

Gary could see I was serious and his attempts to make me change my mind were futile. The divorce was finalised the next day; I just had to wait for the papers to be printed up.

Now I really had to start building a new future for the boys and myself. I was learning a lot at the day centre and started attending various training courses. During the school holidays I did less hours but sometimes took the boys up with me or arranged for someone to have them.

Months went by and my experience and knowledge grew. I'd been working as a volunteer for on average thirty hours a week for over three years. Tom was now in primary school and Adrian at the middle school. Thankfully the episodes of Tom holding his breath were behind us. They'd gone on for over four years, gradually reducing as he got older. Adrian had also had problems with his health all through primary school years. It had taken quite a while for me to realise that he had hearing loss. The school tests had failed to pick it up just as they'd failed to pick up a problem with his eyesight. Eventually, after one ear infection after another, it was decided that he should have an operation; the hospital told us that they couldn't do it for nine months, but Dad arranged for him to go in privately, not wanting him to suffer anymore.

Thankfully the operation was a success and now the physical health of both boys was good. Now I had to concentrate on providing emotional stability and strength.

One day when I went in to work at the day centre, the manager said, "Have a look at this, Marianne," handing me an advertisement for a job.

"Day Centre Manager wanted for North Devon Probation Department," I read and handed back the paper saying, "Hmm... Looks interesting... Are you thinking of applying?"

"No, not me. You!" came the response.

I smiled as I said, "You've got to be kidding. I couldn't apply for a job like that."

"I think you should and, what's more, I think you have a good chance of getting it," he insisted.

I sat down heavily, dumbfounded. I had no academic qualifications other than in hairdressing but here was this man recommending me to apply for a management job. Throughout the morning he kept on and on and in the end, as much to keep him quiet as anything else, I phoned up for an application form.

I walked down the stairs the next morning and there on the hallway mat was a large envelope. That evening I pored over the endless sheets of paper, information about the Probation Department, job description and lengthy application form. "I will not be beaten by this form," I said to myself. I sat down and started to draft out my responses and answers to the points and questions they were making. That night I phoned Dad. He was obviously pleased that I was thinking ahead and trying to plan for my future and that of the boys. Mum and Dad had been very supportive when I told them of my divorcing Gary and although they had always liked him as a person, they deplored his criminal behaviour and were worried about the effects his criminal lifestyle would have on the boys. I'd kept an awful lot of the circumstances and details to myself, not wanting them to know that something that was horrendously bad was in fact far worse. I talked with Dad about the form I held in front of me. Then I filled it out and next day put it in the post.

A few weeks later I was amazed when I was called for an interview. Dad drove me up to Barnstable to have a look around the project and the area.

"Why don't you work with the elderly or children, if you want to develop this sort of career?" Dad asked.

"Dad, I just feel drawn to this sort of work."

"But it would be so much safer than working with criminals," he said.

I knew he was finding it difficult to understand why I should choose to work in this field but a few days later he took me again for the interview. I had a joint interview with all the other applicants and then a personal interview with a panel of three. Two days later I was offered the job.

The boys and I would need to find somewhere to live, but before that I would have to start the job and it was during the summer holidays – what about the children? Without hesitation Jane offered to look after them for me. "You'll need to get off early in the morning, to walk nearly two miles to the station, catch a train and travel to Barnstable and then walk another mile to the Probation Department. You won't be home until late in the evening, so the boys can come and stay with me during the week and I'll bring them over at the weekends." This was a true Christian in action.

It was 'all systems go' arranging with the council about a house. Dad, through his work, knew some of the housing people in the area and put in a word for me. I was told that I was classed as a priority for housing since a job had been advertised but nobody locally had been appointed. Therefore, they were obliged to find me suitable accommodation. We were offered a modern house in a village three miles outside the town.

I found out about childminders and started on a new career, in a new town, as a single parent with two young children. This was not the fresh start I'd expected but now it was up to me to carve out a future for us as a family of three, plus of course Cindy. Never again would I let my children be adversely affected by a man. I would work hard and commit my time to my job and my children. This challenging, even frightening move would be a stepping-off point into a completely different and new life, not just for me, but for Adrian and Tom as well. All the responsibility would be on my shoulders, but likewise my decisions in different situations and circumstances would be solely in my control. No longer would I be *re*-active but rather *pro*-active in forging a more productive lifestyle.

CHAPTER THIRTEEN

A Challenging Time

Gary had now finished his time at the hostel and seemed genuinely pleased that I had accepted the new job. He offered to help us move up to North Devon. I wanted to keep on good terms with him not only for our sons' sake but also because of all we'd gone through together. He was a great help and as we followed the removal van along the winding roads to Barnstaple my stomach turned over as I thought of the ending of one part of my life and the beginning of another.

Adrian and Tom liked their new home. It was quite a small house and they would be sharing a bedroom again. There was a large back garden, which needed a lot of work, and we bordered on to the rolling hills of North Devon. On one side of us we had sheep for neighbours and the garden at the bottom of ours had a goat. The move went smoothly; we didn't have a lot of belongings because Gary and I had split the house contents now we had separated. At the end of a busy day we said goodbye to Gary and he promised to keep in touch.

There were to be a lot of new experiences for the boys, who previously had lived only in cities. They were now six and ten years old and so for the first year would be going to the same junior school in the village. The small building was very different to what they were used to. There was no playing field for football and Adrian was disappointed that he couldn't build on the natural skills he had and those he'd developed. He'd attended many training camps for budding footballers and was clearly talented but there was nowhere to play or practise in this small village.

From the time we moved in and started our new life as a family of three, I realised the importance of spending time with my sons. I had a heavy, demanding work schedule, but I knew I must balance that with being a mother to these two lads who'd had a traumatic and difficult start in life. "Every morning at breakfast and every evening whilst we eat our dinner, the three of us will sit either at the breakfast bar in the kitchen or at the table in the lounge to eat our meals, and we won't have the radio or television on," I announced just a few days after we'd settled in. Adrian's blue eyes and Tom's brown eyes looked back at me. I knew it was important to spend uninterrupted time with them when there were no distractions, and they accepted my statement without question.

7.30am and the taxi arrived to take Adrian and Tom to the childminders and then me to work. I'd been up since before six to give myself time to get ready for work, then the boys organised for school, before we would sit down together to eat breakfast. Our new home was three miles outside of Barnstaple. The only bus was once a week on market day and I had no other way of getting to work than by taxi. I realised I'd have to learn to drive and Dad had said he'd help me with buying a car, but for now I had to pay for a taxi twice a day.

The boys found it difficult settling in with childminders and even more difficult settling in at the school. The local children kept taunting them because they spoke with a different accent and were 'townies'. The village people referred to the fact that we lived, in their words, "on the estate". This was their description of the twenty council houses that had been built some ten years earlier. It made me laugh. They should have seen where we'd lived in Exeter; that was an estate! Hundreds of houses, not just twenty! Adrian and Tom stuck together and gradually made friends with a few of the other children; more importantly, they became closer to one another.

I tried to mix with the local community and thought attending the parent/teachers meeting might be a way of getting to know some of the others in the village. I arrived at the school a few minutes before the start of the meeting and smiled as I sat next to a smartly dressed woman. She turned to me and in a rather haughty voice said, "Oh, hello, are you new?"

"Yes, I moved here a few weeks ago."

"Oh, and do you work?"

"Yes."

"Would that be full time or part time?"

"Full time."

"Oh, and what do you do?"

"I'm the manager at the Probation Day Centre working with serious offenders."

"*Oh!* Well, I suppose somebody has to do it!" she replied, and with that statement she turned her back on me and talked to someone else.

On my first day in the new job, I walked into my office and sat at the desk. "Who'd have thought even a year ago that I'd be the manager of a day centre for the Probation Service?" I thought to myself. I'd enjoyed the interview but soon realised during the joint time with other applicants that they were far more qualified on paper than I was. Margaret, one of the women at the interview, was already working in the centre on a part time basis and I knew that was always a bonus. So I had been really surprised to be given the job and impressed when on my first day, as I was meeting with each of the staff in turn, Margaret came into the office and said, "Before we start, can I just say I'm really pleased that you got the job. I know you're the right person for the work there is to do here and I'll support you in whatever you do." I thanked her and realised just what a blessing she was going to be to the team, to the clients and to me.

Within a few weeks we were ready for the opening of this new facility. The day centre, which had previously been an ordinary probation centre, was now part of a pilot scheme and one of just five of its kind in the country. We were offering the courts an alternative to custody for serious offenders. I'd spent weeks on formulating a programme, presenting it to the court officials, and preparing the staff team.

I walked down the corridor into the kitchen. Every morning the staff gathered here for a coffee but today was to be different. We waited for the first clients to arrive. I'd already met the eight people who were to form the first group to take part in the programme. Prior to them appearing in court for a variety of serious crimes, I had talked with them about what this new programme could offer them. The majority had already completed twelve prison sentences and custody held no concern or fear for them. In fact, it was a place where they felt comfortable; it was the unknown that they found daunting.

Some of the people I'd seen in the past few weeks preferred to go to prison rather than try out the new programme, but others said, "If the court allows, we'll come to the centre."

"Don't think it's going to be an easy option," I said. "If you put one foot out of line you'll be breached and brought back before the courts and then your custodial sentence will be even longer. And while you're at the centre you'll be challenged and confronted in a way that never happens in prison. You'll be made to look at how you are leading your life and the effects it's had on others."

They looked back at me and nodded although they couldn't possibly know or comprehend what was ahead of them.

Now we waited for the eight people to arrive. Their crimes varied from grievous bodily harm and burglary with a weapon, to drug pushing, and drink-driving a stolen car where a pedestrian had been seriously injured, and sex offences. As the group gathered we made coffee, then we sat down and I went through the programme with them.

"Socialisation, literacy, numeracy, group sessions, relaxation, violent and aggressive behaviour and addictions are just some of the issues we are going to be discussing, enacting through role play and applying to your individual lives and then you'll be taking part in a 'hanging court' – but more on that nearer the time." I had their attention and we started that day's sessions.

At the end of the day I waited outside the building for the taxi, tired but fulfilled; it had been a good day's work. At 5.30pm the taxi arrived to take me to collect the children and then go home.

The boys had eaten a snack at the childminder's, after she'd picked them up from school, but now they were ready to eat again. By 6.15pm dinner was on the table and we sat together talking about our day. Tom and I played and chatted whilst Adrian did his homework, and then when Tom went to bed at 7.45pm, Adrian and I could have some time together before he went to bed at 8.30pm. As he walked up the stairs I went into the kitchen to start preparing the dinner for the next night so that all I would have to do when I got in from work the next day was put it in the microwave.

It was a warm balmy evening so I took a cup of coffee out into the back garden to enjoy the peace of the countryside. As I looked up at the tall, sturdy oak tree at the bottom of the garden, I felt strengthened even though the day had been long and tiring. Now I wanted my bed. As I walked up the stairs I had a really strong sense that just like that tree we were now growing in the right direction.

Monday to Friday our routine was much the same: up before 6am, busy throughout the day, a sandwich at my desk for lunch, home just before 6pm, dinner, chat, homework with the boys, prepare dinner for the next day, and then I'd fall into bed at 9.30pm. Saturdays we did the shopping and while the boys played in the fields and dammed the small stream, I cleaned and tidied the house. Sundays we went to church at the Baptist in Barnstaple. I had some kind of inherent sense that it was a good thing to do with the boys. We also went there once a week in the evenings; Adrian was in the Boys Brigade and Tom was in the Anchor Boys, where I also helped out. We became very friendly with Alan and Julie and their daughter Suzie, a family in the church. It was good to get to know others in the area, with whom we could be mutually supportive and helpful.

As time went on I passed my driving test and, as promised, Dad helped me out with a car. Our dog Cindy loved to run in the field and across the sand dunes on the beach. So the first night after I passed my driving test I said, "Come on, let's get Cindy in the car and we'll drive down to the beach near Saunton Sands, and later we'll get some chips." We piled in the car and I carefully drove through the winding lanes to the beach. As I strolled along the water's edge, the boys hid in the sand dunes and Cindy jumped high in the air as she bounded around trying to find them. Later we sat happy and contented on the beach sharing our chips with Cindy, then piled back into the car.

On the way back there was a line of traffic travelling very slowly up a steep hill, the only road away from the coastline, and we joined with the others. I could see that up ahead at the top of the hill was a T-junction and it was apparent that in both directions were blind corners. The car in front stopped and I braked, then pulled on my handbrake.

As the traffic started moving again, I began my well-practised hill start. But something was wrong. My foot slammed harder on the foot brake pedal. Amazed, I looked at the length of cable attached to the handbrake which was now freely moving around in my hand! The car in front had moved away, but how could I do a hill start without my handbrake? My driving instructor hadn't taught me this! The cable had snapped. I sat aghast and with my eyes transfixed on the cable in my hand. *What now?*

The cars behind me carefully overtook, easing their way through the small gap between our car and the hedge. They shouted abuse and glared at me but nobody offered any help. I gently eased the car back down the hill as Adrian slid down in his seat so that he couldn't be seen. "This is really embarrassing, Mum!" he said.

I considered my options. We were now the only car in sight and there was no other route to take. Eventually, I plucked up courage, put my hand on the horn and drove up the hill, praying that nothing was coming the other way across the T-junction. We arrived home safely with me having gained a fear of driving up hills that would last for many a year. Not a good position to be in as a driver in North Devon!

A few months later I awoke with conjunctivitis and called in to see the doctor on the way to work. He prescribed medication and I walked out of his surgery. I was just going out of the front door when a poster caught my eye: "Cervical Smear Test. Book now for this vital appointment." I stopped and paused.

The receptionist caught my eye. "The nurse is already in. You could see her now if you like," she said. I knew that if I made an appointment for later in the week I would be unlikely to keep it, so I smiled back and walked towards the nurse's room.

A few days later the surgery called me for further tests. Seeing my concern, the nurse said, "Try not to worry. Sometimes this happens. I expect it's a problem with the lab."

The days passed; work was hectic. Then one day the phone rang in my office and one of the secretaries said she was putting a call through to me. "This is the doctors' surgery. Could you please call in and see us sometime today?" I made the necessary arrangements at work and during my lunch break called in to see the doctor.

As I arrived back at work after my appointment, I gazed at my watch. I still had fifteen minutes left before I needed to be back in the day centre. I walked into the staff room and sat heavily in a chair.

My senior officer was sat on the other side of the room. "Marianne, are you alright?"

The voice that replied seemed to be a long way away and muffled as if passing through a cloud. "I've just been told I have precancerous cells of the cervix and I need laser treatment," this voice said. It sounded like me but I didn't feel as if I was functioning well enough to put words together and speak them out.

Before I had time to look up he was kneeling beside me holding my hand. "I'm so sorry," he said. He sat quietly with me as we talked through how I was feeling and practical arrangements about my taking time off work.

That night I phoned to tell Mum and Dad. "We'll be up at the weekend," they said. By the time they arrived I had an appointment for the following Friday for the treatment to be done by local anaesthetic at the hospital a few miles from our home. "We'll be up again next Friday and stay over the weekend so that you can rest," they said when I told them.

I looked at them anxiously. "But what about Adrian? He'll be on the end of his week's football coaching and that Friday I need to go and watch him get his awards."

"Don't worry, it'll all work out and your health is the most important thing," Dad said.

And so Mum and Dad arrived a week later. Mum stayed with Tom as Dad and I took Adrian to his football coaching and then me to the hospital. I'd said very little to the boys about my going to the hospital. I knew that they were starting to feel more and more secure as long as I was OK. Once again Gary had let them down badly and not kept in touch, but as long as I was well and strong they seemed to cope. I'd realised that if I had a headache or a bad cold then immediately their security was threatened and they professed to be ill, demanding that I see to their needs. I remembered back to the time when my mum had been taken seriously ill with the cerebral thrombosis and how that had threatened my sense of security as a young child.

As Dad and I walked through the corridors to Outpatients he held my hand tightly. With our family's now normal humour he said, "Don't worry, I won't feel a thing!"

I smiled back at him as I was taken in to the theatre. I didn't feel any pain, only discomfort, but to this day I still remember the smell of burning flesh: *mine!*

Afterwards I linked my arm through Dad's, cautiously walked out to the car park and got into his car.

"We'll go straight home and you can rest," he said.

"No," I replied. "I want to go and see Adrian. Let's go back, collect Mum and Tom, and go to the football ground."

I held on to Dad's arm tightly as we walked across the football pitch and proudly watched Adrian collect his awards. "Come on, Mum, play football with us," the boys said as we walked back across the field. "Not today, maybe next week," I answered. I was all too aware that the local anaesthetic I'd been given was starting to wear off.

Work was going well and having my own car gave us all greater freedom and was so much more convenient. I wasn't earning much; in fact, after taking out travelling costs, childminder fees and work expenses, I had no more money than when I'd been on state benefit, but life was good and I no longer lived in a high state of emotional anxiety. Word had gotten around about the 'hanging court' and now people were becoming very interested in the programme at the centre.

As I gathered together the latest group of clients, I explained, "Each of you will role-play a character that takes part in the court scene, one which you're all familiar with. In turn each of you will role-play the victim and the offender, but in this enactment there is no defence for the offender. The victim will confront you with your crime against them, but in this hanging court you have no defence counsel, you cannot answer them back."

The first client took the stand and the proceedings started. I watched as the man, a hardened criminal who'd already been in prison fourteen times, looked more and more aghast and broken as he became aware of how the impact of his crimes had devastated and destroyed the lives of his victims.

As I sat with him later he said, "I've never really thought about how it was for my victims. They must have been so afraid and still now they must be so angry and traumatised by what I've done to them. This has really opened my eyes."

The programme continued successfully and out of sixty people only one had reoffended ten years later.

The work took its toll on me and then I became the victim of sexual harassment from a colleague. After two-and-a-half years there I decided to move closer to Mum and Dad who'd now moved to Bristol. They had been so incredibly supportive to me and the boys over the recent years, and now they were retired I thought it would be good to be closer to them as they were the only family we had. Once again we made plans to swap houses with someone who wanted to come to a village outside Barnstaple. We found ourselves preparing to move to Trowbridge in Wiltshire.

The caretaker from work and some friends helped me and the boys load the van. Gary was not part of this move and in fact I took great care to ensure he couldn't find out where we'd gone. Even while he'd been once again in prison, he'd written to say he knew where I was going and with whom. Not for the first time he had people spying on me and informing him of my whereabouts and activities. Even now that we were divorced he was still checking up on me. It was as if he was a puppeteer and I was the puppet.

Emotionally he'd had a hold on me for years and now psychologically he still tried to maintain control and yet he failed to keep in touch with the boys, failed to send them cards at Christmas or birthdays, refused to pay any maintenance money. He'd proudly boast, "I'm not paying maintenance; after all, what are the government going to do to me? Send me to prison?' After so many chances and opportunities he was not acting, caring or taking responsibilities of a being a father, his title was in name only, so now I was making a completely clean break. Only a few friends knew my new address and they, along with the Probation Service, had confirmed they would not let anyone know where the boys and I were to be living.

CHAPTER FOURTEEN

Confronted

The house in Trowbridge was larger than the house we'd just left. It had three bedrooms and a large lounge, plus a garage. The garden at the back was also large and needed a lot of work doing to it. Two friends from Barnstaple stayed with us that weekend and by the late evening on the first night I looked around the house in amazement. You'd have thought we'd been living there for years. Everything was in place, shelves had been drilled and put up on the walls, boxes were unpacked and beds were ready to sleep in.

We'd all worked hard and it had been a difficult drive up in the morning. Since the age of sixteen I'd moved sixteen times so I should have been used to it. But that morning, after we'd loaded the van, I found I'd completely miscalculated the odds and ends that still needed to be moved. The boys and Cindy sat squashed in the car for the three-hour drive, surrounded by the extra boxes, the kettle, tea and coffee, dustpan and brush, broom and bags of odds and ends. They both held houseplants on their laps and with other bushes that we'd taken from the garden the car looked like a forest on wheels, with two boyish faces peering through the undergrowth. It was the middle of summer and the car kept overheating; the only way I could keep driving was to put the heater on full blast. I felt as if I was driving through a tropical rainforest!

But now here we were, ready to start the next stage of our life. I had no job but was entitled to claim benefit. To be back on government support again would be difficult and demoralising, but as a single parent I realised that it's not only when children are young that they need intensive attention but also when they are in their teenage years. At this age they frequently need to chat into the late hours of the night. I was aware that they'd experienced far too many domestic problems in the past and as they came to their teenage years they needed to process and discuss what had taken place. Being at home would give me the chance to spend more time with them and give me opportunity to reassess, take stock and consider the way forward. Adrian was now at high school. We'd come up to Trowbridge before the move and looked at the senior schools in the area and although we were in the catchment area for one, we decided that he should go to the other. It was three miles from the house and as soon as he was used to the roads he started cycling. He settled in quite quickly and apart from one incident where he was being bullied he soon made friends and was always in a rush to get to school early so that he'd have plenty of time for football before the bell rang.

Tom went to the local junior school. It was only a few minutes' walk from our house, yet typically for Tom he only just managed to arrive on time. I walked Cindy over the nearby fields and thought of the difference between my two sons. Adrian was sensitive and took things to heart, Tom was laid back and apparently dealt with most situations and trials like 'water off a duck's back'. I was all too aware that for both of them in their own way their childhood had been damaged by the choices I'd made. But during the last few years since we'd been on our own we'd known some good times of security, calmness and peace.

It felt as though in some way we'd been drawn to this town. I'd looked at a number of houses in different areas but this was clearly the one we were to take. I was pleased that there would be more activities on hand for the boys and they would have greater independence as they could easily walk or cycle into the town. We were also just a forty-five-minute drive from Mum and Dad who'd moved up to the small town of Keynsham, between Bristol and Bath, when Dad had retired. I walked Cindy back to the house and as I started preparing an evening meal I had a sense that this was going to be a good place for us.

As the months went by, it was good to have the chance to spend time cooking and making a home for the children. Adrian was now entering his teens and I knew it was important to spend time with him and have the emotional energy to be able to listen to him if he wanted to talk. Tom had always been a good child except for the rare occasions when he was very naughty – and then I used to really despair! Money was tight because I wasn't working but I did my best to provide not only the basics but also a few extras for the boys. I juggled between items for school and needs for the house, trips out and clothes. Presents at Christmas and birthday time were often items to do with their bedroom.

Tom progressed through life always presenting a good image to all those he met. In turn Adrian more than had his moments, although typically they were different to Tom's. Adrian moved from being an exceptionally good child to being a young man who became involved in some of the unhealthy aspects of teenage years. I realised that probably the majority of us go through challenging behaviour at some time in our lives. The important thing for me, as their mother, was to try to be firm when necessary, fair at all times and to love them unconditionally for the individuals they were, even if I didn't always like their actions.

Like all parents, I got it wrong – frequently. I recognised that I did and would make mistakes, but as a single parent, with no help from either of their fathers, all I could do was make what I believed to be the best decision at the time. This stood me in good stead throughout their growing up years. We went through our ups and downs, but I made sure that they knew the door was always open and I never missed an opportunity to tell them that I loved them.

I thought back to the time when I had taken the boys on frequent trips to stay for a day or two with my mum and dad. The boys would be in bed and Dad would start talking to me about my past. I'd sit silently and listen, hearing how I'd disappointed, disobeyed and hurt him and Mum. Why had I done those things when I'd been brought up to know right from wrong, he would ask. He always spoke to me in this way whenever I was staying overnight.

On one such visit, just as on previous occasions, he got up at ten o'clock, after the tirade, and announced he was off to bed. Mum, typically, had sat not saying a word and I'd sat feeling unable to speak. Dad walked off into the bedroom and I followed Mum into the kitchen.

"I know I did wrong in so many ways and that I caused you a lot of pain and I've tried over the years to make up for all the pain I caused you. But I really can't take this anymore. It seems Dad always has to bring up my past."

I was sobbing as I left the kitchen and Mum walked into their bedroom. I heard her say, "You had better go and see your daughter, *now*."

Dad came towards me, surprised that I was crying. "What on earth's the matter?" he asked. I told him how I felt. "But you know how proud I am of you. I tell everyone about you and the work you do and what a good mother you are. And you know that I love you."

"But you've never told *me*," I cried.

Dad hugged me so tight I was fighting for breath. "I'm so sorry," he said.

We cried together and that night marked a changing point in our relationship. From then on, whenever we talked, he always said, "Give my love to the boys and be sure and keep some for yourself." To not only be loved but to be told that you're loved is so vital.

Gradually the boys and I started finding our way around Trowbridge. I heard there was a Methodist church, which had a Boys Brigade, so we went along to check it out. The boys joined and we also found out about the times of the Sunday services, where the boys would also go out to Sunday school for part of the time.

On our first visit I sat between Adrian and Tom on one of the pews. We stood to sing and sat for the prayers, readings and sermon. Then, at the end of the service, a lady walked over to us and said, "Hello! Is this your first time here?"

"Yes," I said. "We've recently moved to Trowbridge. We haven't been here very long."

"Welcome to the church," she answered. "Where's your husband? Is he at home?"

"I don't have a husband," I answered.

"Oh, I'm so sorry. He's died?"

"No," I explained, "it's the other D word. I'm divorced."

"Oh! We've got another one like you. I'll go and find her and introduce you!"

I sat somewhat aghast, waiting to be introduced to 'another one like me'!

"This is Jean," the first lady said.

I looked up and promptly said, "So you're the other one like me, then?" I soon established that Jean was not only divorced but also had two children, a daughter and a son of similar ages to Adrian and Tom.

Over the weeks we started to arrange to meet for coffee and found that we had many things in common. It was good to be establishing a friendship and we started spending more and more time with each other.

We both had very supportive parents but I had never had the opportunity to be without both of my sons at the same time. Now Mum and Dad had offered to have both boys for a weekend so Jean and I booked a few days away in North Devon. I wanted to show her some of the places I knew and also, being in Trowbridge, I missed the sea. I knew I was a person who liked extremes. I'd loved the fast pace and noise of London and I'd loved the peace and relaxation of North Devon, but when I'd lived in the latter I'd had to get to a city at least every six weeks, otherwise I felt as though I was cut off from civilisation.

Mum and Dad came over to look after Adrian and Tom and of course our beloved Cindy. Dad loved walking Cindy over the fields and would have loved to have his own dog except that he and Mum knew that such a pet would put constraints on the freedom they now had in Dad's retirement. Jean's children had been able to stay with their father and so she and I set off travelling back to the wilds of North Devon.

It was Easter time as we drove out of Wiltshire, through Somerset into Devon. Passing the spring lambs frolicking in the fields we felt like a couple of spring chickens let loose into freedom. We stopped for coffee and a sticky bun and then we stopped for lunch.

Arriving in Ilfracombe we found our hotel and booked in. We'd been given a phone number by a friend and had been told that it was a nice hotel run by Christians and that the food was very good. As the lady showed us to our room she told us the time of dinner. We just had time for a quick walk along the seafront before getting back to shower and change for the evening meal. The food was certainly very good and beautifully presented. I felt my stomach stretch as I enjoyed every mouthful. We went for a stroll and then returned to the hotel to have a coffee before going to bed.

We'd talked all day and now we talked late into the night, often breaking out into laughter like schoolchildren and then we'd have to hide our heads under the pillows to muffle the sound so as not to wake the people in the next room. This was the first time in ten years I'd had such a break. Jean and I were acting like kids at a sleepover.

Next morning we arrived in the dining room bleary-eyed. Apparently another thing Jean and I had in common was that neither of us liked mornings! Each breakfast turned out to be a quiet affair when we'd sit drinking strong coffee and tea, trying to drag our brains and bodies into the new day.

As I started the car I really had no idea where we were going but we had all day so I decided we'd just meander through the lanes and enjoy the countryside and coastline. Turning down a lane we came to a place named 'Hunters Lodge', with a sign saying "Heddons Mouth, 1 mile". I pulled into the car park and we got out, following the signs to the mouth of the river. We carried on talking – or rather, prattling away. In fact, we'd hardly stopped since we'd left Trowbridge twenty-four hours before. Except, that is, for the few hours in the night when we were totally exhausted and even our mouths needed to rest!

As I walked alongside the riverbank, I looked up high to the left and right. We were in a deep valley and either side of me the steep hills were covered with bright gorse and heather. It was a magnificent sight but still we carried on talking about nothing in particular. The day was windy and grey, thick clouds were coming in off the sea and there was a wildness to this part of Exmoor, but most of the scenery went unnoticed as these two spring chickens endlessly gabbled and crowed, giggled and chatted.

As we reached the mouth of the river I stopped! Not only were my feet and legs still, but also my mouth! After a while I moved off to one side of the bay. Still silent, I was aware that Jean had moved to the other side of the bay. I sat on a big boulder looking out to sea. Overawed and totally overwhelmed I had become aware that I was in the presence of God! This powerful majestic Creator was not only all around me but right in front of me, closer than the stretch of my hand. I knew I was in His presence. I stayed silent, dumbstruck, as His Being surrounded, embraced and infilled me. Time went by, I was unaware of anything else around me, only Him, the Almighty. Where had He come from? It was as though God had come out of nowhere, interrupted my conversation with Jean and drawn me to one side. Now He was saying, "I'm here, the Creator of the world. Will you sit with Me and get to know Me as I know you?"

Unaware of how long I had sat in complete oneness with God, I got up and slowly started walking back towards the pathway. Jean walked over to join me. Through the tears that were cascading down my face I could see that she too was crying.

We walked back in silence. Not one single word was uttered. We were both clearly gobsmacked. I felt as if I'd been hit over the head with a baseball bat; but not in a way that hurt, just in a way of being woken up. This was my spiritual wake-up call. Who was I? Where had I come from? What had I done? Why was I here? What was I doing? How did I fit into the great plan of life and creation? Where was I going? What was the meaning and purpose of my life?

I sat in the car and after a while turned to Jean and said, "What on earth happened back there? One minute we were chatting away and then..."

I drove back to the hotel. We were much more subdued than we had been the previous night, but following a delicious meal we knew we needed to find a church service to attend the following morning. As we walked around Ilfracombe we tried to understand what had happened. Each of us, but independently and individually, had been touched and affected in a way we couldn't express in words. I knew God had met with me and I had spent time enthralled by His presence. My whole being reeled from the effect of this 'baseball bat' experience. I felt I would never be the same again.

That night Jean and I again tried to find the words that could even begin to describe what had happened at Heddons Mouth. No words in the English language could encapsulate that moment of time. The day had been 'mind-blowing' and I still lay reeling from the spiritual impact that had shaken me to the very core of my being. We had not been talking about anything spiritual. I had not been seeking God or asking questions about creation – *but He had come to me.* It was true that my parents attended church, raised me to go to church and I'd had an interest in Religious Studies at school, but for years my actions and lifestyle had been against everything that the church and God stood for. Paul, on the road to Damascus, had been struck blind. At Heddons Mouth I had, for a short while, been struck dumb. God had confronted me.

Eventually I slept.

Next morning we packed our few belongings and put the bags into the car before going in to breakfast. We'd found a church with a morning service, so as soon as we finished a delicious plate of eggs and bacon we settled the bill and drove into the town. It was a large church and as the preacher walked in I turned to Jean and said, "Oh, my golly... If I go to sleep, give me a nudge." I had taken one look at the very elderly preacher and thought, "This is going to be so boring, just like most of the services I go to."

For me, church was the place to go to and take your children. I felt it was the right thing to do. Just as I'd been brought up to go to church, I now took my children; everyone there was quite sociable and many of them were really nice people. I enjoyed the time and liked to sing and it seemed to be the right thing to do for an hour once a week. But once outside the church building, life was much the same for me as for those who never went there.

I sat waiting to see if I knew the hymns, hoping we were in for a good sing. They were OK, and then I watched as the elderly gentleman made his way cautiously to the pulpit.

"Jesus is the Good Shepherd. Matthew 18 verses 10 to 14. He will seek out even one lost sheep..."

Impact! It was as if the words penetrated my very soul. I knew then that Jesus had sought me out and found me. Yesterday, God had confronted me, and now I was being challenged: did I want to recognise my Shepherd and respond to His voice? Rather than going to sleep, I listened intently to this elderly gentleman, who brought alive this passage about Jesus. Was I prepared to be one of His flock, to follow Him and be led by Him, or was I going to continue going my own way, doing my own thing? Was I going to continue to just get by under my own steam or was I going to follow the One who had created me? *Wow!*

None of it made sense in my head but in my spirit it was all so clear; my life wasn't just about me, I was a part of something so much bigger and now I needed to find out how I fitted into this bigger plan.

I knew that one of the first things I had to do when I got back to Trowbridge was to talk to Edmee; she was the minister at the Methodist church. I knew her quite well because I also did cleaning for her in the manse. She'd been very good to me and the boys, and when I had told her about trying to cover my tracks from Gary when I moved she said, "If ever you need a bolt-hole for any reason and for however long just bring the boys and yourself over here. You've got the key to the manse so you can let yourself in at any time even if I'm not here."

On Monday morning I called her and said, "Edmee, something's happened to me over the weekend. Can I come and see you?" I went to the manse and we talked about my encounter with God and my desire to respond.

"Marianne, I don't believe we can feed you in the way you now need. I believe I must let you move to another church." To say I was surprised by her response was an understatement. Fancy telling me to go to another church! But Edmee went on to explain. "Marianne, it's as if you are a new baby, a new life. Spiritually you have been awakened; it is as if you have literally been reborn. You are full of questions, fascinated by your encounter, and marvelling at the experience. You need to meet with those who will guide you to answers, share their experiences with you and understand the wonder of God's grace."

I looked at this gracious lady and said, "Well, I have been going to the Baptist church occasionally. Maybe I'll see about going there."

She prayed with me in her lounge and I left to consider what I should do.

CHAPTER FIFTEEN

Commitment

It was emotionally painful saying goodbye to the people in the Methodist church. Some had been very kind to the boys and me. One couple had taken us all to the local Bath and West Festival; it was a lovely day out and they'd kindly treated us and paid for all our expenses. I was still managing to run the car, although Dad helped me with some of the main bills, but there was little money left over for other extras. I was now working at the local school in the lunchtimes as a dinner lady and this gave me a few pounds a week on top of my benefits to pay for petrol. I liked the work at the school and enjoyed working with the more difficult children or those with behavioural problems. But we only just managed to financially cover the main bills. To be offered a day out by the kindness of others was very humbling and the boys and I had even had a wonderful week's holiday funded for us by a grant connected to the Methodist church. So with so much gratitude to so many people it was with some difficulty that we moved to another church.

But now it was time to make a change, not in my work, but in my church. I tried to explain to people why I was leaving, but most couldn't understand. I spent hours drinking coffee, saying that I had Edmee's blessing and that I would still be seeing them around the town, but some seemed to take my leaving the church personally. It saddened me that this was the case but I knew I had been dramatically awakened by my Creator; I had questions that needed answering. I was hungry for God's word and knew that my priority had to be building on my relationship with God through Jesus.

I started attending the Baptist church regularly. Unfortunately, this gave Adrian a reason to stop attending church. Quite a while ago he'd given up the Boys Brigade and he'd been going to church under sufferance. Now he said, "I don't want to go somewhere new again; the service at this church is much longer and I don't like the clapping. I'd rather play football." I couldn't drag him to the services so in the end, with regret, I accepted that he'd no longer come along. Tom was that much younger so as a matter of course he came with me.

It wasn't long before I started being involved in the worship group. I enjoyed not only the singing but also the freedom there was at this church in the way you could sing and move. It was as if they worshipped God with their whole being, not just their mouths singing songs of praise. Two guys, Steve and Keith, played base and twelve-string guitar, and individually they were an encouragement and support to me. Paul, the person that played piano at the monthly Saturday Celebrations, was incredibly gifted and I was very blessed in the fellowship of these people. We'd talk about God, Jesus and Holy Spirit in a very natural way and in everyday conversations. This wasn't a religion that came out at church on a Sunday; this was about relationship and personally knowing the ways of God, and I could identify with this after the way in which He had met with me in North Devon.

One Sunday morning I listened intently to all that was being said from the front of the church. It was as if it was God himself talking to me. Later I turned to Jean as we drank coffee after the service; she'd left the Methodist church a short while after me and was now also attending this Baptist church.

"Well, that's it then, isn't it?" I said.

"What's it?" she responded looking at me somewhat confused.

But there was no confusion in my mind. "I must be baptised."

"You must?"

"Yes, didn't you hear? He clearly told me in the word this morning."

"Oh, I'll come round this afternoon and hear all about it," she said as we got in our cars and drove home to have our Sunday lunch with our respective children.

We talked through the afternoon and left to go to the evening service. Then that night Jean also heard the Lord say, "Believe and be baptised." We made an appointment to see the pastor and soon plans were underway to prepare for our total immersion baptism.

A few weeks later I was sitting in the evening service listening to the word of God. By the end of the sermon I was sobbing uncontrollably as I was released from the build-up of undealt-with grief, loss, guilt and a desire for forgiveness. All that had been so crushing was taken from me. My tears could have filled the baptistry as they flowed ceaselessly. That evening God was so amazing; it was as if that deep, dark mess in my life was flushed clean. As I listened to the story of Jonah, I asked God's forgiveness for all the things I'd done wrong. No sin was unforgivable, all sin was equal to Him, and I knew that if I wanted to further experience what I had at Heddons Mouth then the only way was to accept that Jesus had died for my sins.

There had been so much that I had done against God and people, and yet I now knew God had forgiven me. He washed my slate clean. I shed tears for all my wrongdoings, for having sex when I should have said no, for the baby I'd killed, the son I'd given away, the pain I'd put Mum and Dad through, how my actions had hurt others, for the years I'd strayed away from God and His best for me. I could attempt to explain away so many of my decisions and actions, or even blame others, but nothing could justify my past before a Holy God.

Through my acceptance that Jesus had died for my sins, it was as if God took from me all the bitterness and pain of my marriages. I knew that Carl was in God's loving arms. I understood that life on earth was for a period of time and that Carl would never know the painful problems of this world and was forever resting at peace with the One who had given him life (albeit a short one) on this earth. I knew that God accepted and loved me; I was His precious child.

I walked out of the church a new woman, with a sure hope and a certain future in Him. I'd longed for many, many years to have a sense of peace within me and now for the first time I knew what it was to know peace of mind, heart and spirit.

I spent time explaining to Mum and Dad why I was being baptised. As Methodists they'd had me christened as a baby, just as I'd had Adrian and Tom christened as babies. I'd become a member of the Methodist church during my adult years, but now my understanding of the Bible was, "Believe and be baptised."

As I walked into the church it felt like a sauna. The steam from the baptistry hung in the air. It was a lovely summer's evening as I prepared for this special, significant Sunday service. Mum and Dad, Adrian and Tom were among the many church members and friends who attended the service. Jean and I had chosen many worship songs and hymns to be sung before, during and after our baptism. I spoke out the story of my testimony to the people in the church.

My gratitude and thankfulness for God's grace and forgiveness surged within my heart. I had made such a mess of my life, seeking a quick-fix happiness. I had been constantly searching for that 'something' which was beyond words to be my purpose, meet my needs and give me true total fulfilment. For so long I'd been on a quest to fill the void, the cavernous deep gap in my life. Now I understood that the only one who could make me complete was the One who'd made me in the first place. I had been created for a purpose; God had a plan for me and my life; He would meet all my needs and give me a life that was full beyond measure. He wanted only the best for me, not only for now but always.

I entered the warm water and stood as I professed faith in Jesus. As the pastor took me under the water I knew that I was proclaiming that I had died to my old life and that I knew I could only be in a right place with God if I accepted that I was a sinner and that Jesus had died for my sins. That time under the water was in reality so short, yet the moment felt like a lifetime as I was totally surrounded and saturated by the peace of Christ. I now knew what it was to be in His presence and be blessed by the peace of God that is beyond our ability to understand. I came up out of the water and it was as if for the first time I was really alive.

I sang the words of Carol Owens' song 'Freely, freely',[9] which seemed to have been written for me at that moment. Just as I had received God's love, I now had a passion to share that love with others.

Adrian walked purposely and quickly towards me. We had just taken a break in the service to have a cold drink before joining together in communion. As he put his arms around me, I realised he'd made a determined effort to be the first person to get to me after I'd been

[9] You can read the full lyrics at www.worshiptogether.com/songs/freely-freely

baptised. "Mum, I've never seen you look so happy," he said. I rejoiced that Jesus was radiant in my life and that Adrian could see that Christ had transformed me.

I was hungry for times of prayer and Bible study and became aware of a sense of burden. It was a strange feeling, like a concerned thought that just wouldn't go away. It was a new experience for me and 'burden' was not a word I'd ever used before. Strangely, I also knew that it was God giving me this depth of concern. God was causing me to be concerned for homeless people. But what could I do? I may have worked with offenders and addicts in the past, but that had been in a different part of the country. I knew there was no help or support for single homeless people in the Trowbridge area, but there seemed nothing I could do. I didn't know any of the officials in the area, I had no money to provide anything myself and, anyway, I didn't like homeless people!

I still remembered when I'd visited a shelter for the homeless during the time when I'd worked as a volunteer in Exeter. I'd been shown around a night shelter for single homeless men and I could still see myself stood on the pavement outside of the hostel vehemently saying, "I will never work with homeless people." The stench was still in my nostrils; I'd felt repulsed and sickened. I recalled being at Victoria railway station in the early hours of New Year's Day and seeing the homeless people lying on the benches. I remembered thinking that no doubt it was their own fault or maybe they just wanted to live like that.

But God kept increasing the weight of this burden and I knew He was giving me His heart for His people. I talked with others in the town about the homeless situation. Trowbridge, although the county town, was only a small rural town and there were only a few people occasionally that had nowhere to live. But it was also clear that the problem was going to get a lot worse as changes in benefits took place and there were more and more breakdowns in families, people coming out of prison and even those previously in the armed forces not infrequently finding themselves homeless. Also drug-taking was on the increase and clearly that would raise the numbers of people who found themselves homeless.

But what could I do? I talked with God and explained to Him that I thought He had it slightly wrong. "What you really mean is, not that you want me to help these people, but rather that you want me to tell someone else what they should be doing about it," I would say. Night after night I talked and He listened; very occasionally I let Him talk and I listened.

One night I listened as He said, "Marianne, you gave your life to me when you made your commitment. You said, 'Let me live my life according to your will, God, not mine.' Well, Marianne, I'm asking you to help these people."

"But God," I replied, "I don't *like* homeless people!"

I knew I was in the wrong. I knew that we were all children of God and that He cared for the homeless just as He cared for me, that He wanted to reach out and touch them just as He had reached out and touched me. I came to realise that the inevitable was about to happen.

I sat on my bed and said, "OK, Lord, I will do what you ask."

Immediately, it was as if I was flooded with God's love for homeless people. I was instantly given His passionate, unconditional love for a people I was yet to meet. It was as if He had waited for me to be obedient, then He had poured into me His compassion and enabling, to be a servant with a servant heart. As I sat on the bed the picture was so clear I graphically followed the vision He was giving me; a clear picture of a building offering empathy, support and love based on His truths.

"Thank you, Lord," I said. "You have given me a love for your people, you have shown me what you want me to do and I know you will enable and equip me to do this work you have called me to."

CHAPTER SIXTEEN

Action on Homelessness

I was excited by this encounter with God. I'd never had a vision before and it had been so clear. I went to speak to my pastor, but he did not feel led to support a work with the homeless so I went to the leaders of other denominations in the wider church. It was coming up to Christmas and we talked of providing a lunch on Christmas Day, but nothing came of it. Talk didn't result in action.

I turned back to God, exasperated. What else could I do? I was unknown in this town, I'd never worked in Trowbridge in a professional capacity and nobody was taking me seriously. "Homeless? There are no homeless here. We know there's Cardboard City in London and there's a problem in Bristol. But there'll never be homeless people in Bath because that's a very nice city and there'll certainly never be any homeless people in Trowbridge. Anyway it's their own fault they're homeless; either that or they want to be homeless; it's not for us to do anything about their problem." Constantly I heard these comments and thought of how I'd often said the same thing.

One day I'd just arrived home from my job at the school when there was a knock at the door. As I looked at the woman on my doorstep I knew she was canvassing for the local elections. She introduced herself as Ann and when she'd finished telling me what her party would do for the local people I said, "OK, now I know what you stand for, but what about the homeless?"

Without hesitation she replied, "As soon as the elections are over, I'll phone you and we'll get together and see what can be done." She took my phone number and left.

I watched her walk down the road to knock on the next door and thought, "I bet I won't hear from you again."

Within the week we were sitting having coffee in a café in the town. I had been wrong. I was still learning that I should not prejudge people. Ann had been elected for her party and she'd phoned me and suggested a meeting with her and another person called Paula who was a local youth worker. Paula, too, had a heart for young homeless people; she worked professionally and tirelessly and over the years I was blessed by her support and friendship. From that meeting we established ourselves as a steering committee. At last something was starting to happen. We arranged a number of public meetings to assess the local situation, pool information and seek a way forward.

Six months later we were still talking. People were saying, "Until you have the money to build a hostel, pay for staff and do everything that's needed, there's no point in starting to provide anything else."

"Ann, I've had enough of meetings," I said. "We may have walked the streets at dawn and seen a few people that are living on the streets, but so far we're all talk and no action. We know from what's happening elsewhere in the country that it's not going to be long before there are more homeless people in this area. Obviously it's going to take a long time to provide everything that's needed but it's important and necessary that we start doing something now. That way, at least the homeless people know that we know they exist and we're starting, albeit in a small way, to try and help. We need to be about action."

Ann agreed. 'Action on Homelessness' was formed and we set about forming a management committee with all the legal requirements to be a registered charity.

I found a church that was prepared to let us use their church hall one day a week and posters were sent out telling people what time we'd be open and that we required volunteers to cook food and generally help out at this new centre opening for homeless people.

A number of people made contact and before I knew it, my lounge, our only living area, was turned into an office and storage centre. The local community had responded quickly to the appeal for socks, warm clothes and blankets. Often I returned home to find bulging black bags on my doorstep. For the next year the boys and I had to negotiate our way around dozens of black bin liner bags that were full of second hand clothes. It wasn't unusual to find that they weren't clean, so I would wash, dry and put them back into the bags. The phone rang constantly, especially at teatime when people thought they were most likely to find me in. People rang with offers of support and many others with information about someone who was homeless or problems relating to homelessness.

We opened the day centre at the beginning of November. I was still doing the school job so we had to close by 11.30am. But we could offer a cooked breakfast, change of clothes, blankets and advice on accommodation, benefits and other support services. I was well aware that only to open one day a week was very little but we had to start somewhere and we had no venue to operate from on other days.

The second time we were open, a middle-aged man walked through the door. I wondered just how difficult that had been for him. The church hall was up a narrow lane out of the town centre; two sets of large wooden doors were firmly closed trying to conserve the inadequate heating in the church hall. How had he felt coming into a strange place, not knowing who was on the other side of the doors, how he would be received or what we could do for him? As the man came in I looked up and smiled; walking towards him I extended my hand and shook his warmly.

"Hi," I said, "my name's Marianne. Come on in and sit by the heater. Would you like tea or coffee?" I got his drink and then said that we would cook him some eggs, sausages, beans and toast.

He thanked me and then openly told me his story. "My name's Sam, I'm a qualified engineer and I worked for the same company for nearly twenty years. I was made redundant six months ago and then everything started going wrong in my life. I couldn't find another job and my wife was always nagging me. There was less money coming in the house and then there was trouble with the mortgage. She's turned the children against me. I've lost my job, my wife and my children. She threw me out of the house three months ago and since then I've been sleeping rough. I've been catching wild rabbits and cooking on an open fire but the last few weeks I've been feeling so desperate; it gave me hope when I saw your poster in the local library."

Hearing Sam's story, I thanked God that this man now knew that there was hope for him, a light at the end of the tunnel.

Sam ate his breakfast and then I asked him, "Is there anything else I can get you?"

"Would you happen to have a pair of socks?" he asked.

"Yes of course," I said and started looking for socks, shoes, clothing and blankets.

I handed them to him and watched as he took off his shoes and socks. I tried to hold on to the contents of my stomach as I saw part of his foot come away with the socks! Sam had been walking mile after mile to keep up his body temperature. In the wet, his shoes and socks had become soaked. With no dry socks to put on and no way of drying out his shoes, his skin, constantly wet and rubbing, had developed blisters. As he'd walked, the blisters had broken and wept and then, since he was still unable to change or dry out the socks and shoes, the skin had re-grown around the sock material and the two had become as one. As he peeled off his sock he was literally also peeling away part of his foot.

I looked at the raw expanse of flesh. "I think you should go to the casualty department at the local hospital," I said.

"No, I can't," he replied simply.

I thought he didn't know where it was, so promptly offered to take him.

"You don't understand," he said. "I know I'm dirty and smelly. I feel ashamed and humiliated. Once I was a man with a respectable job, a wife, children and a house. Now I am a nobody, I have no one and nothing. I've seen how people look at me when I'm in the town. That's why I spend most of my time in the fields. I'm too ashamed to go to the hospital."

My heart went out to him. This was not his fault; he didn't choose to be in this position. He was a person who had lost all that was precious to him. He was hurting and in need.

I thanked God that He'd opened my eyes and my heart. I knew I was privileged to be alongside Sam. I didn't feel repulsed or sickened as I applied first aid to his feet. I didn't notice the stench as I took away his old socks and shoes. I just felt God-given love and compassion.

God had certainly worked a miracle in my life. He'd given me His love for His people. His compassion was evident. I now had a better understanding not only of God and His Creation but how He had planned for our lives to be. But once sin had become a part of the human race we needed to be provided with a way to get back into our rightful place, in fellowship with God. We were created to be a help and support to one another, to care and live in community. God was now blessing me as I sought to serve Him by serving others.

Within a few weeks we'd been offered another venue, one day a week, in a different part of the town. Now we could provide a breakfast two days a week. Gradually more people started coming in and we told them that we'd be open on Christmas Day for lunch. There were now several volunteers helping on a rota basis and more offered to come on Christmas Day. As we all sat down for our lunch I thanked God for His provision. Just the previous day we had found somewhere for Sam to live, food had been donated and the freezer which we'd been given by the local council was well stocked and would supplement food supplies into the following year.

News was getting around that Action on Homelessness was up and running and actively helping to support single homeless people over the age of eighteen in Trowbridge and West Wiltshire. The local Pentecostal church offered us their church meeting room during the daytime Monday to Friday. Praise God, we could now open five days a week, there was a small kitchen and toilets, and it was central to the town. It soon became clear that the people coming in to use the centre would prefer to come in mid-morning and eat lunch rather than breakfast. I had failed to recognise that for those sleeping rough, they often need to walk around during the night-time hours to keep warm and then fall asleep at around dawn, so don't wake until halfway through the morning. I considered my own situation. I had my small part-time job at the school but that was over the lunchtime. Should the centre be open during the hours that suited me or during the hours that were appropriate for the people who needed the service?

I felt I should be there for them, just as Jesus was there for me and is there for any who choose to come to Him. But to be open and serve lunch would mean giving up my job and losing the money that provided the finances I needed to support the boys and myself.

I gave in my notice at the school. I knew God was saying, "Be my servant and I will provide." I was so excited and blessed to see His hand at work. I'd known a life where I was under the control of others; I'd known a life where I had taken control and directed my own path. Now I was learning what it was to hand my life over to the One who had given me life in the first place; to trust, depend and rely on Him. I couldn't work out how my bills would be paid, how I would manage with the costs of the children, but I did have a belief that if I was truly trying to do what I believed God was asking of me, that all would be well, that our needs would be met and that I would know the blessing of what life was really about.

People brought food and clothing to the centre. There was little storage space so the clothing added to the pile of black bin liners in my lounge and garage. It was evident that sleeping bags were more practical than blankets and in response to an appeal, through the local churches and newspapers, people brought old and sometimes even new sleeping bags either to the centre or my home. Sometimes food would be left on my doorstep with a note saying, "This is for you and your sons to help with your own food costs." A group of people unknown to me decided to make up the financial loss of my schoolwork by pledging an amount of money each month. Faithfully they supported me over the next three years. Jean had become a great help and support in many ways, one of which was to administer the pledges.

I was enabled to keep petrol in the car, which in turn enabled me not only to take food out to people in the evenings, but also to travel to other centres in the south of England and see what they were doing. I had much to learn, but I was aware that God was graciously giving me wisdom, insight and discernment.

I heard of a night shelter that was open in the centre of Bristol and arranged to visit. Dad drove me down into the city centre. It was eight o'clock and there was already a long queue of people waiting to be let in when the doors opened at ten. I went into the disused bus garage that was now being used to provide a hot meal for over one hundred people every night and a bed for the first thirty-nine who claimed one. It was harvest time and there was an abundance of fresh vegetables that had been donated from local harvest festival services. Bread that was left over at the end of the day in city bakeries had been collected and was now being sliced and put on plates. As I chopped vegetables in the kitchen I looked through the hatchway into the large area beyond. Thirty-nine beds with dirty, stained mattresses were in the middle of the old garage. Near to the kitchen hatch were rows of tables and chairs and to one side was a row of toilets. They were the sort that you saw temporarily put up at festivals and fairs. They had no doors on, so there was no privacy.

The lady who was chopping carrots alongside me said, "We have to take the doors off, otherwise they could be taking drugs in there. Also we don't put the bread on the table, otherwise they'll throw it all over the room. And have you read the notice on the door going from the kitchen into the garage area?"

I looked up and saw, "FOR YOUR OWN SAFETY, DO NOT GO INTO THE EATING/SLEEPING AREA UNLESS YOU ARE WITH ANOTHER VOLUNTEER."

The vegetables boiled away making a tasty stew. We sat and drank a cup of coffee as I was told, "We open the doors at ten o'clock. At twelve, those who have not claimed a bed have to leave. We often get a lot of trouble because more than one person states that they've claimed a bed and then people refuse to leave. When that happens we call the police. By two or three o'clock it's generally fairly quiet, then we wake everyone up at six thirty because we need to dish up the breakfast and clear up before we have to leave at eight o'clock.

The doors opened and a swarm of humanity pushed and fought its way to the hatchway. Some threw a bag or blanket on to a bed to claim their sleeping space for the night, others just elbowed and shoved their way around the hatchway demanding to know what there was to eat. I started dishing up the wholesome vegetable stew and handing it to one of the other women volunteers that was at the hatchway. Several people tried to grab the plate and a piece of bread from her. As each got his plate they pushed their way through the crowd to a table. One man looked at the dish that had been handed to him and said, "What garbage do you call this? I'm not eating this!" Inwardly I gasped in amazement as I saw him throw the stew over the woman at the counter.

"What on earth am I doing here?" my voice screamed inside my head. I was mortified at the appalling way people were behaving and how ungrateful they appeared to be.

But God challenged me not to judge. "I grieve when I see My children who have no respect for others and have no respect for themselves," I felt Him say as He looked upon His creation and wept to see the pain of rejection, abuse and lack of love that caused so many to lash out, even at those who were trying to help. What had happened to this person that he currently had so little regard for others and even less for himself? He, like all, had been born as a babe – sweet, gentle and vulnerable, simply needing to be loved and nurtured. What had happened to bring him so low, degraded, angry and bitter?

I thought of the years that I'd lashed out in different ways at those who had tried to show and guide me along His path: Mum and Dad, the teachings I'd received at church, family friends and others. But I had turned my back on their guidance; I'd ended up hurting them and hurting myself. Time after time I'd gone down the wrong path. I'd had a choice as to what to do but I'd chosen badly. Yet God had stood by patiently waiting with open arms. Even though it grieved Him to see how I was living, His love was never-ending. Now I sensed Him saying to me, "Through your actions show the homeless people in Trowbridge My love. Base that action on My guidelines. Show them compassion; be non-judgemental for you do not know their plight. Value them as I value them. Respect them, for they are a part of My creation; they are suffering so give them time and space to value and respect themselves. Sit with them as they come to understand the consequences of their actions and listen to them as they tell their stories. Let them move towards understanding the value of having values/guidelines to live by and the benefits of not only being a part of but contributing to the community in which they live."

I thought back over my own life. If only I'd applied the guidelines of scripture to my life, known unconditional love, felt valued for who I was and had a sense of purpose, then perhaps I wouldn't have become pregnant at fifteen and again at seventeen. I wouldn't have rushed into a marriage that clearly wasn't right, and I wouldn't then have fallen into the arms of another man. But I was already seeing how God could and would use all these situations and experiences. God was bringing about a change, from all the bad and destructive things in my life to good and constructive things. Through Jesus, I had come to know my heavenly Father and had received His love, His joy, His peace and above all His forgiveness. I now wanted to let others know of His grace and mercy. I wanted them to know that there was hope, that life was valuable, that men and women had been created to be respected and have dignity and that when all seemed lost, Father God would be waiting for His child to simply return to Him so that He could restore all that had been taken away.

Outwardly, little had changed. I still worked, but now it was in His strength and according to His will rather than my own. Money was still tight, I received no wages, but God provided and met all my needs. I was still a single parent with responsibility for my sons, but Jesus was my constant companion so I never felt loneliness or isolation. I still had no academic qualifications but through prayer God gave me wisdom and discernment. I had no idea what the future held but I knew that God had a purpose for me and that He desired me to live an abundant life that would stretch into all eternity. I now knew not only that life on earth was for a period of time and that for each of us the length of that time would be different, but that the time in this world was only a forerunner for the time which was to come.

I was jolted out of my thoughts by the screaming, shouting and swearing in the disused bus garage that acted as a night shelter. It was twelve o'clock and two women were trying to persuade people to leave. Fighting broke out at the main door; one of the volunteers was injured and now needed to go to hospital. Eventually there was comparative calm. There were just two other volunteers and me who would be on duty throughout the night. Yelling and friction continued in spates until three in the morning. Many people were suffering from the effects of alcohol or drugs and many also had severe mental health problems. Their minds were in turmoil and their lives were chaotic.

I talked with the other volunteers throughout the night. What were the life stories behind the people who had queued for so long to receive handouts of food and maybe a bed? Many, I heard, had similar backgrounds to Sam; others had been abused at home and existence on the streets was preferable to the life at home; still others had been released from mental hospitals under the Care in the Community Act and now had nowhere else to go; some were former military personnel who were suffering what we now understand to be post-traumatic stress; others were suffering from addictions and I thought back to the time that I'd looked at the bottle of sherry knowing that if I took a drink then I might never stop.

At five thirty we started preparing for breakfast. By nine thirty I was at Mum and Dad's home recounting the events of the night.

Numbers attending the Action on Homelessness day centre were increasing. Volunteers were responding to appeals for help and we regularly met together to discuss how we should develop the charity. Ann, who had been our chairperson for twelve months, now felt it was time for her to commit to other projects. It was clearly necessary to have the right person to replace her. God led me to make inquiries about a new person who had recently moved into the area. Richard was the Area Director of Lloyds Bank and a committed Christian. I phoned his office and asked for an appointment to speak with him. He received me warmly and listened intently as I told him of the vision I'd been given and the work of Action on Homelessness. I thanked him for his time and he said, "I need to think about and pray about what you have said. I'll contact you by the end of the week." It was Monday. By Friday I'd not heard from him.

For quite a time I had been involved in a music ministry team and on Sunday evening we were leading the worship at a local church. Just before the start of the worship Richard walked in and took a seat. As I listened to the scripture message given that evening, I prayed that Richard was hearing the same calling as I was through the Word of God. At the end of the service I walked over to him and he said, "Well, what can I say after that message? I must say yes. Can we meet again and talk in more detail?" My heart leapt and I couldn't contain my excitement as we agreed a date.

Richard was a good balance for me; he was calm, quiet and precise, considering all aspects before taking action, against my more frenetic, talkative and let's-get-in-there-and-do-it personality. I quickly came to love, admire and respect this man of God who committed so much time and expertise to help those whose lifestyle and experiences were a long way from his own. Carol, his wife, became the charity's secretary. Her humour was refreshing, her gentleness relaxing and her faith reassuring. As a couple they blessed me personally in many ways and used their personal attributes and financial blessings in a way that blessed others.

Richard was elected as Chairman, and with Frank, another Christian and ex Bank Manager for Midland who'd already offered his time to be our Treasurer, we were now set up with strong support by the "bank boys" as I fondly referred to them. They were an invaluable strength with their expertise and we were blessed to have their skills. Margaret, Beryl, Mary, Geraldine and others were prompted, I believe by God, to offer help by preparing and cooking meals. Their faithfulness and Christian maturity inspired and encouraged me. Their strength and support upheld me during difficult times that were to lie ahead.

As numbers continued to grow there were always potential problems, but I learnt to see that these were merely situations needing to be resolved. An environment where all were valued and loved unconditionally, just as Christ values and loves us, was essential. I knew that all those helping in the centre needed to be assertive, but not aggressive, in providing boundaries. Our mantra was, "Pre-empt what might possibly happen." That way we were always one step ahead and could deal with situations before they became a problem. I would say to those coming into the centre, "I want you to use this centre, but I will not allow you to abuse it." I believe that if people are allowed to be disrespectful, they cannot in turn respect themselves. As we see the value and worth in others they in turn are able to build a sense of self-worth and self-esteem. Volatile behaviour can easily turn into violence; we needed to be alert and pre-empt what might possibly occur. That approach and prayer protection created a safe environment where people could come for practical, physical, emotional and spiritual support.

Sometimes those coming in seemed to think I could sort out anything and everything. Steve, a young lad who'd been put into care at a young age, came in and told me he'd been sleeping in a field a few miles away. He'd had a tent but the cows had destroyed it. His childhood had been traumatic and now he was abusing drugs and alcohol. A tall, physically strong young man, he could be very violent but I believed the outward aggression was an outworking of his pain. He also used glass, nails, razors and other sharp objects to physically inflict harm on himself, such was his internal agony. The love that God gave me for him, like the others who came to the centre, was like that for my own family. Steve was now sleeping in the ruins of an old building in a town about three miles from the day centre. Frequently he caused problems in Trowbridge and it was wiser for him to stay in Bradford-on-Avon, so I would take food over to him. As I drove up I saw he was sat waiting for me. I handed him some rolls and a flask with hot soup.

"Marianne, you must come and do something about the black duck!" he exclaimed.

I looked up into his face thinking, "He's obviously been taking the 'funny' pills," but his eyes were clear and his face was serious.

As we reached the bank of the river we saw the black duck swim into the water and promptly start to sink. "Do something, Marianne!" he said again. "Every time the duck goes into the water it sinks. Do something."

Knowing nothing about ducks I simply suggested that we move away, in the hope that the duck would get back to the bank. Thankfully, it returned safely and I tried to explain to Steve that I didn't know all the answers, couldn't solve all the problems, but I did care. I told him of the love I had for him.

Knowing that his behaviour was awful, that he was often violent and that most people thought he was useless, had given up on him and wanted simply to get rid of him, he said, "Why do you put up with me?"

My reply was simple. "Because Jesus patiently waited for me and still patiently puts up with me. Action on Homelessness is a result of my recognising that I needed God in my life and committing my life to Him. I care about you and love you because God cares about you and loves you."

Whilst we continued to chat, we watched as five baby moorhens came out of the reeds. Steve told me how he'd been watching these littles ones over the past days, and then suddenly a sixth baby moorhen emerged. I stood back and watched as Steve became so animated and excited at seeing this additional moorhen; it was as if his Christmases and birthdays had all rolled into one. This wasn't a totally bad guy; there was a soft, gentle place in his heart even if he could be aggressive and violent.

Action on Homelessness had recently acquired an office and store rooms so now at long last I was able to move the piles of black bin liners from our lounge and garage.

One day, an aggressive man called Mark, who had recently been released from Dartmoor prison, came into the office. He was looking for accommodation. I knew we needed to come to an understanding quickly so I said, "Either tell me the truth or tell me nothing. I've heard all the stories so you won't pull the wool over my eyes, take me for a ride or shock me. As far as I'm concerned, whatever you have done is in the past. We start from a clean slate." Mark moved into a house we were managing. We went through our ups and downs but he was always straight with me. I constantly thank God that He washes our slate clean and lets us start again.

Hundreds of men and women came through the doors of the centre. Anita was a young girl that I could identify with; my heart went out to her as she became involved with one man after another and became pregnant time after time. I held her hand as we stood by the graveside and looked down at the small coffin of her stillborn baby. Our tears mingled as I held her in my arms. Over the years I watched as this aggressive, insecure young girl grew into a confident, capable and lovely young woman. Little by little she learnt a different way to live her life.

I stood at the gravesides of a number of men who'd sadly died because of drug or alcohol related problems. I'd had such a close relationship with them, their death caused pain and sadness, but I had the blessing of knowing that for a period of time they'd known that they'd been shown love and compassion.

Prayer and action were being combined to provide in a practical way. Action on Homelessness could not solve all the problems people had, nor could it instantly lift people from the depth of destruction of drugs and alcohol, but we could show them that we cared. Our love and compassion was shown in action as we cried with people in emotional and mental pain. Addicts and people who were homeless were seen as the lepers of our society. Jesus had sat with, talked with, and shared with the lepers; so we sat with, talked with, ate with and cried with those who were unacceptable in our community.

One Sunday I was involved in an outreach service in the town park. As I stood on the bandstand with others from the Christian fellowship, I was aware of four people walking across the grass towards us. Three of them were shouting and heckling. I looked down and saw Donny, a young lad who had been coming into the centre for some time. As our eyes met he turned to his friends and said, "She's OK. Cut it out."

One of the lads then came up on to the bandstand; he was clearly unhappy and angry. As we brought the service to a close I went with him, Donny and their two friends to the rooms we used for our fellowship meeting, made them a drink and handed them plates of food from our lunch. As we sat together I heard how the night before, a friend of theirs had torched himself to death in his caravan. Groups of young people, New Age travellers, were staying on a nearby site. That night they had listened as their friend talked of suicide, but he'd spoken in this way before so they took no notice. As the evening went on they had dispersed and continued with their drug-taking, when they became aware that their friend's van was on fire. There was nothing they could do. They later found out that he'd chained himself to the bed along with his two dogs.

Over the weeks we spent much time together. Their lifestyle was not conducive to them attending planned counselling sessions so I knew it was vital to be flexible and we talked things through as and when they came to the centre. The young man who initially had been so angry kept in touch for years even after he moved away from the area.

With a change in circumstances we moved buildings. After three years we received funding and I was put on the payroll but not before the Department of Social Security had thought they'd have to take me to court. Legally I was doing nothing wrong, but they questioned my benefits because they couldn't find a way of recording the number of hours I was doing on a voluntary basis and my employer was God. I was anxious about possible proceedings but if God wanted me to stand in a court of law and say how Action on Homelessness had come about and what I was doing and why, then I would.

I felt as if God was testing me to see if I really trusted Him, because just at it seemed that the Social Security office and I had come to an impasse, a grant arrived meaning I no longer needed to claim benefit and they happily closed the case.

The work was happening at a time when many people, especially those on the fringes of society, carried knives. Over quite a long period of time I would stand at the door of the day centre and as people came I'd ask them if they were 'packing'; if they were then I'd take the knife from them until they left the centre. If they weren't willing to hand it over, and invariably they'd let me know that with some attitude and language, then I'd simply say, "OK then, that's your choice, but you're not coming in here carrying a weapon."

The day centre certainly had its problems, not only with those using the charity but also within the staff. It was clear that Satan was not happy with the witness that was being given regarding God's love and there were times when we were obviously under attack.

I met up with other day centre managers across the country at training events and conferences. Without exception all other centres would regularly need to call for police support, often several times a week, due to violence. In the ten years that I was involved with running the centre I am thankful that we never needed police support. It is true that all staff – volunteers or paid – went through intensive training including a yearly residential weekend and that out of all those who applied to work in the centre I accepted less than ten percent. I know that often people thought it was just about offering food and having a listening ear, but those who came off the streets to access the resources of the centre were very damaged, volatile and vulnerable, so there was a very specific skill set required on the part of all staff to be able to healthily support those who were so marginalised.

I'd come to understand that there are battles in the spiritual realm and not just physically on the earth. Regularly I met with others to pray, read God's word and seek guidance. I never failed to get excited as He showed the direction to be taken. Perseverance to keep on going was found in His strength. Often there was little acknowledgement and even less appreciation, but I knew that I was doing God's will and that was far more important than human recognition.

The day I was able to talk with a volunteer as to how she could become a Christian was a very special day. As we prayed together in the office I thanked God for crossing our paths. Over the years I was to come to experience so very many coincidences, or God-incidences as I might refer to them, where it was so apparent that 'Someone' had brought about a meeting, a particular situation, or a timing that was just perfect. I realise that many people would disregard these situations as coincidental but when on so many, many occasions threads weave together so perfectly, I simply can't accept that it hasn't all been brought about by the One who holds all together in tension and balance.

Lunchtime was always a good opportunity to sit informally and talk with the guys. Unlike at Bristol we were feeding maybe twenty people a day and all the volunteers and helpers would sit down together to eat in a family atmosphere. I was explaining to some of them how we'd recently been able to expand into some rooms above the centre. They were to be used for an office, quiet / counselling room, and storage space. It meant that now all our daytime services could be under one roof whereas for the past few years we'd had the day centre in one location, office elsewhere and storage facilities in yet another place.

I said, "Before we start moving everything in, I want to paint the walls and generally get the rooms prepared."

"When will you be doing the painting?" Dave asked.

"Well, I hope to get a lot of it done tonight," I answered.

"Can we come and help you with the decorating, Marianne?" Dave offered, referring to himself and his friend Brett.

"I'd really appreciate your help but only if you're straight. If you've been taking drugs you won't be any help at all."

I looked directly at him as he replied, "We'll be here at seven."

At the end of the day I dashed home quickly and prepared a meal for Adrian, Tom and myself. The boys were so good about the number of hours I was out of the house. They never complained and always supported me as I tried to support other people. Their understanding and acceptance of what I was doing played a vital part in the time and energy I could give to those who were hungry and homeless.

I drove back to the centre, meeting Jean on the way, who'd also offered to help wield a paintbrush. Dave and Brett arrived shortly afterwards. I was pleased that they'd not been tempted to take any drugs before they'd come and quickly we all set to work.

"Why on earth do you do this job, Marianne? I know that sometimes we can be very difficult. Why do you put up with us?"

I told Dave a little of how my life had been and how God had spoken to me and then how my life had changed. Question after question came from his lips and then, as we stood side by side painting, we discussed the Jesus I'd come to know. It was the early hours of the morning when I eventually drove home. The painting was finished and God had created the opportunity for me to witness in words as well as action.

"WHY? WHY?" The voice screamed inside my head. It was just a few weeks later when I heard that both Dave and Brett had been involved in a horrific crime. Whilst under the influence of drugs they'd held captive and tortured another person who came to the centre. They were both now being detained in prison awaiting trial. They were clearly going to receive long prison sentences.

I drove to the prison and waited for them to come into the visiting room. As they sat down opposite me my heart went out to them.

"Thanks for coming," Dave said.

I looked at him and Brett. "I needed you both to know, I cannot condone what you did, but I still love you and if you want to write and stay in touch then I'll be there and will write back."

There were tears in their eyes as I walked away.

I went back to the centre and, together with others on the staff team, provided support and help for the young man they'd tortured.

Brett wrote occasionally and Dave wrote quite regularly. A year later I received a letter from him saying, "Since you were involved in planting that first seed, I wanted you to know I've committed my life to Christ."

"Praise God!" I cried aloud in the quietness of my office. Even when we're in the very depths God will reach right down to us and hold out His hand – and sometimes it's not until we're in that place that we'll reach out and accept all that He has to give.

It saddened me to hear a new guy who'd just come into the centre say, "I wanted to go into a church to be quiet and sit, but I couldn't find one open." As we talked he told me how his marriage had broken down. He'd left his wife, baby daughter and two stepdaughters and had been sleeping rough for several months. He smelt strongly of alcohol and his language was crude to the extreme.

"I must make the time to talk with him when he's sober," I thought.

The opportunity arose a few days later. I listened as he talked; he was seeking something but he didn't know what. He had a need but he didn't know how, or by whom, it could be met.

I told him about the Christian fellowship I went to and said, "If you'd like to come along we'd always be pleased to see you."

The next Sunday, he walked in just after the service had started. I smiled at him as he took a seat. Then I leapt with joy a few weeks later when he gave his life to Jesus and I rejoiced with praise when, after being reunited with his family, his wife and two teenage stepdaughters also made commitments of faith. His family now serve Christ and his baby daughter is being raised in a loving family that will teach her the truths of God.

Not all the people using the centre had problems with drink or drugs. One young man named Paul had a history of mental illness and often his behaviour was erratic and unpredictable. One summer's night I was asleep in the front bedroom of my house, Adrian and Tom were in the back bedrooms and all the windows were open because it was so warm. Thumping and banging woke me up. "What on earth?" I jumped out of bed. Paul was throwing his body first up against my car and then the front door. He appeared totally demented.

I rushed towards the front door with Adrian hot on my heels. He was angry that anybody should be disturbing us at home and, wanting to be protective, he shouted through the door for Paul to go away. The home addresses of any of the people working at the centre were confidential, but somehow Paul had found out where we lived.

Paul was screaming and shouting, and when I went out to see him he was rolling on the pavement. Gradually he calmed down but as I sat with him a police car drove up. One of the neighbours had obviously phoned them after all the commotion. I watched as they drove away with Paul sat in the back of the car. They were going to take him back to the hospital to receive treatment. Eventually his medication was stabilised and it was a joy when he came to see me with his girlfriend and tell me that he had a job and was now settled in the community.

Frequently I'd find myself confronted with unbelievable horrors and yet I needed to keep my instinctive reaction contained so as not to exacerbate a situation. One such case was with a couple we'd been supporting. They did have a roof over their heads but by no means could it be called a home. She was in a wheelchair and he, as her sole carer, apparently did his very best and always presented himself as being concerned for her welfare. They were involved with a number of agencies, both statutory and voluntary, and all believed that the lady in her forties was physically crippled by arthritis.

On one occasion when they'd been in to the centre and I'd been listening to various conversations, alarm bells went off in my head. That started many months of enquiries and investigation, the end result being that the lady's carer was sentenced to many, many years in prison. He had systematically broken her bones over several decades; she had never received any medical help and so they had simply fused together in their broken state. No doubt due to the trauma, her speech was unintelligible and she had never been able to notify anyone of the horror that was her life. He was all-controlling in his violent abuse. Unbelievably, they had lived off the radar of the medics and, marginalised by society, had slipped through the net, allowing her to be violently mistreated for many years. Thank God, eventually she received the treatment she so badly needed and was able to live in a place where her dignity was respected and she'd be shown compassion, support and care.

I'd never been known for having patience, so it was something I constantly prayed for. When I'd first been given the vision to open a building for the homeless I'd thought it would take about two to three years. Never did I expect to be involved in such a work for ten years. Out of all the places I'd ever lived in, Trowbridge was the town I liked the least, yet it was to be the place I lived in the longest. I came to learn that God has a sense of humour. I'd said I could never work with homeless people and that was what He called me to do. I was a city girl who liked the fast life and then as a person of extremes I'd like to get away to the exclusion of a rugged coastline, yet here I was in a rural town. God had a way of bringing me through, refining me and blessing me in abundance as little by little He started turning me into a more whole and healthier person.

CHAPTER SEVENTEEN

Blessings

As God crossed my path with the paths of so many people, and dealt with issues in my life and the way I looked at things, I was blessed by His touch. He provided for our material needs in unexpected and amazing ways. Adrian had started work at a local factory and now that he was earning his own money had bought himself some fairly expensive trainers. It was good to see him enjoying wearing what many young people took for granted. I'd never been able to afford fashion clothes for the boys and the vast majority of their clothes and mine had been second-hand.

Therefore, I was surprised late one evening to walk into the house and see him sat in the lounge with his work boots on. I listened in amazement as he said, "Someone has stolen my trainers out of my locked locker." My heart went out to him as I thought how my sixteen-year-old son had been working hard, paying for his keep and saving his money to buy something he'd like and now someone had stolen his trainers. His workplace would take no responsibility and he was left feeling hurt and very angry. I upheld him in prayer as I tried to calm his anger.

The very next morning in the post I was amazed to open a card from some friends. It said, "During our prayer time the Lord told us to send you the enclosed money. Use it as you feel led." I looked at the enclosed cheque; it was the exact amount that would enable Adrian to purchase the identical trainers, which were now on sale! *Amazing!* No one else had known about what had happened to him, but God knew and at that time had decided to intervene. Even more amazing, the cheque was already in the post on the day Adrian's trainers had been stolen. Coincidence? I don't believe so. God-incidence? Yes! What an amazing God!

Over the years He provided for us financially in so many ways. On one occasion I was driving to a Christian conference called 'Spring Harvest'. Because at that time I was earning no money, the boys and I were able to go at a very reduced rate. I felt awful as I realised that in talking with God, as I drove, I was complaining about how difficult it was each week to make the money last. Here I was going away for a few days and somehow we always seemed to just manage to pay the bills and buy food.

I apologised to God and said, "I'm so sorry, I know you meet all my needs and I have no right to ask you for what I want, just because that will make my life easier." I was used to being careful with every penny, buying always the cheaper food and accepting that on the last day of the week, before I received my state benefits, that there was just enough food to eat.

Imagine my surprise when I got home a few days later and opened the post. Along with the bills and usual junk mail was a handwritten envelope; inside, the note said, "Please use the enclosed money for you and your family in recognition of the work you are doing in our Lord's name with the homeless." I looked at the four-figure cheque. I was gobsmacked. I couldn't possibly accept this money! I didn't know the people who'd sent it and there was no address so I couldn't send it back but I certainly couldn't cash it. For days I kept looking at it every time I passed the table where I'd left it.

I called in to see one of the leaders of our fellowship and showed her the note. "What's the problem?" she asked.

"Come off it!" I retorted. "What do you mean, what's the problem? A cheque arrives through my door for one thousand pounds along with this note and you ask, what's the problem? I can't possibly accept this."

"Marianne, you must to learn to have the grace to receive," she said quietly.

For a long time, it still felt uncomfortable, but I thanked God for His provision and the way He had laid it on this person's heart to send the cheque. That money helped to support my family over the next three years until such time as I started to be paid.

These are just two of dozens of situations in which God miraculously 'spoke' to people and, knowing their circumstances, asked them to financially support me because of what I was doing.

God blessed me not only with pounds but also with people. One evening I went along to a Christian Prison Fellowship meeting and there I met Brian and Judith. Brian had previously been in prison; he'd been a gang leader and was planning to kill a number of people, when he'd had an encounter with Jesus in his cell. Now he was married to Judith, a social worker, and was doing Christian ministry work in prisons. I started going into the prisons with Brian and was amazed at the blessings I received. Sometimes I was part of a prison ministry team and sometimes on my own, visiting people who were serving a life sentence

I stirred in my bed. I felt snug and cosy under my duvet but outside it was dark, miserable, dank, cold weather. What was I doing getting up at this time on a Sunday morning to drive for an hour to go into a prison? I made marmalade sandwiches and a flask of tea, got in the car and went to pick up Jean. As I drove, we talked of the different prisons we'd been into. Leyhill was an open prison and the men had a reasonable amount of freedom; Earlestoke was near to where we lived and often I'd go there with other groups or on my own to visit inmates; Winchester was a typical city prison with high solid walls; and Broadmoor was for serious offenders who were mentally ill. Not once when I'd been into a prison had I not come out with my 'socks blessed off'!

We drove over to Bristol, parked up the car and ate our breakfast. Brian and Judith arrived with a few other people and we passed through the security to get into the prison. As I watched the men come into the chapel I wondered what had happened in their lives. We held two services: one for convicted prisoners and one for those from the hospital wing and 'rule forty-threes', those who were kept separated from other inmates. As the Bible says, "I was in prison and you visited me."[10] Increasingly I was finding that to follow the teachings of scripture, even those parts that may seem too unpleasant, too uncomfortable, too demanding or just too challenging, brought joy beyond measure. It was a privilege to spend time with these men. I felt

---

[10] Matthew 25:36

so rich, the way they responded to our entering the prison and spending time with them.

Jean and I drove up on to the Clifton Downs at Bristol to finish the remnants of our breakfast. It was now a pleasant Sunday lunchtime. We sat looking out over the grass and talked about the morning and read our bibles. As people walked with their dogs, played with their children and enjoyed the open expanse of the Downs we talked of how our lives had changed since we'd accepted Jesus as our Saviour. It was amazing how God was using us and blessing us at the same time.

"There's something I need to tell you," Jean said. "I've really been praying for the last few weeks about how and when I should speak to you." By now I was wondering what on earth she was going to say. I sat waiting for her to carry on. "Well, a few weeks ago I had what I can only describe as two prophetic pictures. In the first one you were flying off somewhere. You weren't travelling with any other friends, and I was on the roof of the airport and knew that you were going away for a long time."

"Really!" I said rather flippantly. "Was I going somewhere nice?"

"Well, the second picture I had was of you surrounded by brown-coloured children in a desert-like area, but not sand," Jean said.

"Oh, great!" I retorted. "You know that I don't do children." Jean understood that I didn't mean this literally but just never felt that I got on well with young children, and the thought of being surrounded by them was a bit too much. "Well," I said, "it's up to the Lord. I won't say that's not going to happen or I'm not going to do that, because I said I'd never work with homeless people, and look at the work that's going on with Action on Homelessness. But it'll be down to Him to sort all the details out, as well as the major issues, because in no way can I take off, leave this country and be working with children unless it's in His strength and empowerment. I'll wait on Him."

The hours I worked at Action on Homelessness each week grew longer and longer. There was always something to do, some problem to sort out, or someone who needed help. At weekends there were family commitments, cleaning, shopping and cooking. With the prison ministry commitments and being part of several worship groups, life was busy.

I was now attending a local Christian fellowship and we were hosting some evangelists who were staying for a week. I didn't have room to put them up overnight but offered to have one of the families over for an evening meal. I dashed home from work and quickly prepared the meal. I knew the family had two young children so I provided a choice of food to cover likes and dislikes.

As we sat down to eat, the man in the family who was on the leadership of a large Christian fellowship in London said, "What do you do, Marianne?"

I told him briefly about the work at Action on Homelessness, how the Lord had given me the vision and how He was now working through the charity that had been formed.

"That is nothing compared to what you will be doing," he stated.

I sat looking at him, somewhat dumbstruck. Initially I felt hurt that he seemed to be dismissive of the needs of homeless people. But later that week, during a time of ministry in a service, the Lord revealed that at some time in the future I was to be called to another work that would ask even more of me than Action on Homelessness. I had no idea when this calling would come to fruition, but I knew that God had many things to work out in my life and the lives of others before it would be made clear. I left it in His hands, prepared for this to be a time of honing and preparation.

We were always applying for grants to help with the running costs of Action on Homelessness and I praised God as the voice on the phone told me we were to receive a grant for over one hundred and ten thousand pounds. As I told the staff team the news I watched them dance around the room. Then, as I sat at my desk, the voice in my head said, "Now there's going to be a lot of work to do, to put all this money into operation." Plans started being made but I realised that I was becoming more and more removed. What was happening to me? I sat in my office looking at the phone. I knew I should be making a phone call, but my body and my mind didn't seem to be connecting.

Soon I found myself listening to my doctor as he said, "Marianne, you're to take two months off work. I want you to walk out of here and for the next eight weeks only do the things you enjoy doing. I am signing you off with stress. You have what I call Florence Nightingale Syndrome." I stared amazed; the last thing I was, was a nurse! "If you haven't read her biography, I'll let you have a copy of the book," he said.

I returned to my car. No work for two months? What else did I enjoy doing other than work? I felt a panic rise up inside me and at the same time I felt myself close down to people around me. I couldn't function. I spoke to Richard, our Chairman, and told him that the doctor had signed me off for two months. Immediately he was concerned for my welfare and we made plans as to how Action on Homelessness could continue to operate.

I knew that over the last seven years I'd witnessed a lot of pain and problems; I'd worked an average of sixty hours a week plus tried to fulfil my role as mother and daughter by supporting and caring for my family. The working conditions at Action on Homelessness were fairly dire; an inappropriate building that was claustrophobic and totally unsuitable for the work we were doing had added to the stress levels. At national conferences I'd been told that the average time people spent in a job similar to mine was three years.

When one of the men who went to Action on Homelessness started stalking me and used to hang around the church I attended, I spoke with a number of other professionals in the town and we all believed he was potentially extremely dangerous. However, he was unable to receive help with his mental health problem until he acted in a specific way; only then, according to the law, could he be sectioned. Thankfully, that happened sometime later and he received the help he needed. But now I needed to take time to replenish, recreate and refresh myself.

Many people said to me, "Why has God let this happen to you when you're spending time helping other people?" But I'd come to understand that God can use all situations for good. This enforced time away from work was to be a time of real blessing. I needed to spend time with God, in prayer, reading His word, enjoying His creation and the fellowship of others. Brian and Judith were moving house and I happily helped them load the lorry, unpack at the other end and then do some decorating in their new home. God really used that time to rejuvenate me. Many people believed I would never work again, let alone return to work with homeless and addicts, but two months later I went back to work part-time and within three and a half months I was working full-time again.

I'd spent quality time with Mum and Dad talking over many of the issues to do with my past and I now felt strong and healthy. I also knew that it was important for me to take responsibility to lead a healthy life.

I started going to the gym for my physical well-being, receiving appropriate support with my work for my emotional well-being and most importantly spending time with my Lord for my spiritual well-being. I needed to not only spend time talking with Him in prayer but also to spend time listening to Him.

My friendship with Jean continued and we were blessed with some very special holidays that were real times of refreshment. It was good to be able to share all that God was doing in our lives and to think back to that dramatic encounter with God at Heddons Mouth. I valued her support to me personally and her practical support of Action on Homelessness as a member of the committee for several years.

I was just getting in the car to drive to work when Donna, my neighbour, came out of her front door. "Would you like a lift?" I asked, seeing that her car wasn't parked outside her house. She got in, and knowing her interest in poetry, I showed her some Christian poetry books that I was using for something I was doing at work. "If you like, I'll put them through your letterbox when I get back from work," I offered. She seemed interested and I was encouraged at this opportunity to share with her. We'd had a few brief talks in the past and I'd come to know her a little better when she worked at the day centre as a volunteer for a while, but now there seemed to be a fresh inquiring within her.

Donna knocked on my front door a few days later to ask some questions relating to the poetry that was all based on scripture. I said, "If you'd like some more of your questions answered there's an Alpha Course[11] running in the town which is specifically for people interested in finding out more about the Christian faith. I'll get you the details if you like."

The next day I handed her a leaflet with information about Alpha. She read it with interest and said she'd like to go.

"Are you happy to go on your own or would you like company?" I asked.

"It's OK. I'll go on my own."

I smiled as I said, "Alright, let me know what you think of it."

---

[11] The Alpha Course, now known simply as Alpha, is an evangelistic course which seeks to introduce the basics of the Christian faith through a series of talks and discussions.

The next evening, fifteen minutes before the start of the meeting, Donna knocked on my door. "Do you think you could come with me?" she asked. I was pleased that I had no other plans. My heart leapt with joy when she committed her life to Jesus, and when some time later she applied for and got the job as my Administration Officer I was ecstatic. She was my neighbour, my friend, my sister in Christ and now my colleague.

God used Keith and Steve in a very special way one evening. As we rehearsed some music for the following Sunday they became aware that I was in a lot of pain. "Can we pray for you?" they asked.

"Yes, if you like," I agreed.

"Do you mind if we lay hands on you?"

"No," I answered wondering what on earth was going to happen to me. At this time, I hadn't been a Christian long and nobody had ever prayed for me like this before.

As you might recall, I'd had problems with my back for a long time. One side of my pelvic bones had shifted when giving birth to Aidan and was now permanently out of place, putting a severe strain on the bottom part of the spine and the surrounding muscles. Over the years the discs between the vertebrae in the lumbar region had worn away causing bone to rub on bone and create bone spurs. Frequently the pain was unbearable. The constant taking of painkillers made me feel depressed and at times all my muscles went into spasm and I was completely unable to move.

As Keith and Steve prayed I thought, "Should I be feeling anything? What do I say when they've finished?" When they all said amen, I simply said, "Thanks very much."

That night as I got into bed I didn't feel too bad, so for the first time in months I didn't take any tablets to help me sleep. Always a restless sleeper, I'd had months of disturbed sleep because even with the pills, every time I turned over I felt pain.

When I awoke I became aware that I'd just slept right through the night. I wriggled my toes. No pain! I shifted my shoulders. No pain! I sat up, put my legs over the side of the bed and stood. *No pain!* Praise God! Only occasionally did I have problems in the future and then I always knew it was when Satan was attacking me. Without fail the power of prayer, in different ways and in His timing, has healed me. I was learning to trust and rely on God but it wasn't always easy.

CHAPTER EIGHTEEN

A New Season

One place I'd always wanted to visit, even long before I became a Christian, was The Holy Land. I'd always had a love for the Jewish people and two of the most memorable films I'd ever watched were Masada and Exodus. The plight of the Jewish people over the centuries had affected me deeply. Now as a believer I wanted to go to the land where Jesus had walked, the country of so many biblical events.

Jean and I discussed the idea of going on a pilgrimage. What sort of tour should we go on? What time of year? When could we afford to go? Eventually our questions were answered, our plans were made, our cases were packed and we were off. Excitement was an understatement! Due to an early start, Jean had stayed overnight, and after just a few hours' sleep we were on the coach to Gatwick Airport.

We stood in the queue waiting to check in our luggage. As I handed in my cases I answered the questions put to me by the airport staff; security was tighter for Israel than for many other countries. I'd heard on the news of troubles, but knew little of the problems other than Arabs, Palestinians, Jews and Israelis always seemed to be fighting. I'd seen the pictures of young children and youths throwing stones and thought, "Why don't their parents have more control over them? They're 'yobbos'!" But I gave it no more thought as I set off to visit the land which is home to Judaism, Christianity and Islam.

Landing at Ben Gurion Airport in Tel Aviv, my heart seemed to flutter and tears came to my eyes. I stood like a sardine on the bus that ferried us all from the plane to the terminal. Now was the anxious moment; as the carousel moved into life, would I see the cases that I'd parted with over eight hours before in London? Thankful as always to be reunited, I lifted my luggage on to the trolley and followed the rest of the group to the coach.

The travelling had been tiring and I was thankful to get into my bed soon after we'd booked into the hotel. Bleary-eyed next morning, I sat quietly at the table eating my breakfast, listening to the chatter all around me. Never a morning person, it was taking me a while to wake up, but as I boarded the coach my excitement grew. I walked around Jerusalem constantly aware that I must keep with the rest of the tour party as we entered the narrow passageways of the souks. We had been warned by our tour guide to keep a cautious hold on our bags, particularly in the crowded areas. People jostled, pushed and shoved as they went about their business, and groups of tourists looked anxious, amazed and bewildered as they were shown around the sites.

Every place that held any significance had a church. I listened intently to all the information coming from our guide. Dates, occupations, invasions, wars; this city had never known peace. I was mesmerized by all the history, too much to contain; my head was in a whirl. Sights, sounds, smells, my senses were straining. The people were so colourful, the noise from the mosques so overpowering and the smell of spices and hot bodies so overwhelming. I hurried on, not wanting to lose sight of familiar faces. Narrow pathways, pushing people, tired feet, throbbing head... oh, for a bit of space; a quiet spot; a cold, refreshing drink!

O little town of Bethlehem, how still we see thee lie. Neither the Christmas card scene nor the image of small neat homes in the hillside met my eyes. "Beware of your bags; stay with the group," I heard as I entered the Church of the Nativity. So this was where Jesus was born. Amazing, awesome, awful! There was no time for peaceful reflection, for time to ponder at God's gift to the world, for time to consider the implications of His birth. We quickly sang 'Away in a Manger' then were back on the coach to get to the shop and buy the keepsakes of this experience.

I walked into the Church of the Holy Sepulchre. So this was where He died.

Crowds massed around me. "I feel faint," I said to Jean.

I went over to the tour leader and he said, "Make your way out of the church and we'll see you as we come out."

"Excuse me, please; excuse me," I said as I tried to create a path through the people and hoped I wouldn't faint and make a fool of myself.

I was thankful to see the others as they came out of the church and I took Jean's arm as we were led out of the old city. As we waited outside Jaffa Gate I could feel my temperature rising rapidly. Where was the coach? I sat on the pavement waiting, fearful that I was going to pass out or start vomiting in the street.

"The coach can't get through. All the main roads are blocked off because Warren Christopher is in Jerusalem for the peace talks. We'll either have to walk or get taxis back to the hotel." I listened as our tour leader gave instructions to the group. All I wanted was to get back to the hotel, lie down and have a toilet close at hand.

The rest of the ten days I was in bed. I lay on the back seat of the coach as we travelled from Jerusalem to Tiberias. There was no toilet on the vehicle and I prayed that I would be able to hold on to the remaining contents of my stomach. I'd been so ill in the last hotel, I felt weak and increasingly frightened. Would I ever feel well again? As soon as we were checked into the hotel I went to bed.

The following day the tour leader came and said, "If you're not feeling better by lunchtime, phone down to reception and they'll call a doctor to see you. I think they're likely to take you to hospital. When we get back from our day out I'll find out where you are."

I lay in bed listening as one by one the bedroom doors closed. As I imagined them making their way to the lift I felt the tears start to flow down my cheeks. Never a good patient, I was scared about what was wrong with me. I knew I had an extremely high fever, was dehydrated and could not keep even water down. My body was weak and my legs kept shaking; my head was banging and my back ached as if it were broken. Frightened and alone, I cried out to God.

"Don't worry, my child, I am with you. You cannot depend or rely on people, but I am your God. I am always with you and you can always depend and rely on me. Trust in me and not in man. I am with you, my child." He was so close to me as I heard His voice. The tears stopped, my heart was calm and my fears subsided.

The doctor called. "You need to go to hospital," he instructed me.

"Please just give me something to enable me to keep down water; I know I'm dehydrated." I'd never liked hospitals and I certainly didn't want to be admitted to one where I didn't understand the language. This was not how I had expected this holiday of a lifetime to turn out; hours spent in bed and drifting in and out of sleep. Watching television, I saw little of the land where Jesus walked, but I did hear and see quite a lot of the land as it is today. Television programmes showed me the current issues of the day and I started to become aware of the Palestinian people and the land of Palestine as well as the land of Israel.

I was so thankful to get back home to Trowbridge. First thing next morning I saw my own doctor. After tests he told me, "You have Shigella; it's a Middle Eastern dysentery. It's highly infectious."

The next day a person from the Environmental Health Department came to the house and I was given a prohibition order. "You mustn't handle any food that is to be eaten by anyone else. All your towels etc. must be separate to anyone else's in the house. Meticulous hygiene must be observed and you will have to present frequent samples to the doctor until you are clear."

I felt like I should ring a bell and call out, "Unclean, unclean!" Obviously my ill health was nothing compared to that of a person suffering from leprosy but in a very small way I could have some empathy with those whose health issues separate them from society.

It was almost six months before I felt fully well. Even after I was clear of the main effects, I suffered from severe ulcers and generally very poor health. I certainly would never forget that holiday. But within weeks of landing I wanted to go back. I'd missed so much and yet I'd gained so much. Maybe I hadn't seen all the places on the itinerary, the sites recording events of two thousand years ago, but I had been made aware of the land today and its differing people. Also I'd learnt a very important lesson in my faith: I cannot depend upon, rely on, or trust man – man makes errors and fails – but I can depend on, rely upon and trust in God. I'd felt alone and let down when I'd been so ill, and in the past I'd felt rejected and abused, but God is faithful and we can overcome all if we allow Him to work in our lives.

Throughout much of my life I'd put my trust in 'man', be that others or myself, but now I knew what is was to trust in God. In the middle part of the Bible it says:

It is better to trust the Lord than put your confidence in man,
It is better to take refuge in Him than in the mightiest king.

Psalm 118:8

People can and do change. "You're exactly the same and yet you're so different." Gary sat opposite me in my lounge as he said the words. It had been years since I'd seen my second husband. When I'd left North Devon I'd carefully covered my tracks; I didn't want a repeat of all the things we'd gone through and it was necessary for the boys and me to have a clean break. Now here he was sat in my lounge. After six years he'd found us.

Dad had phoned a few days before. "You'll never guess whom I've just been speaking to on the phone," he said.

"Gary," I answered, as a statement not a question.

"How did you know that?" Dad asked.

"Because it's coming up to the anniversary of Carl's death and even though Gary and I have been divorced for years, I just know how he thinks and what he feels."

"Well, he told me he'd tracked us down through the phonebook. When he found out you'd left Barnstaple he tried to locate us in Plymouth. Since then he's been trying to track either you or us. He thought we might have moved back to the Bristol area, and found our number in the telephone directory. He asked after you and the boys. I told him you were all well and that we'd seen you just yesterday afternoon."

"Oh, Dad," I said somewhat despairingly, "if you've told him you saw us during an afternoon that means we can't be far away from you; it won't take him any time at all to find us now."

"I didn't think of that," Dad confessed, "but he has given me a number where he can be contacted in Bristol and he'd like you to phone him."

Late that evening, after the boys had gone to bed, I rang the number. We exchanged news and pleasantries and I knew there was no point in holding out on him. He had always been determined and got what he wanted. Now he was so close he would keep on until he found us. I decided it was better to be amicable than hostile so invited him to come over.

And so he visited and it was two thirty in the morning as I responded to his statement that I was exactly the same, yet so different.

"I've become a Christian, Gary."

"But you've always been a Christian," Gary retorted.

"No, I was brought up in a Christian family, I used to go to church and I believed in God, but I've now made a commitment in my faith and accepted Jesus as my Lord and Saviour." I went on to tell Gary just some of the things that had happened over the last few years.

"I wish I could find what you have," he said.

"You can," I replied. "What God's done for me, He can do for you; what I know, you can come to know; it's what God wants for all of us. It doesn't mean I don't face any problems, but I do know that Jesus is with me in any difficulty and that He will enable me to overcome."

Gary sat and listened. We talked throughout the evening and he said he'd like to see the boys. We arranged for him to come back after breakfast so that I could prepare them first.

Adrian and Tom sat surprised as I told them that Gary had made contact, was in the area and would like to see them. I hoped this would be a positive time for the children, that at long last Gary would rightly accept his responsibilities as a father.

We spent a lovely day together. Gary had been happy for me to join him and the boys, understanding that I was anxious about letting them spend the day with him on their own after all that had happened.

"I'll keep in touch," Gary said as he left. "It's the beginning of March now. I'll phone you and we'll make arrangements to meet up over the Easter." He wouldn't give me his phone number or address. As so often had happened when we'd been married, he needed to be in control and wanted to know all about what I was doing, where I was and with whom, but I was never to know about where he went, what he did and with whom.

It was the week before Christmas. "There's somebody knocking at the door, Mum," Tom called.

It was dark as I opened the door and saw Gary on the doorstep. We hadn't heard anything from him for nine months.

"Hi, I thought I'd call and take you all out for dinner," he said boldly. It was as if he'd only been by the previous week. He was acting as if he'd always done what was right for the children, as if nothing was untoward.

I was past being shocked or surprised. So many out-of-the-ordinary things had happened in my life that no new situation phased me. "Wait there a minute. I'll see what the boys have to say."

I closed the door and called up the stairs to Adrian. "Adrian, Gary's here and would like to take us all out for a meal. Would you like to go?"

"No, I'm not going anywhere with him. He's let me down too many times. He's always made promises and never kept them. He thinks he can just turn up as if nothing has happened. No! Now he wants something and I'm going to let *him* down and say no."

"OK, Adrian, I understand. Tom, would you like to go?"

"Yes, I would, Mum. What can I have to eat?"

"Anything you like, son," I said. "Gary's refused to ever pay maintenance; as far as I'm concerned you can have everything on the menu."

Again I went with Tom and Gary, not just to get a free meal, but because I was always anxious about Gary's motives.

Gary chose not to stay in touch. He continued to walk away from his responsibilities and deny himself the joys of being in a relationship with Adrian and Tom. I had to accept that we all have the right to make our own choices. I had decided to keep Adrian away from Phil, his blood father, for his own safety until he was old enough to look out for himself; he then decided he didn't want to see Phil. Gary had the choice of being a father to the boys or not; he chose not. In many ways it made the boys and me closer but I always regret not having provided them with better fathers. I had chosen to marry these men and have children with them, but now my sons were denied the opportunity of being in a loving relationship with their father. When Tom made a confession of faith and became a Christian it was a sheer delight for me to see him made whole by God his heavenly Father who would never let him down. At his baptism I sang 'Father of the Fatherless'[12], a chorus that speaks of the love that God has for His children. I praised God that where man fails, He will meet all our needs. He knows what is best for His children, He loves unreservedly and unconditionally. There is no better father for my children than our Almighty God.

---

[12] Graham Kendrick; Make Way Music (1992)

God continued to provide for us and I found when I emptied myself of myself that He would fill me to overflowing with His strength and gifts by the power of the Holy Spirit. Action on Homelessness continued to thrive and expand. After seven years in the small inadequate premises we moved into a large building which had previously been a clothing factory and warehouse. The agency had sufficient money to employ more staff and Action on Homelessness became known as "the best in the west". The service provision was good, the agency operated professionally and, more importantly, God was being glorified as His project was meeting the needs of those who were homeless. Heroin and hard drugs were being used prolifically in the area, people suffering from mental illness were on the increase, survivors of abuse were sadly becoming very common and people who would mutilate their own bodies was not unusual. The pain of humanity, sin and sickness was evident; man's inhumanity to man was all too clear.

I'd enjoyed a ten-day break with Mum and Dad travelling through Europe to the lakes of Italy. It had been good to have this time with them, particularly as it was becoming obvious that my mum was entering the early stages of dementia. Now, three years on from my last trip to the Holy Land, I was preparing once again to travel there on a pilgrimage. Jean and I had again saved hard, people had been praying that I would know good health, and I had been praying that I would know God's heart and see through His eyes.

4.00am – not usually my best time of day! I awoke with bright alertness. "Humility," God said clearly. I reached for my bible, not wanting to wake Jean, yet wanting to find the scripture passage to which God was leading me. I read Deuteronomy 8.

"OK, Lord," I said, "I accept your word and wait to see what it is you will reveal to me."

What a way to start this pilgrimage! We were staying in a hotel at Gatwick because of an early flight and the fact that we had to book in three hours before departure. I'd expected to get up at six in the morning – but to be woken at four? God certainly had a way of jolting me.

The overwhelming feeling of being home was unexplainable. Each day throughout the fortnight God revealed more and more that this was the land to which I was to come, not just for a pilgrimage but to live and work! *What!* How? When? Where? Questions spilled from my mouth.

"I will reveal all," God said to me, "but know that I have called you to this place. It is for here and these people that I have been preparing you these last years."

God revealed to me in my spirit that the prophetic picture Jean had had of me all those years ago was in this land. The children that I was surrounded by were Arab-coloured. I recalled the words of the man whose family I'd entertained for dinner, who had referred to the work I was doing with the homeless as being nothing compared to what I would be doing. During the pilgrimage God showed me time and again through His word that I was to trust and be obedient to His calling.

I spoke with John who was the spiritual leader on our tour. He said, "Marianne, it is clear to many people that God has been speaking to you. Seek confirmation when you return to England; I'll be interested to know what happens."

I landed in the UK physically fit and spiritually challenged. The first Sunday service I went to was at Mum and Dad's church.

"I wonder if any of you know anything about the Jewish New Year?" The lay preacher opened the service with a question that astounded me. She could have said good morning, welcome, or any one of a hundred different things. I sat up straight and pinned back my ears; I had just been part of the Jewish festivities for their New Year in Jerusalem. Throughout the service God used this preacher to confirm my calling.

During the next weeks God spoke through different people clarifying and clearly confirming where He was calling me to be. I was careful not to speak to anyone beforehand, as I didn't want them prompted into saying something, but as they spoke into my situation I revealed to them what I knew God was calling me to do.

I spoke with Adrian and Tom separately, telling them how God had been speaking to me and that He had now called me to leave England and work in the Holy Land. "You have my support and you must do what God is telling you," said Adrian. Both boys were clearly understanding all I was trying to convey to them; more than that, they wholeheartedly supported me. I was encouraged by their response and my heart glowed with love and pride for my sons. My marriages may have been disastrous, but the fruits from those marriages were a joy and blessing. It reminded me of how God works; He can bring something good out of that which was bad.

I looked back on my own life. God had created me, my parents had lovingly set me on the right road and nurtured me, but then I had fallen by the wayside and gone astray. I was dried up and dying, seeking instant fun and constantly searching fulfilment in the world, but then my eyes were opened to God's glory. His light and truth led me back on to the right path and then by His grace I had flourished. Redeemed, I was back on His pathway and travelling with Him.

I spent much time in prayer thanking God for His patience as He continued to confirm the calling and allowed me to cast aside any anxieties. My main worry had been Dad. For the last two years I had spent almost every weekend with him, supporting him as my mother's dementia worsened. I was on the phone every day so that he could use me as a sounding block and let off the pressure of the day. I knew that it would be difficult for him to hear what I was going to say and I asked many people across the country to uphold him in prayer.

Christmas celebrations... where would we all be next year? But this year we'd be together as a family and I started to make the preparations. Over the last ten years I'd often worked over the Christmas, spending time cooking and talking with the people at the day centre, then rushing home to spend time cooking and talking with family. This year there were enough staff at Action on Homelessness for me to be able to spend all the Christmas festivities with my family.

I love to cook and prepare meals; it's therapy for me and a double blessing when people enjoy the food. Just a month ago I'd organised a weekend of celebrations and meals for Mum and Dad's Golden Wedding Anniversary. It had been a great time with friends and family although sadly it was marred by the fact that Mark, my brother, and his family didn't join us. For years he'd been estranged from Mum, Dad and me. It caused much pain and heartache, but as always we all have choices and it was his choice. Even so, everyone enjoyed the weekend and it was a joy for me to see people relish the food laid out before them.

Now I stood in the queue at Tesco's listening to mothers shouting at their children, women complaining that there was no longer a certain type of green bean on the shelf, and watching as fretful families wandered the aisles adding more and more food to their trolleys. This was the season of goodwill and the time to celebrate that God had sent His son as a baby, to be born in a humble stable. He was born into a world of violence but, as the Saviour for the world, had come as the Prince of Peace. Yet here were people shouting and complaining about not having the right beans on their dinner table! Materialism and human desires, needs and greed were all too evident.

Mum and Dad were coming to stay for four days, as was my mum's sister Sheila. I'd rearranged the bedrooms to accommodate them; now I was at the store early in the morning to get the supplies we needed before going to work. Tonight I had a meeting and would have to dash away from that to collect Sheila off the coach. Plans were made, preparation accomplished and prayer was in action for me to tell Dad on Boxing Day about God's new calling on my life.

Seven of us sat down to an enjoyable Christmas lunch. Adrian's girlfriend and I cleared away as Mum, Dad and Sheila listened to the Queen's speech on television. Later we took Sheila over to the house that Adrian and his girlfriend lived in to see their two Doberman dogs. Sheila loved animals and it was nice that Prince and Reggie were now part of our family. Cindy, our beloved Alsatian, had been put to sleep a few years back; she was still regularly part of our conversations and Mum had painted a beautiful picture of her just a few months before I'd held her in my arms at the vet, whilst she administered the injection. Adrian attempted to restrain his boisterous 'boys' as they tried to climb up on Sheila's lap. It was good to spend time together, enjoying the frolics and the fun.

Boxing Day morning… I knew this was the day to tell Dad of all that God had been laying before me over the last months, but I also had some idea of how difficult it was going to be for him to hear what I had to say. I'd always known that Dad had emotional baggage about the Jewish people and the Arabs. He'd been in Palestine during the time of the British Mandate at the end of the Second World War and had personally been on the receiving end of much violence from both peoples.

I felt that the best moment to tell him would be when we were on our own taking a walk. I prayed for good weather and, amazingly, it was a clear, bright, dry day. Now, how to broach the subject of us going out together just on our own without Mum and Sheila?

After lunch we sat in the lounge drinking coffee. Sheila was chatting away and Mum was nodding in agreement.

"Get me out of here. Say that we're going for a walk. Say that you need to talk to me." I could hardly believe the words that Dad was mouthing to me across the room. Without knowing, he had given me the opening I needed. God was clearly at work.

Our shoes were on and we were out of the door. Walking arm in arm, Dad and I chatted generally and I sent up arrow prayers that God would give me the right words to say to him.

"Dad, I think you're aware that my last pilgrimage was no ordinary holiday. Five years ago I became aware that God was preparing me to live and work abroad. I know now that I am to go to the Holy Land."

Dad didn't falter in his step and after a minute or so he said, "I'm going to miss you like hell, but you have my blessing."

Praise God! Dad was accepting of what God was calling me to do. I knew it was going to be difficult for him, Mum's condition was continually deteriorating and I knew he would also be anxious about my safety in a land where there were frequent troubles, but he had given me his blessing. Over the next months he and I continued to discuss the implications of my leaving the country. I knew I was being called to live by faith, have no regular income and to trust and rely on God for everyday needs including food. Dad found this difficult to understand and he also struggled with why God should be calling me to a new work when there was still much to be done at Action on Homelessness. I said, "Dad, I believe we are called at different times to different things. God has worked through me for ten years to establish a project that would help homeless people; now others can continue that work. I am coming into a new season in my life; it's time for me to be involved in a new work."

CHAPTER NINETEEN

Obedience

Donna, my neighbour, friend, sister in Christ and secretary, offered to come with me to the Holy Land for two weeks as I went to 'knock on doors' and see where God was leading me. It was a blessing to have her company and prayer support as I took this step holding on tightly to God's word and promises. I thanked God for the numerous confirmations I'd had affirming that this is what He was calling me to do; I had no doubts and knew I must just wait for His timing to reveal where and how. Since I'd returned from the pilgrimage, I'd spent the last six months reading and enquiring about agencies that might accept volunteers. I read through the list with Donna as we sat on our beds in Jerusalem. We'd been told of someone that would provide us with fairly cheap accommodation and having arrived at Ben Gurion Airport, we had picked up a hire car and now found the house where we would stay for a few nights.

Over the next few days I systematically checked out the information I had about various agencies, but I just knew in my spirit that none of them were where the Lord wanted me to be. The borders into the West Bank were closed due to recent problems and I felt that it was time for us to go north.

"I feel we should move on up to Tiberias," I said to Donna. "I don't know of any organisations there, but I believe we should use this time wisely, as a gift given by God. I don't think we should spend any more time here. Let's move on to the Galilee area and wait on God."

Donna was the one insured to drive the car and as we made our way up through the Jordan valley we marvelled at the scenery of the desert.

I'd fallen in love with this bleak, hostile terrain last time I was in the country. Now as we drove Donna said, "I don't want to have to do this journey again." The road was tedious to drive but eventually we came into the rich fertile land surrounding the Sea of Galilee.

I'd stayed in contact with someone I'd met when last in Tiberias and now Donna and I called on him to say we were in the town.

Omar was pleased to see us. "Where are you staying, Marianne?" he asked.

"We've not booked in anywhere yet," I said.

"Leave it to me. I'll phone a friend at the Scottish Hospice."

That night Donna and I looked out of our bedroom window over the lake and next morning we saw the sun rise over the water.

The hostel had a private garden on the lakeside. We stepped into the cool, clear water and knew God's presence as we swam in the very waters that Jesus had calmed and walked upon. We weren't alone; not only was God with us, but also another girl whom we found out worked as a volunteer in the hostel. We chatted with Elaine as we swam and heard of the work she was doing.

Next morning, just as Donna and I were coming out of the dining room, Elaine approached us. "I don't know if this is right or not, but having talked yesterday I feel led to tell you about a residential school for blind children in Bethlehem. If you're interested in going I could arrange time off and come down with you."

Before I could say anything, Donna replied, "We must go!"

I looked at her. "But that would mean not only driving back through the desert, but returning again the next day – and you know what you said about driving that road..."

"I still think we should go," she insisted.

"What about the borders?" I said to Elaine. "They're closed."

"No worries," she said. "They opened again yesterday."

Arrangements were made and we were soon underway. It gave us a great opportunity to find out more about life in the land from Elaine's point of view. "We'll need to leave the car in Jerusalem, because it's a yellow plate and you're not insured to drive it on the West Bank," she said. I knew nothing of the yellow plates for Israeli cars and blue plates for Palestinian cars. Our hire car company had simply specified that we could not take the car into Palestinian areas, saying that it would not be safe. Elaine went on, "Blue plate cars are not allowed into Israel but if you own a yellow plate car or have special arrangements with the hire company you can take a yellow plate car into Palestine." It all seemed very complicated as we drove into Jerusalem, parked the car and then waited by the roadside for something Elaine called a 'sheroot', a van that would take us to Bethlehem.

Eventually we arrived at the school. Immediately I knew this was the place. I talked with Helen, a blind Palestinian Christian lady who ran the school. We had lunch, played with the children and I left saying, "I suggest we both pray about whether we think it right for me to come and if it's God's will then I'll expect to be back in three months."

Donna and I spent the next few days looking around the Galilee, amazed at how God confirmed through two different people that it was right for me to go into Bethlehem whilst we were still in Tiberias. Both these people 'happened' to be staying at the hostel and just 'happened' to know of and had had involvement with the school in Bethlehem. I was still learning, and awestruck that God amazingly puts people across our paths, but that it's right for us to constantly seek wisdom and discernment as to whether it is of God or not.

I believe other forces can be at work and will try to bring confusion and temptation. One such situation clearly crossed my path with Omar, the man I'd met in Galilee on my previous trip. I enjoyed this man's company and he talked of our being married and my living in Tiberias. I had been on my own for sixteen years and the idea of being in a relationship and married was very appealing. Since my second divorce I'd committed my time to Adrian, Tom, Mum and Dad and work. Now I knew there was a chance for me to be in a relationship with a man I had come to adore. I kept praying and seeking God. I remembered the passage in scripture he'd given me early that morning before starting out on the pilgrimage where He revealed that I was to move to the Holy Land. Deuteronomy 8 talks of not forgetting God and being obedient. Physical and emotional longing can so easily become foremost, but I accepted peacefully, when it was revealed, that Omar was not to be part of my life. God was now first and uppermost for me and once again in my spirit I knew that He clearly said, "This is not part of my plan." Maybe one day God would provide me with a husband, but one thing was for sure: I only wanted a partner if God ordained it. His plan was perfect and He knew what was best for me. My thoughts on what would make me happy had not always been for the best, so now with much sadness yet an absolute surety I obediently walked away from the possibility of a relationship with Omar.

Seven o'clock in the morning found me sat at my office desk typing out my three-month resignation. Donna and I had flown back to the UK the previous day and I now knew it was time to start closing down the chapter in my life of working at Action on Homelessness.

I handed the letter to Richard, my chairman. It wasn't altogether a surprise for him, but even so I guess we all wondered whether the day would ever come that I would walk away from the agency that, following the vision from God, I had initiated, brought into being and, with invaluable help and support, built up into quite a large charity that was known, used and valued throughout West Wiltshire. But this 'baby' was now up and walking on its own; it was time for me to hand over to others.

Leaving the UK was clearly going to have a major impact on my family. Adrian asked if he and I could go away for a few days on a trip down memory lane. We duly travelled around North Devon and Exeter revisiting houses we'd lived in, places we'd visited and the crematorium where Carl's ashes had been scattered. The time away allowed me the opportunity to talk through with him, as I had already done with Tom, the realities of the troubles that could occur in the West Bank. We talked of the possibility of me being in the wrong place at the wrong time and being killed, and we chatted through the implications of such a tragedy in the physical sense but also that I was doing what I believed to be right. Adrian understood that I firmly believed in the passage from the Bible that says in Philippians 1:21, "For me to live is Christ, to die is gain."

Gradually word went around that I was leaving. I cried with some of the people that had used the centre over the years. I would never forget those I'd spent so much time with. It had been a privilege to share in their pain and pleasures. Nearly a quarter of my life had been spent with people who were homeless, addicts, suffering from mental health problems and others in the area of West Wiltshire. Plans were made for my departure. I sold many of my clothes at car boot sales to pay for health insurance, booked my air ticket and arranged for Adrian and Tom to live in the house and pay the bills.

I was two weeks away from flying when I fell down the stairs and broke my ankle. It had started off as such a good day, although Donna had knocked on my front door in the afternoon and found I was suffering from a headache. "Come in later and have a cup of tea," she said. With my head throbbing, I hadn't thought this unusual, although normally we didn't wait for invites; we just called in on each other.

A few hours later I walked into her house and found her with the family and Rachel. Food had been prepared and obviously they had planned some fun and games. I looked at them strangely as I was being told that they had a few little gifts for me but that for each one I would have to do a forfeit. Never before had I been caught out in such a way. Even my surprise fortieth birthday party had been planned by me! It said much about me that I needed to be in control and in charge even if that was by delegation. It had been a whole new experience of "letting go and letting God". We laughed together as I completed the forfeits. Everything had been cleverly worded in rhyme and put me into a situation that was out of the norm or unfamiliar. This was to prepare me for life in an unfamiliar place where everything would be outside of my normal experiences.

At the end of a great day, which included going to church wearing clothes that didn't match and odd shoes, I went into my own house to see the decorating job Tom had done on his bedroom. "It looks fantastic, Tom. You should feel very pleased with your first wallpaper-hanging experience." I picked up some empty boxes and walked down the stairs. Then halfway down I started moving quicker than I had planned!

I fell heavily and felt the sickening pain in my ankle. Tom was beside me in an instant. "Don't move, Mum," he said as he checked me all over and asked if I'd knocked my head. He calmly took control, carried me to the car and drove to the local hospital.

"We have no X-ray equipment here at night. You can either come back in the morning or go to the Royal United Hospital at Bath," the nurse said.

"We'll go to Bath," Tom replied. It was already nearly one o'clock in the morning and I was worried about him being tired and driving. "I'm OK," he assured me. "I think it's important to get your ankle X-rayed. I can't believe it's broken, not when you're just about to fly to Palestine."

"Well, it's in God's hands," I answered, "but before we go to Bath, can we go back to the house and ask Donna to activate the prayer chain?"

Tom knocked on her door, waiting for her to come down from bed. She stood laughing as he told her what had happened; she was convinced that I was trying to play a joke back on her for all that she'd put me through during the day. As she realised Tom was serious she dashed to the phone and started ringing around asking people to uphold me in prayer.

Back in the car Tom cleverly asked me to recount the message I'd heard at the service that night as we drove to Bath. His tactics were good and helped keep my breathing even and my mind off the pain in my ankle.

The doctor looked at the X-rays. "I'd like to get a specialist to look at these," she said.

I sat waiting. As the two doctors looked at the film they confirmed it was a most unusual break. Tom came with me as I was wheeled to the plaster room.

"You go on back, Tom, you must be tired," I said as they laid me face down on the bed.

"No, Mum, I'll stay until you're on the ward."

I looked at him as he watched them manoeuvre my ankle back into position and apply the plaster. Tom was clearly fascinated at the whole procedure and quite unperturbed. I later upheld him in prayer as I opened up the Gideons bible by the side of my bed, knowing he was driving back to Trowbridge at around five in the morning. I thanked God for the peace in my heart and the lack of pain as I drank a cup of tea that the night sister had kindly brought me. I didn't understand why this had happened but I knew He had me in the palm of His hand and there was no need to be anxious.

The next day two porters arrived to wheel me in my bed down to the X-ray department. I'd previously given it no thought, but then I remembered that earlier on during the Sunday evening church service I'd been praying about the situation with my brother being estranged from the family. I knew he worked in the hospital as a porter and found myself asking those who were taking me down to X-ray if they knew him.

"Yes, we know Mark. Does he know you're here? We'll leave him a note at the Porters' Lodge. Who shall we say it is?"

"Oh, just say his sister is in the hospital."

Later two other porters were pushing me back to the ward. "Excuse me, Mark, can we just get by?"

I looked up at the man who moved to one side. *It was my brother.* I hadn't recognised him; it was twelve years since I'd seen him. I said nothing.

Mum and Dad sat by my bed. Dad was coming out with our family's normal warped humour. (Many would think we were either sick or insensitive but we always made each other laugh and it had a way of boosting us up and preventing us from getting into the 'poor me' syndrome.) I told them of my conversation with the porters and just as I finished recounting the events, Mark walked on to the ward and came to my bedside.

As he briefly hugged Mum and Dad and took my hand, I recalled that the previous night I'd asked for prayer ministry regarding my brother. It saddened me that I was leaving the country, not knowing when I'd return, and that I was not reconciled with him.

He was working, so every so often had to keep leaving the ward to collect patients. As he came back in the second time, Mum looked at me and said, "Here comes that man again. Do you know him?" Dad and I looked at each other and tears welled up in our eyes as we realised that due to Mum's worsening dementia she did not recognise Mark as her own son. I prayed that Mark would respond to this contact and stay in touch with Mum and Dad. Out of something bad, my broken ankle, God had brought about something good, an opportunity for him to come back into the family. I was well aware of the heartache that Mum and Dad had endured over the years since being estranged from Mark and his family. They and I had tried many times in numerous different ways to bridge the gap between us, but to no avail.

As with other areas of my life and people I pray for, I accept that God will prepare the way for reconciliation but it is always the choice of each individual as to whether they take that step. God will not force anyone. He has given us free will. The choice is ours. I realise that for relationships to be healthy both parties have to commit and sometimes, for a host of reasons, however much one party desires the contact and is committed, the other feels differently and therefore a relationship is untenable. It is so identical to our relationship with God. He lovingly desires us to be in fellowship and harmony with Him. He has bridged the gap, through the sacrifice of His Son. His desire is to reunite and restore, but we will always have the choice whether to have that relationship with Him or not.

God brought about a miraculous healing on my ankle, to the extent that some weeks later the registrar couldn't even see on the X-rays where the bone had broken. He had to check against earlier film as to where the injury had occurred. I thanked God for the extra time he'd given me with family and friends. I attended the two leaving events that had been arranged at Action on Homelessness with my leg in a plaster cast. I was given permission from the hospital to be let out for a few hours to meet up with staff, local supporters, dignitaries and others within the town.

It was a strange experience to be wheeled into the day centre when I was under the influence of strong painkillers and clearly drugged. People had gathered, nibbles had been prepared and I was very moved by the kind things various people said about what I had done in the town for disadvantaged people.

I could not stand to speak but replied, "Firstly, I'd like to thank God for entrusting me with the vision and enabling me to do the work He called me to. Secondly, I'd like to thank my family; without the support of Adrian and Tom and my Mum and Dad, I could not have given the time and energy. Also I'd like to thank the many staff, committee members and members of the public who over the years have worked ceaselessly. It has been teamwork and I've been privileged to be part of that team."

I was bizarrely given the 'freedom of the town' in recognition of establishing Action on Homelessness and all that I'd been involved with since. I appreciated the gesture of the award and evidently it means I have the right to take a flock of sheep through the high street!

A week later, after my discharge from the hospital, Dad drove me to the centre to say goodbye to the clients I'd worked with. This was, for me, by far the more important meeting where I was to have the opportunity to say goodbye; in no way does this disrespect the dignitaries but for me it had always been about the clients, not the authorities. As Dad drove up outside the building, two of the guys came out to the car. Dad was left to wheel in the wheelchair as, somewhat mortified, he watched them carry me in. I was deeply moved as it signified that the people I'd tried to support over the years now literally supported me. I was humbled that some whom I'd not seen for many years had made long journeys to come and say goodbye. I cried.

My parting from Adrian and Tom was unbelievably painful. Having gone out for a meal just a few nights before I was to leave the UK, each gave me precious gifts: Tom a gold chain and locket containing his photo; Adrian his most treasured possession, his football medal. Leaving my two sons, detaching myself from the small family unit that had gone through so much strife but shared such a depth of love, was extremely difficult.

At that final moment of parting, I kept getting out of the car that was to take me to the airport and running back to Adrian. Time and time again, I could not leave. It was as if my heart was being ripped apart by a blunt spoon! I knew I was prolonging the agony but it was so emotionally painful to say goodbye. As once again I exited the car and went back to him, he put his arm around me and walked me firmly away from the vehicle. "Mum, this is what God has called you to do. You've given Tom and me life and love; you have raised and nurtured us well. We are OK. We love you and respect you." With that he turned me around and started once again walking me firmly back to the car. "Go now, Mum. We support you in what you're doing." What strength and character! What support, encouragement and affirmation! I was on my way to the next chapter of my life.

Rachel had offered to fly out with me for two weeks to see me settle in. We sat at Gatwick drinking coffee with Jean. She'd come to see me off, to see her prophetic picture come to fruition, of her stood on the airport roof watching me fly off. She'd already been awestruck at seeing the photos of the children at the blind school, identical to those in her picture of me sat with brown-skinned children in a desert-like area. "I think they're calling your flight to return to the desk," Jean said. We'd already checked in our luggage, so picking up our handbags we made our way back to the desk.

I looked at the letter I'd just been handed. "The advice of the British Government is that due to troubles in Israel you do not fly at this time. Your air fare will be refunded in full." Tears flowed down my face; it was a wonder that I hadn't gone rusty with all the tears over the last few weeks. The three of us made our way to the airport chapel; at a time like this the only thing to do was pray. Had I got it all wrong? Was God bringing about this issue with the flight to stop me going to Beit Jala? Or was this the enemy wanting to prevent me from going because this was God's agenda for me? There were many questions that needed answers and they needed answering fast!

We entered the chapel and I fell on my knees. The stillness that entered my spirit in the midst of this confusion and stress was tangible. I knew that God was with me, that he would have me go. I was at peace – beyond understanding. *I would fly.*

As I exited the chapel I thought of the practicalities. Rachel had a lot of my possessions in her luggage. If she decided not to fly, then many items I needed would not arrive with me in Beit Jala. I knew that in no way must I influence her decision; the potential risks were far too great. Rachel's face expressed her anxieties as she came out of the chapel and together with Jean we stood in silence. I clearly knew I should still fly but Rachel was unsure. I hadn't reminded her of the luggage situation, not wanting to put pressure on her. As I looked up she made a dash back into the chapel.

A few minutes later Rachel emerged absolutely transformed. "We go," she said boldly in an unusually confident, calm voice. "I've just prayed that if I was to go, God would give me His peace, and instantly He filled me with a peace that I can't even put into words!"

We now needed to hurry to our departure and again I cried as I hugged Jean. We'd been friends for many years and had gone through many 'life issues' together, including by far the most significant spiritual experiences. As I waved goodbye I had no idea of when, or even if, I'd see her again. I sat on the plane, obedient to God's calling. I was on my way to Palestine.

Chapter Twenty

Grow in Me, My Child

The plane was less than half full. Many people had decided to heed the Government's advice and we'd waited for their luggage to be offloaded. As we stood on the runway waiting for take-off I thought of Jean up on the roof. It was cold, windy and wet, a typical November day. Rachel and I felt peaceful as we took off.

Arriving in Ben Gurion everything seemed normal; the Western concerns about Iraq didn't seem to be unduly worrying the Israelis. I soon came to realise that both they and the Palestinians are so used to such troubles that it was almost the norm. Rachel and I booked into the guesthouse we were to stay in for a few days in Jerusalem, prior to going up to the Galillee and then on to the school near Bethlehem.

I phoned Adrian as I'd arranged. "Hi, darling, it's me."

"Hi, Mum! So you're still in London?"

"No, Adrian, I'm here in Jerusalem."

"But you can't be. It's been on the news that all flights are stopped and Britain is evacuating all her subjects."

"I know, Adrian, but I managed to get the last flight out."

There was silence on the other end of the line for a moment, then Adrian spoke meaningfully. "OK, Mum. Tom and I support you in what you're doing."

Previously I had chatted through with both of the boys what I was doing and why. We had talked about the fact that I was coming to a country that was often under threat as well as having local troubles. I'd explained that I believed this was what God was calling me to do, just as I'd believed He'd called me to set up the charity working with homeless and addicts. Adrian, Tom, Mum and Dad had always been not only supportive but encouraging. They knew it was important for me to be in God's will, wherever that might be. They knew my love for each of them was absolute, but they also understood that God was first in my life; after all, He had created me in His own image and made me His own.

I put the phone down, aware of my family's concerns. I prayed that they might seek God's strength and peace.

I showed Rachel around the various sites over the next few days and then we went to the school. That first night I experienced several moments of panic. This was all so different to being here on a pilgrimage or knocking doors. I was very aware of a mosquito buzzing around the room and kept putting my head under the covers. It was unbelievably cold and everything suddenly felt very alien and abusive to all my senses. In prayer I placed myself at the foot of the cross and asked God to take me unto Himself.

I woke in the morning to discover that both my eyes were so swollen that they were almost closed. My face was an explosion of swellings. I had twenty-seven mosquito bites on my face! Just one incredibly annoying, minute insect had pumped its poison into me and I was swollen beyond recognition. My body's defences started fighting the infection but I felt really ill. What on earth was I doing, allowing myself to be put through this? Rachel looked at me with concern and questioned what I was going to do. I felt so miserable and poorly I simply wanted to be out of the situation.

Having thrown myself on God's mercy I decided to check yet again if this was where He wanted me to be at this time. "God, if I've got it all wrong, please let there be a seat on the plane that Rachel is booked on in a week's time to go back to the UK. If on the other hand I've heard your voice rightly and here is where I'm to be for Your purposes, then let me know Your peace and grace." I phoned the airline. The flight was full!

Ever since coming to faith and trying to be a faithful follower of Jesus, my understanding has been simple. If God desires me to do something for His purposes, He'll make a way even when there appears to be no way. I understand and expect that the enemy will often try to thwart that plan from being realised, but if I simply hold God's hand

He will see me through and throughout; even though it might not be easy, I will know that precious gift of His peace.

Gradually the days became easier and I slowly started to become accustomed to the Arab way of life. Culture shock was an understatement. I was now treated very differently to a foreigner on holiday. I knew I needed to be sensitive and tolerant to local beliefs and traditions. It was not for me as the Western Brit to come into their land and say, "This is how you should be doing it!" I vowed to listen, listen and then listen some more before I ever spoke my opinion or made a statement. Humility and peace were to be my key words and actions. I was constantly in prayer for God's grace and guidance.

Helen had not been in the school when I arrived; she was travelling the Americas and would not be back until Christmas Eve. I set out to get to know the staff and the children, to watch and to listen. I was immediately drawn to Nisreen Kunkar, Helen's secretary, a young girl of twenty-two. She radiated Jesus. I knew that the staff team were a mix of Christians and Muslims and my heart especially warmed to her over the days.

I sat with her in the office and we started talking about our families. She told me about her mother and three brothers.

"What about your dad?" I asked.

"He was killed at the beginning of the intifada," she said and started to tell me about the events surrounding his death. As she spoke, tears fell down her cheeks.

I walked across the room and took her in my arms, our tears mingled. I had so much to learn. Although I knew a little about the Israeli people and the Jewish way of life, I knew nothing of the intifada and even less of the Palestinian people and their struggle throughout more recent history. As we cried together I listened to Nisreen telling me of their current dire life circumstances.

I enjoyed being with the children and started making plans for Christmas. I decided to introduce them to Christmas stockings and busily started making, by hand, sixteen stockings. I bought small gifts to go in each one and then set about making a fireplace to hang them around. I'd never had the skill of my mother and had no artistic leaning, so I knew it was truly of God when I was inspired and created a reasonable-looking Victorian-style fireplace out of cardboard, crepe and metallic paper. As we prepared for Christmas I would share with them the Christmas story of Jesus born in a stable just a mile or so from where we were. I could say how Jesus loved them and grew up to be a man of peace and that was His hope and heart for their country.

Life was physically quite difficult after Western comforts; the food was vastly different and I craved mashed potatoes, baked beans, egg and bacon and many other delights I took for granted in England. Their diet lacked variety: rice and fatty meat were the staple diet; occasionally chicken was a welcome change. I became frustrated at the state of the roads. It seemed as if all of Bethlehem and the Beit Jala area, where I was living, was under construction in readiness for the millennium celebrations. Even in these winter months, dust and sand got into everything. As I got ready for bed, I put on my ankle-to-wrist thermal underwear and pulled over my head a floor-length wool-mixture nightshirt. I climbed into my zero temperature rated sleeping bag and then pulled up five blankets. It was cold! Then I settled down to sleep in a room I was sharing with a severely mentally and physically handicapped girl.

Throughout the night the girl would scream out; she was doubly incontinent and would gnaw on her deformed hands as she twisted and writhed in her bed. I would feel guilty at being frustrated at my constantly disturbed nights and lack of sleep, when clearly her body and mind were in such distress. I remembered that the Bible says, "In *everything* give thanks,"[13] and thanked God for a comfortable mattress and that I knew He would give me the strength in body, mind and spirit to be His servant.

I learnt to look at things very differently to the way I had when I lived in England. A people that didn't have the wealth or materialism of the West surrounded me. Many lived in refugee camps. I heard their pain, anger and frustration. What did I know of their plight? Nothing! But I could listen and stand beside them. Never had I known how it was to have a member of my family shot by soldiers who were occupying my country, or to have armed men forcefully entering my home week after week. I started to think what it would be like to have your country occupied by one foreign power after another. I thought back to Dad and how he'd been part of the British forces during the time of the British Mandate at the end of the Second World War. In this land

[13] 1 Thessalonians 5:18 (KJV); emphasis added

healthcare was largely non-existent; 'old wives' tales' were the order of the day so frequently I would see people putting butter on burns and wrapping children up warmly in layers of thick blankets when they had a fever. Health and safety was also largely non-existent: cars had no MOTs; electrical wires would trail dangerously; young toddler children would play on the flat roofs of their homes with no walls or railings to protect them from falling; food would be reheated many times over and then left uncovered on top of kitchen cupboards for hours, allowing flies to settle and spread their germs; often due to limited water supplies, hands would be unwashed before handling food in close proximity to open toilets. The basics that we took for granted in the UK were not part of the lifestyle here in the West Bank.

"The Americans and British are bombing Iraq." Seham, one of the care staff at the school, woke me with the news. Britain was bombing Arabs in another country but to the Palestinian people these were their brothers. Never before had I considered the implications of all the politics and powers of the Middle East. The issues, though clearly complex, had been apparent for many thousands of years and yet were unknown not only to me, but undoubtedly to the vast majority of people in the West. How would the Palestinian community react towards me when my Government was aggressively targeting their fellow Arabs? I felt humbled as local people were still friendly towards me and didn't hold me in contempt.

Helen returned to the school and I learnt more of how she, as this daughter of a well-known wealthy Palestinian family, had been educated in England. Helen, as not only a disabled person, but a disabled female, had unusually been afforded many benefits that others in her culture would not have received. She was a vehemently strong, direct single lady who controlled the ways of the school and how it operated. The children were a delight and treasured every touch of human warmth and compassion. They were taught by the older students who likewise were partially sighted or fully blind. Most of the children were either orphans or had been disowned by their families because of their disabilities.

My role was primarily to assist with their physical needs and also assist Helen in the operation of the charity. I was to be her driver, not only in the local area, but also as and when she wanted to go into Jerusalem or farther afield. Helen had acquired a yellow-plated car that gave her access into Israel. This was highly valued, setting her apart from, and making her superior to, the vast majority of the Palestinian population. Palestinian cars are blue-plated and only allowed to operate within the West Bank. The legal agreement with Israel and the insurance company was that the car could only be driven by either an American or British driver and so I was to escort her to many places driving on 'the wrong side of the road'. Within the West Bank no one upheld any of the rules of the road but, thankfully, I enjoyed driving and believed myself to be quite good at reading the road and predicting what other drivers might do. It was to stand me in good stead on many an occasion! Helen also wanted me to assess how the school could obtain funding support from the UK. She was aware of the contacts I had back in England and was constantly mentioning her need of money from the wealthy West.

It soon became apparent that I would have to return to England every three months because of my visa. I made the arrangements and thanked God for the provision to see my family on a regular basis. It was a blessing to go home to see Adrian, Tom, Mum, Dad and friends. But God had doubly blessed me; He had also provided me with a family in Beit Jala.

I was excited and looked forward to going back to the UK, savouring the delights of smoked bacon and Stilton cheese, but I was also sad to be leaving Palestine and the Palestinians. My three months were up, my visa about to expire; Christmas had come and gone. I'd packed my bags and was waiting for a car to take me into Jerusalem.

Nisreen was sat in the office. As I went in to say goodbye she said, "Everyone who comes here leaves and we never see them again."

I took off my cross and chain. Viv, a friend who worked with me at Action on Homelessness, had given me the crucifix just before I'd left the UK, saying, "I don't have any cash to give you but this is gold, and gold speaks volumes in all countries and cultures. By giving you this, if ever you need to buy your way out of a problem you can use this."

I'd worn it constantly since I'd been in Bethlehem and now I handed it to Nisreen saying, "Nisreen, I'd like you to wear this whilst I'm away. You know this is precious to me; it was given to me by a friend who has a concerned and loving heart. I am concerned for you and love you. I will be coming back so you wear this whilst I'm gone and then you can give it back to me when I return."

She looked up, removed her own cross and said, "As long as you'll wear mine in exchange."

We were making a vow to each other that I would return.

I knew I was going to miss this girl. I'd met her family a few times and their hospitality overwhelmed me. Just before Christmas I was invited to attend the Christmas Celebration of the Bethlehem Bible College. I was amazed to find myself at the Bethlehem Hotel enjoying a sit down dinner. That night I briefly met Zuzu, Nisreen's eldest brother, and then on New Year's Eve I was invited to their home for a barbecue.

Family, food and fellowship in abundance surrounded me on the roof of their home. "What's wrong?" Zuzu asked me, his face showing concern.

"Nothing," I answered. "I'm just watching you and your family; your lifestyle, attitude and interaction are very different to Western ways."

"As you see, we have nothing,' he said.

I tried to explain that to some extent I understood that statement, but that also in some ways they had everything. As a people they treasured every moment they spent with one another, making their own entertainment. It was a joy to watch Zuzu with his brothers, sister and mother, grandmother, cousins and neighbours as they laughed and talked, sang and danced together. They had no need of electronic gadgets, expensive trips out or the abundance of materialism. They simply savoured being in the company of each other.

My ten days back in the UK went all too quickly – a brief catch-up with my parents and sons, a number of prearranged talks, and several shopping trips to acquire items that would be useful back in Beit Jala. I was grateful to Jean who had undertaken the task of forwarding regular updates of news to people in England. She also set up talks for me to give to groups whilst I was on return visits. One of the things I would share with people was the lack of items that were so much taken for granted in the West, such as the crayons, drawing paper and scraps of materials that I had so struggled to find when making the Christmas stockings for our Victorian fireplace. Medication and toiletries were limited, to say the least, as was clothing. Books and toys were difficult to obtain and there was little choice. Baby thermometers were just one of the vast number of items that were unobtainable. So I would go with a long list of items around the town and purchase as much as possible in the knowledge that Monarch, the airline I flew with, had kindly agreed to triple my weight allowance in response to my request and information on what I was doing in Palestine.

All too quickly I was once again flying out of Gatwick, preparing myself for the many hours of interrogation that I would get on landing in Israel. As I landed and queued to go through Passport Control, I wondered if I would be pulled to one side again. I was – escorted to a different part of the airport under a very obviously armed guard. Israel has one of the best, if not *the best,* defence force and intelligence services in the world.

I eventually arrived back in Beit Jala, the town that nestles alongside Bethlehem, and went to Nisreen Kunkar's home to visit, staying for the night. I shared her large double bed and soon we were lying looking at each other, somewhat bleary-eyed, and talking about my time away. My time in England had been frenetic, speaking in different churches, all too brief times with Adrian, Tom, Mum and Dad.

"Move in here," Nisreen suddenly said.

"I can't do that!" I exclaimed.

"Why not?" she retorted.

"Because I'd be taking up your space and your privacy."

She looked at me strangely. I had yet to fully comprehend that space and privacy are not part of the Arab culture.

"We are Arab; we no understand your British need for space and – well, at least stay over again tonight," she replied.

Two nights became three and three became four. "Bring your things up here and move in," Nisreen said again.

"It's all very well you saying that," I said, "but what about your mum?" Esperance had always been delightful, welcoming, hospitable and friendly, but it seemed an awful imposition to move into her home.

"Mum loves you; she says you are her sister. She wants you to move in." Nisreen's statement amazed me.

"But what about your brothers?" I asked. Zuzu at twenty-four and Nisreen at twenty-two also had two brothers, Basheer aged eighteen and Majeed fifteen.

"You're family," she said. "They want you to live with us."

I drew breath, unable to understand such love and acceptance. "But you know I'm here as a volunteer. I live by faith. I can't pay for my keep."

"We don't want anything from you. We just want you to live with us."

I moved in, overwhelmed and thanking God that He had brought such a family across my path, not so much for the provision of a home in which to live but more for the provision of a family to love and be loved by.

I was aware that Esperance's family had been evicted from their home in Jerusalem with only a few hours' notice by the British forces at the end of the Second World War. Her family had lived in the home for many generations but they were to make way for the Jewish people who were coming to establish the State of Israel. She and her family were placed in tented camps in what was to become known as the West Bank. This was the woman who now called me her sister and was asking me to become an integral part of her family, even though she knew my father had been a part of those British forces!

The night I'd arrived back at the school followed not only over sixteen hours in transit and travelling, but also many hours of interrogation by the Israeli Defence Force. I had been advised by many Christians in the land to always say I was simply going to Jerusalem, but giving this information to security forces would clearly have been an untruth. At all times my aims were to speak the truth and live in peace, so I would always be very open and honest as to where I was going and why. In practice this made the journey time much more tedious and taxing so I would always arrive at the school tired and somewhat drained.

I was therefore a little surprised when, upon entering the school, even before I'd taken off my coat, Helen asked me how much money I'd brought her from England. Before leaving Beit Jala, Helen and I had talked about the planned talks I was to give whilst in England and, if people offered any financial support, I could tell them what would be required for the students at the school. Helen had said that four children needed beds, books and pens would always be appreciated, and money for clothes was a constant source of concern. People had given incredibly generously, many specifying what they would like the money to be spent on, and in accordance with UK charity law knew I would endeavour to ensure that the money would be spent as they had intended. Helen vehemently voiced that I was to hand the money over there and then, and she was going to spend it on the car.

It soon became clear that my position in the school was untenable. I knew from the recorded mileage that the car in question had been driven by someone else whilst I was away and since there were no other British or American people in the area to drive the car, it had been driven contrary to the insurance agreement within the State of Israel. I was unable to hand over the money to Helen.

It was a very painful decision to stand in the place of truth and honesty when Helen subsequently refused me any contact with the children. I had built up special relationships with the children and had become extremely fond of them and the staff. I left the school and came to realise that it had simply been a stepping stone into the country, that I was to move out into a wider work as a Christian in the land. I was awestruck to then realise that God was one step ahead. In leaving the school, I no longer had accommodation provided, but already I had moved in with the Kunkar family so I was free to work, witness and serve wherever God may lead. As always, He also had His hand on all the details.

I contacted the people back in England who had kindly given money for the ministry at the school and informed them of all that had taken place. Their support and affirmation as to the decisions I'd taken were a great encouragement. They said as the money could not be used as planned for the equipment at the school, I was to use it for whichever new work God was leading me into. When people graciously give money to help others it's always a great responsibility on the part of the person who is administering it and I felt very humbled by their response.

I came to realise the amazing awesomeness of God in placing me in the Kunkar family. Their father had been the first person to be killed in the first intifada. He had been shot in the back, just a few yards from his home, whilst simply going to a neighbour's house to try and sort out some form of schooling for their respective children. As soon as the Israelis occupied Beit Jala, as in other places they closed all of the schools. As Nisreen's father was the first martyr, the family was very well known throughout the country. As I became increasingly integrated into the Palestinian community, I discovered the power of the typical conversation opening, "Who you? Where you live?" "My name's Marianne. I live with Kunkar family in Beit Jala." It opened many doors that would otherwise have been closed.

Yet again I was to witness how God causes our paths to cross with those of other people for His purposes. I was introduced to a man called Nasser, a Muslim who had been imprisoned during the first intifada and was in a cell with a deaf man. He came to realise the dreadful plight for those who were deaf. They were often treated worse than animals, chained outside their homes or abandoned. Nasser vowed that when he was released he would dedicate the rest of his life to seeking out and helping those who were so afflicted. Nasser asked if I would help him, and though yet again I had no specific previous experience, I sought God's guidance and the teaching of Holy Spirit to show me what He would have me do.

Nasser took me with him on drives into the desert, often quite long journeys, whenever he heard of a deaf person, who was often shackled outside the home. He would then encourage the family to release the person and allow them to come into Bethlehem where they could attend a centre that Nasser had established. This centre was located in a hollowed out room in the hillside just outside Bethlehem. The running water was a dribble coming out of a pipe. The toilet was little more than a hole in the floor and the seating was a few plastic chairs. This was a haven where deaf people could meet with others who suffered the same plight, establish ways to communicate – there was no Palestinian sign-language – and start building up some life and social skills. It was my privilege to assist Nasser, and I was humbled by the way the constantly expanding group welcomed and accepted me.

Nasser was also a frequent attender at the 'peace talks' between members of the Israeli and Palestinian communities. He would invite me along but it seemed absurd that since they were generally held in Israel the only way he could attend was by crossing the border illegally, running the risk of being shot by Israeli soldiers. We went anyway, while I constantly prayed for our protection and was fascinated by the coming together of these different peoples.

Nasser would frequently tell me of the past troubles, though giving no details on his involvement with Hamas. He was always kind, courteous, sharing and polite towards me. I would be invited to all male Muslim meetings, where their own women were only allowed to come as far as the doorway to pass over the coffee, water and cakes. I was always treated with nothing but respect, yet I always had a feeling that if he was ever called to take my life he would have done so without a further thought. That's just the way it was.

One day we were sat drinking the thick, almost syrup-like strong coffee, when we got on to the subject of the ongoing problems between Israel and Palestine. Suddenly, a visible blackness came over Nasser; he thumped his hand on the table and said, "I will never forgive them." This change in his appearance and the ferocity as he spoke was so 'out of the blue'.

After a few minutes his demeanour returned to his norm and I quietly said, "I am so sorry for all your pain. But if you cannot forgive, then you can never move on."

"Maybe so," he said, "but that is how my people and I feel."

One day, just as I arrived at the centre, Nasser said he'd heard about a person who was deaf and disabled physically and mentally, living – or rather, *existing* – not far from Manger Square in Bethlehem. As we walked up the hillside I was completely unprepared for what I was about to witness. Nasser made contact with the person who had phoned him. The man explained how he'd found out that his nephew, thought to be in his early twenties, had been dumped in a trash skip. He'd rescued him and had been giving him food but was at a loss as to what to do with him. He took us to a padlocked wooden door about three feet high that was covering the entrance to a cave. As he was unlocking the padlock we were aware of a howling noise that sounded like a wounded animal. He opened the door and inside on the floor was a young man whose body was twisted and deformed, writhing about in his own excrement and urine. He was unable to see and could only feel for the plates of food that had been put on the floor for him.

That evening when I got back to the family, Esperance asked me why I was so quiet. I left the room, broke down in tears of distress and anger. How could a human being treat anyone like this, let alone one of their own?

Nisreen came in and sat on the bed beside me. As I voiced my anger she replied, "That is how it is here. Many of the Palestinian people believe that deformity or any sense of disability has been brought about by God because of sin within the family. Many of our people either won't, or don't know how to, care for someone because of the implications of recognising the person."

Nasser found great difficulty in locating a place for this young man to go. Eventually he told me he'd found a small group of nuns in Gaza who would take him in and care for him. I was aghast; this wouldn't happen in England. But I wasn't in England; I was living within a society that believed, "It is what it is." Everything that happens is "Insha Allah", the will of God. There was little thought by many to serve each other or to show care and compassion by their actions, and there was no state provision.

On my return trips to the UK, I made contact with the British Society for the deaf and various groups of people with hearing impairment to see how I might better support those back in the West Bank.

One day Nasser and I drove out to Hebron – a known hotspot for trouble between Palestinians and Israelis, but we wanted to meet with a number of men in Hebron who had established a similar support group. On the way there we were stopped by an Israeli soldier who was outside of his own territory. His rifle pointing at our faces through the open windows of the car was quite a salutary moment. After a productive time of networking in Hebron, as we drove home we were stoned by Palestinian youths. Such is the trouble in this afflicted land.

I became aware that Nisreen and her family believed that life in the West, and specifically in the UK, was perfect and that they had no quality of life in the West Bank. When I felt that this 'grass is greener' belief was becoming very unhealthy I decided to try to make arrangements for Nisreen and her brother Zuzu to come over with me to the UK for a few weeks. Initially it was necessary for us all to go to the British Consulate which is in East Jerusalem. The difficulty is that to get there we had to travel through West Jerusalem, which the Israelis don't allow Palestinians to do without a permit. This was clearly going to be quite a dangerous journey so I contacted friends back in England for prayer support. We knew that there was no way we could talk the Israeli soldiers into letting Zuzu through the checkpoint – being a young Palestinian and therefore surely a terrorist – so he had to walk a four-mile detour over the hills around the checkpoint. However, we hoped that maybe they would let Nisreen, being a female and travelling together with me. It worked; she was given clearance without a permit, but she was humiliated and ridiculed by the soldiers in a totally abusive way. I was shocked and angered as I watched and heard how they spoke to her and treated her. Nisreen took my hand, kept her head lowered and just said, "This is how it is for us here."

We made contact with Zuzu who was angered at what had happened to his sister but we pressed on towards the Consulate. Now they were travelling without permits and it has been known for Palestinians caught without these papers to be shot. It was therefore with a sigh of relief that we reached the Consulate building in time for our appointment.

I explained my circumstances and that, "I'd like to take these two young people to England for a few weeks," but I saw concern come over the Consulate's face as he read files on the desk.

"We're not able to give permission," he said. "Zuzu has already been refused entry into the UK." His mother had applied for him to live with his aunt who is resident in Worthing, Sussex, shortly after his father was killed in the Intifada. Esperance had been concerned about Zuzu and hadn't wanted him to get caught up in any acts of retaliation.

I explained that neither Nisreen nor Zuzu had ever been in any trouble, that they were both former students of the famous Bethlehem Bible College and this trip was simply to show them that life is not *all* perfect in Britain.

Eventually the Consul agreed to give them a visa as long as I stood guarantor for them. We were grateful to him and I punched the air as we left the office. Now all we needed was to get the absolutely necessary permits from the Israelis so that they could travel through Israel to get to the airport. This was no mean feat; there were constant delays and it was literally the day before our flight that they received the papers required. Now we needed to organise a yellow-plated cab to collect us from the West Bank and take us to the airport.

Done! We were on our way! All the family and extended family and friends waved us off; this was a major event for the local community.

We'd been travelling about forty minutes and were just a short way from the airport when suddenly we were surrounded by flashing lights and torches shining into the car, bringing the taxi to a halt. When our eyes adjusted we could see that we were literally surrounded by military vehicles and all the soldiers were aiming their weapons on us.

"OUT! OUT! OUT!" we heard.

Immediately the taxi driver exited the car. Zuzu was literally dragged from the vehicle and I prayed earnestly as he was manhandled into a nearby cabin. I knew he would be strip-searched and suffer awful indignities. "Dear Lord, please let him remain calm and not retaliate," I prayed.

In the meantime, Nisreen was ordered from the taxi with a rifle in her face, and all her luggage, so carefully packed, was emptied on to the pavement. I tried to get out to stand beside her but another soldier shoved a rifle in my face and said, "You stay. Who you?"

I explained that I was a friend of theirs, that I'd been living with them and that now I was taking them into the UK and that we all had the necessary documentation. He turned his back on me, barring the door, preventing me from getting out.

An hour later we were underway, shocked and rather battered, not physically but definitely emotionally. Arriving at the airport, time was no longer on our side. Although we had allowed several extra hours for any eventuality, we still had to go through airport security. Suffice to say we were all interrogated, searched – personally and our luggage – and were the last to board. People were staring at us and comments such as, "They're Palestinians," could be overheard.

As we taxied down the runway Zuzu took hold of my hand and said, "Thank you, Marianne. I never thought this day would or could ever happen."

Landing at Gatwick and walking through the terminal, Nisreen and Zuzu's eyes were wide open. I showed them around various sights over the next few weeks and when I later asked them what they liked best, without hesitation Zuzu swiftly came back with his reply, "Driving around in the car with no checkpoints and all the green fields." He was sat in the back constantly clicking his camera at green fields.

"When you get those developed," I said, "don't go asking me where each green field was!"

He laughed but continued to use up roll after roll of film.

Clearly they couldn't go home without seeing London so we duly had a day looking around the capital city. Early evening found us walking up Regent Street, where Zuzu made comment on yet another person curled up in a doorway. At that same moment a limo cruised down the road. "Marianne," Zuzu said, "this is not good. Here you have a person with no home and there you have a person with very expensive car. We do not have this in Palestine."

I could only agree.

As we cut through some of the streets we saw a collapsed teenage girl surrounded by some friends. They assured us that they had called an ambulance and that she had reacted badly to some drugs she'd taken. As we walked on Zuzu said, "Marianne, this is not good. We do not have this in Palestine."

I could only agree.

As we arrived at Trafalgar Square we came upon a large crowd of very scantily dressed girls and I heard, "Marianne, this is not good. We do not have this in Palestine."

I could only agree.

Then as we walked towards the tube station there was a very vocal large group of lads cursing, swearing and falling around drunk. "Marianne, this is not good. We do not have this in Palestine. I am proud to be Palestinian."

As I agreed, I thanked God. Bringing him and his sister to England had been successful. They had seen that not everything in our society was wonderful. Although back home they had very little and there was even less for them to look forward to, they did have a lifestyle that many in the UK lost some time ago. Nisreen and Zuzu were blessed by simple pleasures – spending time with family, singing and dancing without being intoxicated, and they did have a roof over their head albeit shell-pitted. They might not know tomorrow, but they valued today. Now we could return. No longer did they have rose-tinted glasses in their beliefs of the wealthy West. They could be rightly proud of their own culture.

The centre within Bethlehem grew and gradually it was accepted that women would also be encouraged and welcome to attend. This was a major breakthrough, as within the culture the men and women rarely met with each other. A group of friends of mine came out from the UK and we ran several workshops so that people could learn crafts and skills which would enable them to earn money from tourists. I thought of the millions of people who visit this land and particularly Bethlehem, the birthplace of Jesus. People saw all the tourist sites yet had no idea of what was happening just a few streets away. I thought about how the lives of one group of people could be so adversely affected by another group of people; how claims of land, power and control devastated communities; how people's beliefs, religion and history set out to destroy others whose faith and walk of life was different.

Once again my visa was about to expire, and with plans to establish a space for teaching 'English as a foreign language' following requests from the local community, I set off for the airport, looking forward to ten days in the UK and time to meet up with friends and family before preparing to return and start the new project. As always, I had just a small holdall in readiness for a much weightier return journey. Little did I know that it would be over a decade before I would once again walk in the Holy Land.

I've come to know many people who have been out to the Holy Land on short term mission – a time of blessing for them and I'm sure they were a blessing to others. I thank God for the opportunity He's given me not only to live in the land within a community, but to have had the opportunity to spend time on *both* sides of the border. I've lived with a Palestinian Christian family, worked with Palestinian Muslims and spent time travelling on vacation, socialising and at peace meetings with Israeli Jews, Messianic Jews, Muslims and Christians. Having experienced such a breadth of relationships, I've had the opportunity to hear the life stories of the different peoples and have been able to experience the true reality of living in the land. It was a privilege and blessing for me to have the opportunity to get to know and spend time with the Kunkar family. They enabled me to gain a better understanding of the Palestinian issue as I listened to their pain and saw their plight.

Chapter Twenty-One

Go into All the World

Hard as it always was to leave Nisreen, her family and her people, it was wonderful to get back to the UK. I had numerous talks planned to bring people up-to-date with all that was happening and now to tell them about the new project.

I had been just a few days back in the English culture when my mobile phone rang. It was my friend Jean. "Are you watching the TV?" she asked.

I told her I was at the home of a mutual friend of ours and, no, we were just chatting; why?

"The West Bank has erupted!" she said.

I quickly turned on the television to see that Ariel Sharon had walked on to Temple Mount where the Al Aqsa mosque is sited and was reputed to have said, "The Temple Mount is in our hands." This had provoked an intifada (Palestinian uprising). The place was not only in chaos but many had already been killed. I knew this would not only shut down all the borders but that there would be no flights for a significant time going into Ben Gurion airport from the UK.

I immediately phoned Nisreen and after many attempts found out that Beit Jala was on lockdown by the Israeli Military and that the Palestinians were once again incarcerated with no resources going into the West Bank through Israel.

My heart broke not only for her and the family but also all those who were now going to struggle with unbelievable hardship. I felt frustrated at being so far away from my Palestinian family and questioned God as to the timing of my return to England. I believe He knows all things throughout all time and so would have been aware of what was to happen in Jerusalem and the immediate retaliation by the Palestinians. Why could I not be there to stand in support of those who had opened their home to me? My questioning of God was to go on for many years but in the meantime it was all too apparent that even though the very little I owned was in Beit Jala, I was not going to be able to re-enter the land for some time. I quickly set my mind to finding a job to pay my way in the UK.

The next six months saw me involved in yet another work that I had previously always said I was not able to do. I realise it's not strange for God to often place before us opportunities we'd always thought we could not, or would not, do! I started working with an agency supporting people, children and adults with profound disabilities. What a privilege! Initially I felt somewhat daunted at trying to build a relationship with people who were often unable to speak, comprehend, talk and often had major difficulties with mobility. Often they had severe mental incapacity and were locked inside their own world. Initially I felt fearful that I would be unable to know how to meet their needs but gradually, as I was enabled to get to know each one as an individual, I became aware of how to value and respond in the way of assisting and caring. Each person I worked with taught me so much; it was humbling to spend time with them.

One example is Sally. She was autistic and unable to speak, appeared to comprehend very little and was locked inside herself. She never responded to any external stimuli – her face wouldn't register a sudden loud noise – and she appeared unable to smile or frown, show anger or pleasure. Often people who have autism struggle with any new experiences, environments or out-of-norm situations. Sally was such a person so we always did the same activities – until one day...

It had been decided by the team manager that we would take the group trampolining. Each member of the team was paired with one of the group and I was paired with Sally. Once a week we would go to the sports centre and within a few weeks all of the group became more familiar with the trampolines and started bouncing up and down. Not Sally. Week after week she would sit near, but not beside, the trampoline and I would sit beside her. If I tried to move our chairs closer she would simply move them back. It took many months of patience and perseverance to slowly edge toward these strange pieces of equipment until eventually she was able to lay her hand on top of the trampoline. This was a real breakthrough. I was encouraged to persevere. Several months later not only was Sally stood on the trampoline but the day arrived when she and I started bouncing! She appeared calm and at ease and then... her body raised from the trampoline by about eighteen inches and her face beamed a smile from ear to ear.

I was so enthralled at seeing this first ever facial expression but my natural reaction had to be contained; for me to give her a hug would not have been appropriate or helpful as she was extremely hesitant of any physical contact other than hand-holding. But, *oh Sally!* What a joy! I could liken it to seeing a baby take their first step, but that wouldn't be fair. With most children we expect and wait for that day to come, but this was so unexpected and beyond anything anyone had ever hoped for. Sally continued to smile whenever she was on the trampoline. Joy of joys!

My time with the agency was short-lived. For many years I'd seen in Christian magazines an advert that said, "Ladies required to make tea, serve cake and chat to military personnel." Well, that seemed to have my name on it; I'd always loved feeding people and chatting was my middle name! I phoned for further details and was told that the charity had cafés on several bases and they were particularly looking for people to go to Cyprus or The Falkland Islands.

I was invited up to Glasgow for an interview and was met at the railway station by a gentleman on the committee. I was told they would assess me over the weekend – I was to stay with a lady committee member – and there was to be a formal interview on the Monday with the full committee. As the gentleman drove away from the station towards the ladies' house, he spoke about their need for a team leader in the Falklands and, might I be interested? True to say, I had been thinking I rather fancied Cyprus: sun, sea and something like a prolonged holiday, I thought! Not surprisingly, I couldn't have been more wrong. As I'd already come to realise, God has a way of taking us to places we're not naturally comfortable with. Just a few weeks later found me having my Yellow Fever jabs before flying off to The Falkland Islands to head up a team consisting of civilian paid workers, military volunteers and those who worked for the Christian charity.

It was not an easy decision to go to the other end of the world. My mother's dementia had deteriorated and there were many people in my parents' church who were appalled that I should be leaving my father. But Dad and I had many talks and he supported me and affirmed I should go. To all intents and purposes, even though it is a 'live theatre' I was safer down in the Antarctic than in the West Bank, and he felt he had the help from friends and agencies to support him as the carer for my mum.

This was also going to find me in the bizarre situation of living on a military base, yet I'd always declared myself to be a pacifist. In addition, as a person who'd struggled with authority I was to be given the same ranking as an officer, a Squadron Leader. God surely takes us out of our comfort zones, but I knew this was His guiding. Throughout all my journeys since coming to faith I've always waited on God to confirm, confirm and confirm, by laying a fleece as described in the Bible, being given a 'word in season' from another person, or by a message spoken through a sermon or teaching. Yet again the confirmations had come in, and Adrian and Tom came to Brize Norton to see me fly out on the military Tristar.

Saying goodbye to the boys, now grown men, was once again difficult. It would be at least six months before I would be allowed leave (R&R[14]) to return to the UK. Yet, amazingly, Tom would soon be joining me down in The Falkland Islands. On hearing that I was appointed to be involved in this mission he said he'd like to join me. When I told him that the position was for mature ladies he said, "Apart from being sexist and ageist, what other reason is there for that?" I suggested he get in contact with the committee and ask for an interview. Before I flew out we discovered he would be the first ever young man to be appointed by the charity and would be joining me in the Antarctic in just a few weeks' time.

The plane touched down in Ascension Island to refuel and as passengers and crew disembarked I had a glimpse of how it was as a civilian to be surrounded by men and women in uniform. Once again I was an oddity; just as in Beit Jala where I had been surrounded by Arabs, now I was surrounded by the military, a fish out of water. "Lord, I thank you that you are with me, that you've brought me to this

---

[14] rest and relaxation

time and place. May I continue to know Your will and heart's desire." Constantly, ever since I'd come to faith in Jesus, I offered up 'arrow prayers'. Talking with God without it necessarily being apparent to others was now a part of my norm. I was learning to take time to listen to Him, so that I wasn't simply on a one-way conversation, and was constantly and continually amazed at the clarity of dialogue. This is not to say that I always heard what I wanted to hear, but I did recognise that it was what I needed to hear!

Some eighteen hours after leaving the UK we touched down at the base in the Falklands, where I was met by an elderly lady who had been holding the fort until my arrival. After a warm welcome, she said, "I'll take you straight to the café and show you the ropes because I'll be leaving with the Tristar when she takes off in forty-eight hours' time." With just two days' induction I found myself in yet again an alien environment, heading up a small team of mission workers who were permitted to be on base in this live theatre.

Our role was to provide a café for any military personnel and civilians on the base, or from the islands, who would like to use the facility. The Oasis café was the only authorised place on the base that was smoke and alcohol free. It was also known as the Christian café attached to the forces' church which served both Catholics and Protestants. The Padre was an Anglican and I met with him shortly after my arrival. We immediately found much in common and I valued his ministry. His wife and young children were on the base with him and it was always a joy to be invited up to their 'home' for an evening. My military quarters were quite stark and Spartan, but I was provided with my own bedroom with en suite, a luxury on a military base and compared to Beit Jala. The mission team also had the use of a small lounge and galley kitchen which was a wonderful blessing.

Once again I couldn't have been more wrong in my assumptions as to how life would be. The advert for ladies to make tea and chat which had sounded so restful was to be far from the reality. True, when I'd first arrived to manage the café they only averaged half a dozen customers at any one time. My challenge was, how could we possibly introduce Jesus to people if we had such little contact with those on base? As I'd looked around the café it was apparent that there was little to appeal to today's twenty-plus-year-olds who were immersed in military culture. There was little to attract them away from the mess bars and many corners that provided illegal alcoholic drinking spaces. The menu in the Oasis café was far more suited to Victorian personnel with instant coffee and Victoria sponge as the highlights. No surprise that they weren't queuing up at the door!

Within a few months I'd ordered uplighters to take away the starkness of the strip lighting, appealed to the camp C.O. who had graciously found a few sofas and easy chairs (very scarce on base) to provide some more comfortable seating, and changed the menu. The smell of smoked bacon for sarnies, garlic bread, chilli and mocha coffee were amongst the items now available and with the café door open on to the longest corridor in the southern hemisphere the delightful smells wafted their way to draw people to the café. In no time at all, the norm was a queue out into the corridor as people gratefully waited for appealing food that was a welcome alternative to that which was provided in the mess. In addition, we played contemporary Christian music as a change from the tubular bells and panpipes that had previously lingered on the café airwaves.

Now we had an appealing, attractive setting relevant to the time and culture, within which we could build relationships with the customers. Our day would start at 7am with prepping food followed by team prayers, then more food prep in readiness to open the doors at 10am. We had only a small team of staff including two paid part-time civilians, so our working hours were very long. The café closed at 10pm and then we obviously needed to do the clean down and be partially ready for the next day. We were open six-and-a-half days a week, closed only on a Sunday morning for church attendance. For me, the paperwork, till-tallying, rotas and invoices were all too time-consuming, but the best time, the purpose of it all, was that spent serving endless cups of coffee as I listened to concerns and was involved in conversations with military personnel.

Once again I realised how little I knew, let alone understood, of those within our society whom I'd had no contact with. By listening, I crossed the bridge to where they were. Then, as that rapport built into a relationship, they would ask, "Why have you come down here as a volunteer to serve us?"

"It might seem strange," I'd say, "but it's because I believe God told me to."

That then brought us to a place halfway across the bridge, where I could chat about Jesus.

Always in the forefront of my mind were the words of a very wise vicar whom I'd come to know quite well and who had a parish in Winsley, not far from Trowbridge. "Listen before you preach!" I realise I'm very passionate about Jesus and long to let others know about His saving grace so that they too might come to a place of peace and reassurance, not only in their lives now, but for all eternity. But I also understand that there is no reason as to why anyone should listen to what I have to say if I've first failed to listen to them.

Tom arrived on base a few weeks after me and was a great help. He frequently manned the café for many hours after official closing times so as to be available for the Military Police who would be on duty throughout the night and patrolling the corridor. He would keep the café door open till the early hours so that they could call in for refreshment and take well-earned breaks. Tirelessly Tom would hump boxes from the stores to replace stock and was a tremendous support to me and an invaluable member of the team. His appointment, although unprecedented, was very appropriate; he was the only person on the team who was in the age group of the majority of our customers. As a young man who had made a commitment in his mid-teens to be a disciple of Jesus, it was precious to have him on the base and a part of the team.

It was also whilst Tom and I were in The Falklands that we received a letter from Adrian saying that whilst he'd been alone in his bedroom he'd had an encounter with God and he now acknowledged Jesus as his Saviour. I'd waited a long time for him to come to this realisation and make a profession of faith but never had I thought I'd be at the other end of the world.

Throughout my time serving on the military base I always sought to honour God, be obedient to His call and serve as He came to serve. Undoubtedly there were many difficult times, not least when 9/11 changed the lives of many people directly and, probably true to say, most of humanity albeit indirectly. I was in Cyprus at the time on R&R. Jean had researched holiday accommodation that was able to provide me with literal rest and relaxation from what was normally an eighty-hour working week. I was more than aware that ministry was a lifestyle and vocation, but I was exhausted due to the opening times of the café that were required by the military authorities and the far too few staff that the charity had available to assist us.

I'd left for my two weeks' R&R knowing that the team would be down one member but also realizing I needed the vacation. Jean and I were on holiday in Cyprus, sitting outside a tavern, waiting to order a coffee and tea after a delightful meal. When the waiter came up I confirmed that I would like tea.

"Ah, you English so you would like tea with milk?" he said.

"Yes, I am English and, yes please, I would like milk, but I am used to drinking it black and very sweet because until recently I was in Palestine and that is how they drink it," I replied.

"The Palestinians, they bomb Pentagon," he retorted and duly showed us to a television where, like most of the rest of the world, we stood transfixed, looking in horror at the scenes of devastation. As the world went into numbed response, we frantically tried to phone our families. Not yet knowing how events would develop, we were concerned for those we knew in the UK. I also thought of all those military personnel that I knew on the base and wondered what effect and impact this would have upon them...

CHAPTER TWENTY-TWO

Study and Serve

Due to the charity's procedures, I found myself back in the UK and able to catch up once again with family and friends. Mum had now reached the stage with her dementia that she was in a care home. Thankfully, Dad had been able to get her into a residential home not too far from where he was living. He'd tried for a very long time to meet her needs but her advancing forgetfulness, wandering and at times violence became understandably unmanageable for him. It took Dad a long time to get over the feeling of having failed her and not being able to cope, but he drove into Bath every day to visit and would sit for hours beside her, holding her hand. She was no longer able to hold a conversation but would repeat the same few words over and over. Thankfully, she seemed at peace within her spirit and for that we could be grateful.

It was time for me to take stock and see where God was going to lead me. I've always loved islands, the sense of getting away that they provide and the culture that they infuse. Jean and I drove on to the ferry heading towards the Isle of Wight – maybe not an exotic location but an island all the same. Each day we would drive up on to the headland, reading our bibles, discussing passages and considering what God was saying – to His people back in the days it was written, to His people today, and specifically to us.

By the end of our few days away I couldn't believe what was stirring in my spirit and what I sensed God was calling me to now do. "Go to college, God? You're having a laugh!" How could I possible go to any Bible College? I'd left school at fifteen and had no written academic qualifications. No college would accept the likes of me on to a course. Jean and I talked about it, around it, through it, over it and under it! I couldn't see how it could be possible, but I did now know a God for whom *all* things are possible. Well, all I could do was push a few doors, so to speak, and see what happened.

In the meantime, I managed to get agency work at Mum's care home. It was a privilege to care for her, along with other residents, even though she no longer knew me as her daughter. I was simply another face who came in to help her maintain her dignity and tried to meet her needs.

Over the next week I made the relevant enquiries and duly turned up at an open day that just happened to be taking place at 'Christ for the Nations' in West Sussex. I was offered an interview and asked why I wanted to attend Bible college and obtain a Practical Theology Diploma. As I explained some of the journey I'd been on with God over the more recent years and the testimony of my former years, I also spoke of my passion to better understand the Bible, to have the opportunity to be taught scripture and learn more about God the Father, Jesus the Son and the Holy Spirit.

"We'd like to welcome you to this college and we have a space for you on the next two-year course starting in a few months," said the principal.

"But I have no qualifications. I left school by 'arrangement'. I'm not clever," I hastily said.

"But you love Jesus and want to know Him more; that's our primary required quality and concern," came back the reply. *Wow!*

Now it came down to the nitty-gritty: would I be able to cover the eighteen thousand pounds in costs for the two years' residential fees? I hardly had eighteen pounds let alone eighteen thousand! I was asked if I might be able to get enough money for the first term of the academic year. I worked out the costs and calculated that if I did twelve-hour shifts six days a week, every week for the next few months, I would be able to make the payment. But once having started the full-time course I'd only be able to work part-time at best. They agreed they were more than happy to take me on the course and stand with me before God that somehow He would enable me to make the future required payments. These were people who knew what is was to fully trust in

God, that He will provide, when we believe we are called according to His purposes.

He did! Sure, I had to do my part, but one way and another I was able to complete the two years' study and fees were paid. I managed to pick up several part-time jobs during term time. I was employed part-time as college cook for fifty-plus people when our full-time cook had her days off, was sick or on leave. Also I managed to get an evening job as a waitress and bar worker at a local Christian Conference Centre and during college vacations I resumed the twelve-hour shifts six days a week at the residential home where my mum lived. Halfway through the course I began repeatedly having unbelievably horrendous attacks of pain and finally it was established that my gall bladder would have to be removed. Even though that curtailed some of the hours I could work, by God's grace I not only paid for the fees but came out of college with my Diploma in Theology. Sadly, Mum was far too poorly to be at my graduation, but Dad, Adrian, Tom and friends attended and we could all give God the glory.

I – the one who hadn't passed her eleven plus, had not even sat her O Levels, had never read an entire book until she'd become a Christian at the age of thirty, who'd been the black sheep of the family time and time again – was the student voted by the student body to be the Valedictorian. *Wow again!* I'd not known about the vote, having been off sick after the major operation to remove the gall bladder, and in truth I'd never heard of a Valedictorian, let alone known what one did! Well, now I was to be it and do it, so I thought I'd better check it out! I came to realise that it was a huge honour and felt very humbled that my fellow students should have chosen me for this privileged role. This academic title is used in the USA, Canada and various other countries. The Valedictorian is the student appointed to deliver the closing speech at the graduation ceremony and has been chosen by his or her peers due to being the highest ranking among the graduating class. Well, one thing was for sure: I didn't have the highest marks in our class! Indeed, I'd had to get extra tuition with one of the subjects because I just could not understand the lectures. So to have this title bestowed upon me was beyond my comprehension; all I could do was seek God as to what He would have me say.

Day after day I prayed, and then one night I woke in the early hours and put on the light. I always had pencil and paper beside my bed. I started writing and half-an-hour or so later turned off the light and went back to sleep. 7am and my alarm call woke me. Sleepily I picked up the piece of paper and read what I'd written during the night.

I was quite blown away – not at the words I'd put on paper but at the content. I kept looking at three key words. The problem was I didn't have a clue as to their meaning! Out came my dictionary and as I looked up the words, the sentences made sense. I now knew I hadn't written this speech, God had! It fitted perfectly with all the workings of the college, the staff and students, and all the experiences and learning God had brought us through during our two years together.

One day when I had been in the library, our college pastors came in and handed me a rolled-up newspaper saying, "We've been praying and believe that God has a certain job in mind for you that is advertised in here. We haven't highlighted the advert, but have a look through and see if your spirit is prompted by one particular ministry position."

As I flicked through the pages, I spotted an advert for a Lay Pastor at the Methodist Church in Grays, Essex. All I could do was laugh; I knew immediately that this was where I would next find myself living and working.

I travelled up to Essex a week before the interviews for a 'recce', duly attended the interview and was then offered the position. Part of the salary package was for me to be resident in the Grays manse. Although I didn't own one piece of furniture, the manse was well furnished. I also received some furniture from friends downsizing, and a few pieces from college. All items colour-coordinated and I could be based in a very welcoming, warm home that could offer hospitability to many. *Wow, yet again!*

CHAPTER TWENTY-THREE

Family

Life as a church pastor was a privilege and responsibility. I know there are those who think that church leaders only work once a week, on a Sunday, but the reality couldn't be farther from the truth. People have very different ideas on what 'church' should be. Some say it should be there to provide support, provision and care to the local community and farther afield, some say it should be a place of worship for those who live locally and believe in Jesus as their Saviour, others say it should be both of these and more. Whilst I was in college I learnt that the original root word for 'church' was 'ecclesia', a Greek word meaning 'those set aside with a common purpose'. Therefore, it was simply a word used for any group of people that held a belief or ethos in common. Church has come to be thought of as those who either liberally or evangelically hold a belief in Jesus as the Son of God and call themselves Christians.

For me as a pastor, my role was to encourage those who attended the church to better understand the Bible, the calling and equipping that God had upon their lives, and how they could more fully understand His forgiveness, mercy, grace, redemption and restoration, and in response seek to be a follower of His teaching and put that into practice in the way that they served others within the community. It was for me and the church family to seek to be 'as Jesus' to those we met, not simply to be a community centre offering social support. As the Bible reminds us, faith without works is dead,[15] and therefore our aim was to

[15] See James 2:14

act out what we believe, but also to know that we are justified by faith, not our good deeds.[16] In other words, we cannot earn our place in heaven; no amount of me trying and striving to do the right thing will suffice. This all acts as a continual reminder to me of how wonderful God is; we are offered salvation as a free gift because Jesus became the once-and-for-all sacrifice for our sins and therefore has made it possible for us to have full communion with our Creator.

As I was not an ordained minister, my position in the Methodist denomination was rather unusual. Each Christian denomination has a slightly different set-up regarding their roles, rules and regulations, also regarding their specific beliefs on how they interpret the Bible. Some choose to think it can mean all things to all people, that they can pick and mix according to their feelings and circumstances a bit like liquorice allsorts! For me, the Bible is quite specific and when I read it in context I believe God is clearly showing and telling us how we, as those who have been created by His hand, should live in accordance with His purpose and plan. Anyone who creates anything has brought about the creation for a specific reason and purpose; when that creation is used in an inappropriate, unacceptable way, it becomes damaged and can no longer fulfil its original purpose in a fully meaningful way.

After being at Bible college, my heart was to share what I had learnt with anyone who might have that same desire to better know God. Being a pastor also meant that I longed for those who as yet knew nothing of God and His Son Jesus to question, through my actions of concern and love for them, "What is life all about?" Questions are wonderful ways of seeking to better understand, as long as we take time to listen, read, ponder and consider. It's so easy for us to map out what we are going to do, how we're going to do it and where we're going to do it. But life doesn't always turn out as we have planned. As I had learnt to my cost so many years previously, my actions brought about consequences which resulted in me taking decisions that would affect not only me but others. But maybe our character is built on how we handle the unplanned, how we respond to the unexpected.

My son Adrian went to Australia for his thirtieth birthday, where he had a wonderful time catching up with two friends who had emigrated and were establishing life in a culture quite different from that of the

---

[16] See Romans 4:3

UK. He loved it and it wasn't many days after his return that my phone rang.

"Mum, I need to start doing something with my life. I need to try and get some qualifications." Adrian had left school at sixteen and had worked in various factories. "I think I'd like to do a course in painting and decorating; they need people with that qualification in Australia, so once I've got the relevant exams I could apply for a visa and work down under. What do you think, Mum?"

I told him I thought it was a really good idea; a trade would put him in a good position for the future, be that in Oz or in the UK. "If I can help, let me know. Maybe you'd like to see if there are any courses up here in Grays, then I can put a roof over your head and make sure you have food so you won't have any basic living expenses. You could pick up a part-time job in addition to the course; that way you'll have personal spending money whilst you're training."

It seemed that in no time Adrian was living with me in the manse. The arrangement worked well and he thoroughly enjoyed his course. It was lovely for me to have the time to further deepen our relationship.

Whilst I'd been at Bible college, on several occasions Adrian had mentioned about going to Athens for the Olympics, so when he mentioned it again during one of our phone calls I said, "That would be a wonderful experience. Whom are you going with?"

"I'd go with you, Mum," was his reply.

You could have knocked me down with a feather! I was so surprised and then somewhat dismayed because all my money was paying for my Bible course and there was no way I could afford such a trip. "Well, darling," I said, "that's a lovely thought but I'm really not in a position to afford that just now."

"It's OK, Mum," he replied, "I'm already doing double shifts. I'll be able to cover the cost of flights, hotel and tickets, if you can manage to save for your own spending money."

Without doubt we had the most wonderful, memorable experience and I was impacted by his generosity, not only of money, but also of spirit.

I'm sure that after Adrian moved into the manse he made it his focus that at least once a day he would make me laugh. For me, humour is a treasured part of life, and Adrian and I share the same type and sense of humour. People's humour varies greatly, even within families and certainly within cultures, but to laugh is healing and healthy and as long as it isn't at the expense of another, I believe that the more that we can laugh in life, the healthier we truly are. As they say, "Laughter is the best medicine."

After some perseverance Adrian obtained a job at the local Asda store and quite often I would go down to do my shopping just prior to him finishing his shift so that I could drive him home. One day as I entered Asda, I spotted him working in one of the aisles and said, "I'm just picking up a few bits, so I'll be ready at the end of your shift if you'd like a lift."

"OK, Mum, thanks. I'll probably see you at the checkout," he replied.

It didn't take me long to pick up the few items I needed. I headed for the tills and started taking items from the trolley and putting them on to the conveyor belt.

"You've got some nice food items here; are you making something special for tonight's dinner?" asked the girl on the checkout.

I looked up at a smiling face and found myself replying, "Well, I think I'm quite a good cook, but we're on 'spag bol' this evening and I have to admit my son makes the best 'spag bol' ever. You'd be welcome any time to come up and try it."

Adrian came alongside me and started reloading the trolley. Then, as he was pushing it towards the car, he said, "I just don't believe you, Mum. You invite anyone and everyone up to the house and now you've asked the girl on the checkout. She's the girl I believe I'm going to marry!"

To say I was astounded is an understatement. "What?" I said. "I wasn't aware you'd been out with anyone since you'd moved up here."

"No, I haven't," he admitted. "I've not asked her out but I've been making enquiries. She's not in a relationship and hasn't been for quite a while but she's got three girls. I need to be sure about what I'm doing before I start getting involved in their lives; I don't want to mess any of them about."

Within weeks the girl on the checkout was sitting in our dining room eating the 'spag bol' that Adrian had just made. I quickly recognised that Natalie had the sweetest heart and from that moment 'sweetheart' became my name for her. Adrian's plan had been to qualify from college and travel down to Australia, but his life took a very different route.

Later that year I was once again in Asda pushing the trolley up and down the aisles looking for bargains when I spotted a teddy bear all alone on a bottom shelf. I reached down and picked him up thinking, "How cute!" but then spotted his T-shirt which said, "NO. 1 DAD." I popped him back thinking, "Ah, he's not for this trolley then..." and carried on walking up and down the aisles as I picked up other items and put them in the trolley.

I spotted Adrian in the freezer aisle and headed towards him to tell him I would be able to give him a lift home at the end of his shift.

He looked up. "Hi, Mum," he said, "or perhaps I should call you Nan... I've just found out that Natalie and I are going to have a baby!"

For a moment I was so surprised that I found myself still pushing the trolley but in a somewhat dazed, silent, unresponsive manner! It took me a few minutes to recover before I said, "Just a minute..." I pushed the trolley back to the first aisle, found the teddy, put him in pride of place in the trolley and walked back to Adrian. "This is for you, then. You'll make a great dad, darling."

My mind was racing, rapidly considering all the potential problems he might face. A baby on the way and three girls – Holli, Katie-Rae and Chloe – who would no doubt become his stepdaughters would be a heavy responsibility; there would be large regular costs and who knows what other difficulties might lie ahead! All his plans to go to Australia were probably unlikely to happen and – oh, my gosh... But now it was time to support him in whatever way I could and embrace the addition of Natalie and three granddaughters – Holli aged nine, Katie Rae aged five and Chloe aged three – plus the forthcoming baby into our family.

Some months later, the baby was born. Even though Natalie had already had the three girls this birth proved to be very different! As soon as Adrian realised there were complications he phoned me and I said that I would drive up to the hospital. Even though I knew I wouldn't be allowed into the maternity wing, I'd wait in the car park and at least he would know I was nearby. Also I told him I'd set the prayer chain in action and, literally within minutes, people all over the country were praying for them.

In the meantime, Natalie was left without painkillers. The nursing staff in the delivery room were incompetent and didn't even know how to switch on the equipment they were trying to use. As Adrian got back to her he realised how terrible the situation was and in very explicit language told the nurses to get out and get a doctor. After some debate, but with Adrian's clear insistence, eventually Natalie and the baby started to get the medical care they needed. The nurses fetched a doctor who immediately insisted that Natalie be given pain relief and then within minutes managed to help her with a normal delivery. She then found out that if Adrian hadn't yelled for the doctor when he did, then her and her baby's life would have been seriously at risk and an emergency caesarean would have been their only possible hope of survival.

Within hours of the birth I was driving this precious family back to their home. As we got into the house Natalie took herself to the bathroom, Adrian went to the shop and the baby started to cry. I called out to Natalie, "What would you like me to do, sweetheart? Leave him in his chair and let him cry, or pick him up?"

As she came out of the bathroom she said, "Mum, you can pick him up if you'd like."

As I took him out of his car seat I said, "I'd never pick him up without asking you first, sweetheart."

"Oh, Mum, you don't have to ask. You're his nanny; you can pick him up anytime you think he or you would like a cuddle."

"Ah, thank you," I replied, "but I'd not pick him up if he was asleep."

Again Natalie retorted, "Oh, Mum, he'd soon go off again and probably wouldn't even wake. You cuddle him whenever you'd like."

I considered how amazing this precious family was; I'd even been asked to give them a list of baby names that I liked from the Bible. The name Luke was decided upon and then I found out that he was also to have the name Carl, as Adrian wanted him to be called after his own brother who had died of a cot death all those years before.

All of them, over the next many years, were to experience some incredibly tough times, but they all held together as family. Humour has been one of their most precious qualities along with the strong desire to be a truly supportive family abounding in grace. Although at times I've been dreadfully concerned for each and every one of them, in my love for them I've also tried to be supportive, offer a listening ear, and counsel from my training and life experience.

Acquiring three Essex granddaughters overnight was a steep learning curve for me. I'd had little to do with very girly, lacy, flouncy girls and, it has to be said, I didn't quite know what to make of them or do with them! God was being so good *yet again!* He took me out of my comfort zone and added another item from my I-don't-do list! Over time we all got to know one another better and better. 'Sweetheart' Natalie is very giving, gracious and generous with her desire to embrace and share love. I was amazed at her openness in sharing her newborn babe. Adrian took to fatherhood like a duck to water. His commitment to Luke, the girls and Natalie was absolute.

Tom, my son from my second marriage, married Cheryl and branched out into his own life with his wife and their daughter Lucy.

After staffing positions were rearranged in Essex, I moved to Chichester to take up another position as Pastor within the Church of England. Denominational hierarchy will always be a contentious issue for me, as I believe that before God we are all equal and that each person simply has a different role and part to play within the body of Christ. There are no positions, better than or superior to, as there is only one head: Jesus. We all have been given different gifts and abilities and when we come together rightly, in the way God intended, we have a fully functioning, effective body where the members not only support one another, but can also be effective and a blessing to the local community and our wider society. Sadly, all too often we're too intent on doing our own thing for our own status and don't connect positively with others; the result is that we are as if dislocated, appearing to be connected but not properly joined, and we are then far less effective.

At the church in Chichester there were many people with learning difficulties and those suffering from mental health problems. Once again I felt righteous outrage at how both of these groups of people were and are marginalised by our society. Care in the community may work for the few and may work for the workers and politicians, but many who are suffering are left unseen behind their closed doors.

During my four years of ministry in Sussex, I tried to bring those who were marginalised into the heart of the community and the forefront of the church so that they would no longer be standing in the wings, but taking their rightful place centre stage, equal with everyone else. It was my privilege to oversee a group that throughout the week offered practical and spiritual support to those who felt they had been side-lined and, I believe with God's guidance and under His direction, many came to know just how precious they were in the sight of God and had a greater sense of being a part of the church family.

Day by day I had come to realise just how dysfunctional families could be. I thought back on my own family, my relationship with my parents and how it had changed numerous times over the years, the babies I'd had and lost, the broken marriages with those extended families and being estranged from my brother, such sadness and pain in the lack of wholeness, and I thought on my father now turned ninety years of age and all the changes he'd seen happen in his life.

My mother had died whilst I'd been living in Essex. Dad had visited her almost every day whilst she'd been cared for in a specialist home for people suffering from dementia and in the latter days of her life he struggled to let go of the woman he'd always loved and honoured.

Dad died rather unexpectedly whilst I lived in Chichester. He was poorly for just a few days and was taken into hospital. At one point I spoke over the phone with the nursing staff, who told me that the doctor had just completed his rounds and they were expecting to discharge my father in a few days as he was doing so well. Then, literally five minutes later, the phone rang again. I was in a meeting but felt prompted to take the call. "Can you please come straight in?" the nurse said. I explained that I was over three hours' drive away and she then gently told me that my father had just died.

I rang Adrian, regretting that I had to tell him about his grandfather's death over the phone.

"I'll be leaving here within half an hour, Mum, and be on the next train down to Chichester to be with you." He dropped everything to travel for many hours to come down and support me.

I phoned Tom, who was only about a twenty-minute drive from the hospital, again letting him know as gently as possible. I asked him if he was able to go to the hospital to start going through all the necessary procedures and that Adrian was on his way down to me and we'd drive up tomorrow.

When a family member dies I think most of us get carried along with the system that is in place; this was certainly the case for us. I'd preached at Mum's funeral and would do so again at Dad's. Both my parents had talked through with me their plans for their funerals many, many years earlier. Now, at this time of shock, mourning and in the very early stages of adjusting to being without my parents, I found their forward planning of great assistance. Dad had certainly done all he could to enable this difficult process to be as easy as possible for me.

Emotions were understandably quite raw at times and there were misunderstandings and upsets. Family life is rarely permanently plain sailing.

Chapter Twenty-Four

Manna and Quail

Throughout most of my life I'd rarely had more than a few pounds in my pocket. I had started fulltime work at the age of fifteen working forty-eight hours a week, and throughout my life had worked for wages, or voluntarily, or at home as 'Mum' for long hours each week. At times I'd been grateful for some financial support from the State but most of the time I managed independently. My work had ranged from scrubbing floors on my hands and knees for many hours early each morning in offices, to managing a large charity, to helping those in countries experiencing conflict. Throughout, God had always supplied sufficient unto the day, but at times life had been extremely difficult.

I could think back to the days of pounding the streets knocking on doors to try to earn enough money for Aidan's layette. I could think back to the days when I'd made biscuits without sugar so that my sons wouldn't want to eat too many, yet had something to nibble on. I could think back to having sold my bathroom scales so as to be able to buy a loaf of bread. And I could think back to having sold the majority of my clothes to get health insurance when I went to the West Bank. Now life was going to take another turn as I inherited money from my parents.

I firmly believe God's timing is perfect and it was a blessed surprise to me that when I found myself at the end of my work contract in Chichester and with no roof over my head, I was in a position to buy a property. This decision wasn't without its strife but as I was now homeless and without work, I felt I could start a ministry providing an oasis for those who needed rest and relaxation.

Throughout my life, especially in latter decades, I had occasionally thought, "I'd love to live by the sea. If I could see the sea that would be wonderful and if I had a balcony that would be absolutely amazing." After some waiting and searching I was able to purchase such a property. Dad had been adamant that he wanted me to be, in a physical and practical sense, secure and settled in the latter part of my life. I knew I was amazingly blessed to be in this position and naturally sought to share that blessing with others. The property could offer numerous options and would, if ever it were necessary, be able to provide a home for not only me but also Adrian, Tom and their families.

'Manna' is a word we read in the Bible and talks of God's provision to His people. The gift of inheritance from my earthly father was provision for me in my time of need, thus I called my new home 'Manna House'. Quail were also God's provision to His people as they walked towards the Promised Land, so the annexe at the bottom of the garden was called 'Quail Cottage'.

Many friends and friends of friends came to stay. I always intended that the house, my home, could be a place of refuge and retreat for those who had a need to take some time aside from the stresses of the world. Here in Manna House they could relax and take time to let God restore them during a time of recreation.

When Adrian, Natalie and the children came to stay the house became quite full, especially since from the outset Adrian and Natalie had taken the decision that they would not sleep in the same room when under my roof. They had lived together for many years and had had Luke but they both felt strongly that when either I was with them or they were with me, they didn't feel it was appropriate to sleep together. I know many people found this very strange, unusual and even quite bizarre taking into account my earlier lifestyle and that they normally lived together as an unmarried couple, but they felt strongly that it was respectful. Even though I'd never made mention of it myself, it is true that their sharing a room would not have sat happily with my current thinking and beliefs, so I was grateful for their understanding and sensitivity.

Therefore, it was wonderful that their wedding was planned within a few years of my move into Manna House. What a special, precious day! The ceremony took place at a local hotel overlooking the bay and

Adrian had asked if my church pastor could come and pray for them and give a blessing on their union. The sun eventually shone; Natalie was looking radiant, if somewhat nervous; Holli, Katie and Chloe were beautiful bridesmaids; and Luke was incredibly smartly dressed for his role as his dad's best man. Adrian planned and organised what in some ways was a simple, small ceremony and celebration, but his thoughtfulness and attention to detail made it a perfect day and after a night in the hotel they came back to Manna House where during future holidays they would then share a bedroom.

As I entered into this completely new season of my life, it came as something of a surprise to find out that I had significant health problems. As I started the process of coming to terms with my physical and mental restrictions and limitations, I read, "I am accepting of, but not resigned to." These words by Elizabeth Babbs were to be so very helpful as I learnt by God's grace to be accepting of my current situation, yet refused to allow myself to become resigned to, or dwell in, my physical and mental condition. It was a timely reminder that through my Dad, I could value God's provision during my earthly life, but ultimately my physical life was absolutely in my heavenly Father's hands. What a life I'd lived! But God certainly wasn't finished with me yet!

Adrian, Natalie, Holli, Katie-Rae, Chloe, Luke and I now all live together in Manna House – three generations sharing, supporting, helping, valuing and loving. We are family, with the ups and downs of everyday life but committed to each other. Each one of us has our strengths and weaknesses; we value the former and graciously seek to understand and be better accepting of the latter. We all get along together because we grow in grace to embrace each other despite our differences. I've been blessed by the great joy of this family dynamic. It's my privilege to be able to be a part of their lives. I enjoy their fun, questions and cuddles and am overwhelmed by their uncomplicated ability to love. They have embraced me into their lives and for that I am forever grateful.

This sort of living arrangement was, and is, very common in the Middle East, Greece, Africa and many other cultures, but here in the UK it is a little more unusual. Yet with compromise, understanding, sensitivity and yet more grace, it works well and I believe is of benefit to each individual. I've been used to living in very different types of accommodation as well as cultures so that prepared me to be quite flexible. I have learned much from the children, with their acceptance and non-judgemental attitude.

We soon established how each one of us could recognize our weaknesses – our own and those of each other – but also that in being a cohesive family unit, overall we were strong. Each one could be an individual, yet collectively we would be a magnanimous and harmonious unit. Without doubt there are some very strong personalities within this family unit yet it has been said by many other people who have spent time with us that it's clear to see that each person knows their place and is valued for who they are. No one is perfect but each is treasured. Respect for and of each other, and a considered understanding and belief in core life values, has been paramount and enables us to live in harmony.

I think back to holidays in Greece and remember the scenes of Granny either sitting on the doorstep or on a white plastic chair as she looked after the young children in the family whilst their mum and dad worked. I don't sit on the doorstep or on a white plastic chair, and rarely do I look after the children – in reality, they are more likely to look after me – but perhaps I have something to offer the wider family; in helping with homework, being a listening ear, showing interest and being available for cuddles; we are a very tactile family. They offer me so much: energy, humour, companionship and an endless supply of cups of tea. One of the family's sayings is "caring is sharing" – we care and we share, just as God cared and shared of His abundance with the manna and quail.

One major aspect of family life is the constant change. Nothing ever stays the same for long; children grow and change, they develop their personalities and we observe character being formed. They learn how to socialise and they acquire new interests and friends. Parents struggle with work/life balance, the stresses of being tired and yet being available, understanding and compassionate to the family's needs. They can feel pressured from all sides and can do little to relieve that pressure, but they can also know the joys of each other and the children in their care. As a grandmother I am abundantly fortunate to be surrounded by love, and I adore Gizmo the family cat. I can spend time one-on-one with each of the grandchildren when we talk about the meaning of life and ponder on their life's path. I can be in the hub of the family with many a diva moment being enacted by one of the granddaughters, but can also retreat to my own room when the exuberance of youngsters gets just a little too much.

The sometimes manic busyness and the constancy of change can be overwhelming but I soon came to realise that "I ain't seen nothing yet!" It's at such times when it's so precious to have the assurance that God never changes, that when life is like a pack of cards thrown up in the air and we have no way of knowing which way they are going to fall, that God is always the same. He is constant, never wavering; He is our rock and our anchor.

Chapter Twenty-Five

Restoration

My health – physical and mental – was notably starting to deteriorate. Non-alcoholic liver disease, non-age-related mild cognitive impairment, two arthritic hips and M.E. with chronic fatigue were now known to be the result of something which was causing inflammation throughout my body. The medics were floundering in the dark as to what was causing the inflammation and they had little they could offer by way of treatment, other than helping me find a way to manage my enforced drastic change in lifestyle. For two hours on two days per week, at the most, I could undertake a small activity like driving the mile to town, and I could spend no more than an hour meandering around the shops. Many weeks I couldn't even manage that and it wasn't unknown for me to be too fatigued to eat, shower or perform the most basic living tasks; but I thanked God that I was strong in spirit and that I knew that would underpin the effects of physical and mental decline.

I held the belief that in aspects of health my spiritual well-being was of first importance because that was eternal, my mental health of secondary importance because if my head was clear I could work out how to manage and cope with situations, and my physical health the third priority because my body was only temporal. As for my emotions, I sought to remind myself that I am called to live by faith which is not based primarily on how I feel. I have found over the years that it's very easy to feel down because of circumstances, but in time circumstances change, so I aim to focus on and choose to live by faith in what God has done and is doing in my life, rather than by the little that I can see and understand.

Due to the liver problem and chronic fatigue I needed to balance not only each day, but each week and month. To avoid a complete inability to function I found it necessary to plan in significant rest periods, often for many days, prior to and following even a short appointment or activity. It was after one such appointment at the M.E. clinic when I received a phone call from the administrator at our church.

"Marianne, I've been trying to get hold of you. A lady has phoned the church office asking if I could let her have the contact details of a Marianne Edwins. I have told her we won't give out personal details and I've asked her what it's in connection with. She said she's unable to say and has given me her mobile number. She said her name is Vivien and, would you please ring her?"

I only knew of one person called Vivien. She had been a volunteer at Action on Homelessness and we'd lost touch years ago. I couldn't think why she would have gone to such efforts to track me down.

I already had a lot going on in my mind and my body was feeling weary following the clinic appointment, so I took my cup of tea and went up to lie down on the bed. My mind was closing down and my body was not responding to even simple tasks so it was time to rest in a darkened room. Then the home landline rang. This in itself was unusual as most people who would use the landline would text me first to see if I felt well enough to take the call. So as I reached out to get the handset I felt rather annoyed, expecting to speak to a recorded message or an unrequested call from P.P.I. or an injury claims company.

"Hello," I said somewhat curtly.

A lady's voice on the other end of the line said, "Hello. I'm sorry to trouble you but could I please speak to Marianne Edwins?"

The way she spoke seemed formal and unfamiliar so I immediately became a little guarded. "Yes. Speaking." Again I spoke rather abruptly.

"Would your full name be Marianne Anita Edwins?" the lady asked in a very pleasant voice.

What was this about? Clearly this was no ordinary cold caller, but was it some kind of scam or fraudster who'd obtained my details? Now I was *really* on my guard. "You seem to be asking me an awful lot of personal questions. Who might *you* be?"

"You won't know me but my name is Vivien and I realise this is a very strange phone call for you to receive. I am sorry but I'm trying to locate someone. Please could I just ask you a few more questions?"

"OK," I replied, now extremely guarded.

"Do you happen to have anyone with you?" she asked with a tone of voice that I could possibly believe was out of concern for me.

"Yes," I replied, thinking that was probably the wisest answer and knowing that Adrian and Luke were downstairs.

She then asked me my birthdate which I refused to confirm or deny. She apologised for being so intrusive but then asked if she could possibly ask me a few more questions. I told her she could but I wouldn't necessarily answer them!

"Might the date 'the 6th of July, 1971' mean anything to you?"

"It might," came my reply. *What on earth?* Dulled yet screaming questions were flying through in my mind.

"And would the name Aidan mean anything to you?"

Almost breathless, I said, "Yes." My head was fast-tracking back forty-four years ago to the baby I'd given up for adoption. It was as if I was motionless in time, transfixed into a memory of my past life.

"I'm Aidan's wife, Vivien," the kindly voice said. "I am sorry, this call must be an awful shock for you, but we've been actively looking for you for a long time."

I paused before saying, "I've moved twenty-seven times in my life and changed my surname several times as well."

"Yes," Vivien replied, "it hasn't been easy trying to find you. Would you be OK to chat for a little while or could I ring back at some other time? Aidan, or Andy as he's called now, is not here at the moment, though he knows I'm ringing you. He's been trying to locate you for quite a while. He's always known he was adopted and I'm making this contact in the hope of being an initial bridge between you."

Fifty minutes later I got off the phone and walked downstairs. Adrian was in the lounge having just come in from his late evening shift and was eating his dinner with Luke sat beside him. As I stood in the doorway he looked up at me and said, "Mum? You OK?"

More than a little hesitatingly I said, "Yes... I'm... fine. But at some time in the near future we need to talk."

Adrian muted the TV and looked at me with questioning concern.

"Not now," I said, looking at Luke.

Immediately Adrian turned to Luke who, even though he had no school the next day, was already pushing past his bedtime. "Up to bed, son," he said and, as Luke started to object, "I need to talk with Nanny. Come on, up you go!"

Luke came over and gave me the usual bend of his head, for me to kiss him on the top of his head and say goodnight, and with that he went up the stairs.

Then I started to relay the unfolding of the events to Adrian, from when our church administrator had called with the bizarre message through to the conversation I'd just had with Vivien.

"Was that the phone call you just had on the landline?"

"Yes," I said.

"But you were laughing..."

"Yes, she's a very nice lady. We've just had a lovely chat and then been laughing because Andy's passion is football and he supports Liverpool. I've just explained that you're a fanatical Spurs fan!"

"Could be worse; he could support Arsenal!" Adrian's prompt response was typical football humour and I continued to relay more of the conversation Vivien and I had just had.

The phone call with Vivien had ended with her saying, "I realise this must have been an enormous shock for you. I'm sure you now need time to think through how you feel so I can either ring you again in a few days' time, or you could ring me when you feel ready, or if you decide you don't want any further contact we will both respect that and not contact you again."

I said that I thought I would call her as and when my energy levels allowed.

Adrian, Natalie and I talked through into the early hours of the morning. Natalie was in floods of tears, constantly hugging and cuddling me and saying how wonderful it was and that she was *so* happy for me. I was still dazed, awestruck and fluctuating from speechlessness to a seemingly endless use of words that totally failed to express my feelings. Eventually we went to our respective bedrooms and all too soon I once again found myself coming down into the kitchen. As I came through the door and turned the corner I saw Adrian just switching the kettle on to make a drink.

"Morning, Mum. Get much sleep?"

I just stood looking at him through glazed eyes and replied, "Morning, son. Not so much!"

"Me neither," he said. "Eventually I got a few hours of sleep, but the second I woke up my first thought was, 'Mum's now got the last chapter for her book,' and the second was, 'Thank God he doesn't support Arsenal; that would have been a step too far!'"

Like me he had woken to the thought that this could be the last chapter of the book I'd been putting together for over fifteen years. Now, so clearly, this phone contact from Viv was bringing full circle a part of my life and would make the perfect final chapter.

Throughout the morning I couldn't settle and took myself off for a stroll along the seafront. It was early into the afternoon that I texted Viv's number and said that I was at home if she was able to ring, so that we could continue the conversation from the previous day. Before long the phone rang.

Vivien kindly asked me how I was and as I started chatting she said, "Andy is right next to me. If I hand the phone over to him, would you feel able to speak to him?"

I agreed and then realised she was passing the phone to the son I'd not heard from for forty-four years. The last I'd heard from him was the sound of his crying when he'd wanted milk. Now I heard his voice. "Hello."

My breath caught. "Hi," I said. "This is really strange!"

We then chatted for nearly an hour. I told him that he was the important person in all of this and that he could ask any questions he wanted to. Even so, he was quite tentative as he asked me if I had ever thought of him during the last forty-four years.

"Yes," I said, "I have. A lot. Though, in all honesty, not every day."

"Could I ask you another question? – but if it's too difficult I quite understand if you'd rather not answer."

"Of course. You can ask me anything," I said.

"How did you cope with that?" he asked.

"Oh, that was simple," I replied, then realised that this son didn't know me or the way that I would talk by making a statement and then going on to explain my reasoning, so I quickly explained, "You were put in a box and placed on the top shelf. If I hadn't done that I couldn't have gone on living."

With great empathy he sensitively said, "I can understand that. I don't want you to think that I have any animosity towards you. I've been curious for a number of years about my birth mother but it's also been a fifty-fifty thing and I've also wondered if my birth mother might want to be found."

That call was to be just the beginning. Over the next weeks we exchanged many emails and talked for hours on the phone, enabling us to start the process of getting to know one another. I heard of the love, kindness and grace of his Christian parents who attended a Methodist church and had told him from the beginning that he was adopted. Andy said how his mum was thankful to me for having given him up for adoption so that she could be his mother and love, raise and nurture him. I heard of the good and happy life that he had lived and that it had been since he'd become a dad that he'd thought more seriously about looking for me.

I was euphorically buzzing!

Adrian and Natalie and a few close friends helped me talk through and process all that was happening – many times a week. I had numerous moments of 'leaking', unable to control the flow of tears, and on one occasion I totally imploded. Just a few days after the first phone call with Andy, I was overwhelmingly distraught at feeling I wasn't good enough for him to contact me. Adrian gently but very firmly talked with me and helped me set my feet firmly back on the Rock. I went off to church and knew that God's grace would sustain me, that I could be confident, not in myself, but in my Saviour.

I treasured every email, every smallest piece of information and every second of the minutes and hours of hearing Andy's voice on the phone. As I listened to him say, "I see this as an adventure that lies before us," I was smiling, rejoicing in the cosmic wonder of the moment and the time to come.

Yet another aspect of my life's journey was before me. Like the gem of a diamond, with so many facets to explore, now I was being given the opportunity to come to know about the life my son had already lived and to share with him in the time yet to come. But that was not all, there was even more: his family with his wife Viv, for me another daughter-in-law, and their two sons, for me two more grandsons, Callum and Alfie.

Within weeks of sending and receiving emails and a few photos, Andy was asking if we could meet up. Reading his email, it was unclear as to whether his suggestion was for me and him to meet or for him, Viv and the boys to meet with me, Adrian, Natalie, Holli, Katie, Chloe and Luke; he'd now explained to Callum and Alfie about me and the family in Weymouth, but I had yet to talk with my other grandchildren who had absolutely no idea that I even had another son!

I realised this was going to be a 'conversation-and-a-half' and first of all I'd need to wait several weeks for Holli to join us in Weymouth, because one thing was certain: I couldn't tell the other grandchildren before her!

Holli, who'd stayed in Grays to complete her A Levels, arrived hot from a cruise and having just received her A Level results. Her first evening home we talked about her exams and her holiday and all the time it was in the back of my mind that I was about to give her information about me that would be completely contrary to the Nanna she knew.

The next day Holli was out in Quail with the rest of the children when I called up and asked her if we could have a chat. As she was sitting on the floor in my bedroom she said, "What have I done, Nanna?"

"Oh, darling, it's not what you've done, it's what Nanna did." I told her of all that had happened in 1971 and then the events of the last six weeks. At eighteen years of age, anxious not to upset me, she lovingly asked questions and accepted without condemnation what I had done in my teenage years and said how thrilled she was for me and asked when we would be meeting up. As she left my room I asked her to ask Katie to come in to see me. A similar conversation took place with Katie, who said her heart was pumping so hard with love for me that it was beating all the way from the lounge to Quail and back! Both these granddaughters were so amazingly accepting, gracious and loving, failing to think badly of me and overflowing with happiness for me. They were both eager to meet up with Andy and his family, and I explained that they were coming up in a few days and that he and I would meet together on our own first of all and then the Plymouth family and Weymouth family would meet up together on the beach.

I then decided to speak with Chloe and Luke as a 'job lot', a 'two for one' scenario! Luke was thrilled at the thought of having two more boy cousins much the same age as himself, even though it meant he would no longer be able to say he was my favourite grandson simply because he was my only grandson! And Chloe was perhaps the greatest surprise, since even though she was only eleven years of age she was full of questions both then and on a regular basis since.

Both Andy and I were well aware that regardless of how this new contact worked out, this was life-changing not only for me and him but also for Viv, Callum, Alfie, Adrian, Natalie, Holli, Katie, Chloe and Luke, and so it was with some nervous apprehension and excitement that we were within days of meeting up.

As we approached the day when we'd all meet, I thought on all the conversations I'd had with Andy both by email and phone and I thought about Adrian, totally marvelling at how he had reacted and responded throughout this seven-week period. With Andy's sudden 'Jack-in-the-Box' appearance, it would have been completely understandable if he had felt threatened, insecure, jealous, annoyed, distrustful or even dismissive. It says so much about his character and our relationship that actually he was one hundred per cent supportive, intuitive, cautious and constantly loving in his support towards me. I'd told both him and Tom about Aidan from their earliest years but naturally over time we'd only voiced occasional reference to their half-brother; but Adrian knew instinctively of the cavernous hole in my heart and was beyond joyful that Andy had made contact. He kept saying, "This is absolutely momentous, Mum."

Rightly and understandably so, Adrian was initially cautious and protective, not only of me, but also of Natalie and the children. As the male head of the house he was concerned to check that we weren't at risk physically, mentally or emotionally. He also said, very candidly and wisely, that if the contact with Andy and him didn't 'click' or was not comfortable for Natalie and the children, then they wouldn't maintain contact with him, however, he would be very happy for me to build a relationship with Andy's family and it would simply mean that I had family in two different places.

Saturday morning duly arrived, the day of our meeting face to face! I'd checked and rechecked what to wear, even having a 'fashion show' the previous day with the grandchildren giving me marks out of ten as to their opinion of which outfit I should wear. Decision was made and after very little sleep I was up early and started to get ready. Suddenly, due to the weather, I completely changed my mind on what to wear and came down into the kitchen. The children were buzzing and constantly came up very close to me, with their face inches from mine, asking, "How are you, Nanny?" My heart was in my mouth. Never at any time in the last forty-four years had I thought that this day would or could ever happen.

Andy had said they'd be up for 11am and we planned to meet at a pub where if the weather was fine we could sit outside, and if not, the seating inside wasn't too close so as to be overheard. I had no idea how I would react when I first saw him. Would I cry, be dumbstruck, retreat into myself, hug him and not let him go, or be quite calm? I arrived early and pulled into the carpark with enough time to prepare myself before I came face-to-face with my adult son whom I'd last seen as a baby just days old.

As I checked my phone I noticed a text saying, "Hi, Marianne. In Weymouth, so will see you soon. Regards, Andy." I sent him a text to say I'd just pulled into the car park and instantly received a message back saying, "Just outside, walking in." There was no time to gather myself; I could only pray, step out of the car and walk towards him!

We hugged briefly. It was unexplainably momentous! Emotions beyond words! Memories brought to the fore! The wonderment of joy bubbling up within me like a shaken bottle of champagne!

As I tentatively embraced my son, the man whom I'd last cradled in my arms as a baby just days old, it was as if the cork on the bottle had popped and all my pent-up emotions of the past forty plus years were released – and yet they were... contained! I moved through the day as if anaesthetised to the enormity of the occasion. All the fizzing, exploding emotional bubbles stayed firmly inside! Typical for me, I kept a very firm lid on all my extreme feelings, not daring to release such deep emotions for fear that once I let go I would be emotionally out of control. I came to realise that because of all the memories, heartache and unbearable agony of all the factors surrounding Aidan's birth and adoption, I would need to filter and process my feelings over a long period of time.

Once before I'd had a momentous moment, when I had met with God and came to know that I was forever His child. It was as if being in His presence we had come face to face and throughout the rest of my life I would process the enormity of that experience. Now I was in the presence of my child, meeting once again face-to-face with my son. This man, forever child of mine! I would forever in my mind replay this day.

We bought coffee – though I wonder if I actually drank mine – and sat outside talking. Andy gave me chocolates along with a photo album containing some photos which spanned the years of him as a toddler, young boy, teenager, young man and then more recently. I was thankful for the sun which enabled me to wear very dark sunglasses; it was almost as if, though utterly thrilled to be sitting here with him, I could also keep myself a little distanced, so as not to give in to the overwhelming urge to keep touching him and endlessly stare upon this, my child.

After some time, and with both of us getting several texts asking, "How is it going?" we phoned our respective families. Viv and the boys joined us at the pub and then we drove down into the town and met up with Adrian, Natalie, Holli, Katie, Chloe and Luke by the clock tower.

For the next twelve hours everyone talked, played, laughed and ate. At eleven in the evening they left Manna House to return home. Having waved them off, Adrian and I stood outside the house, even though there was a severe storm, and for over half-an-hour we talked about the events of the day. Now my tears were falling like the rain; my raw emotions were starting to flow.

This first meeting of what has become known as 'the eleven' could not in any aspect have gone better. Andy had been quizzed at some length by Holli and Katie whilst we'd been on the beach. He had been open and willing to answer an unending list of questions. The younger children had all played well together both on the beach, in and out of the water, and when they were back in Quail Cottage. Whilst eating in the evening, and with the children off playing, the adults chatted candidly about family issues, values and beliefs, and it was such a blessing to find that we all held core values relating to family, behaviour of children and fundamental ethics. It was surprisingly wonderful to observe that Natalie and Viv were very similar in their personality types and so thoroughly enjoyed one another's company. Andy and Adrian also held similar beliefs on fatherhood and the raising of their children and both were fanatical about their respective football teams and enjoyed sport in general.

I have an absolute belief that God brought about not just a miracle in enabling Andy and Viv to trace me, but also the miracle of His grace, in the opportunity for me to know restoration by having a relationship with the man who had been the baby that I had given up for adoption. The unfolding months showed how so many strands had been and were being woven together. The detail and enormity of circumstances were so complex that there is no way for such complexities to have been simply coincidental or even within the ability of man to construct. It was playing out like a perfect tapestry, with all the workings and ends on one side, whilst a beautiful picture was being created on the other. Such, I believe, is the walk of our lives; on one side we see our mistakes, struggles and the hard work that life's journey can be and on the other side we see how the awesome journey of life can come together to create something wonderful and beautiful, a scene to be admired, valued and treasured.

Afterword

Reconciled

How can it be that the one I gave away
Has chosen to find me and, I hope, to stay?
That which was mine became loved by another,
Yet once again I am to be as if a mother.

Aidan is Andy, with wife and two sons,
A family united embraced and at one,
By grace restored, always the bridge,
Now part of one family in love we forgive.

Always forever held in His hand,
Bound by a thread for the sake of man,
Reconciled in truth and always to be
Family together for all to see.

Harmony, completeness, covered by love,
Dwelling in unity, a gift from above,
Living in hope, a child of His care,
Always and everywhere upheld in prayer.

Download Free Supplementary Material

If you are interested in reading some of my thoughts today on the various circumstances that I found myself experiencing throughout my life's journey, then please visit:

www.onwardsandupwards.org/product/child-of-mine

...or scan the QR-barcode below with your smartphone:

You will be able to access a free download, which discusses:

- how I view my life decisions and experiences retrospectively;
- the reality of those situations within our society both then and now;
- questions and challenges placed upon our communities and the likely effects on individuals – physically, mentally, emotionally and spiritually.

There are also a few points to consider personally or, alternatively, to use as a starting point for discussion or Bible study within a small group setting.

Download your FREE copy today!

What Shall I Read Next?

Publisher's Recommendation

My Mighty Son
Virág Wheeler-Mezei
ISBN 978-1-911086-54-3

"This is the story of a journey that few of us have to take; it is only for the bravest. Virág and James are two young people who are talented, bright and attractive. Soon after their beautiful marriage and reception in a castle in Hungary, they came to live in one of the loveliest English cities ... After a while Virág became pregnant; no one could have been more delighted and thrilled than the two of them. Luki – or Luke – was born. Luke seemed a very healthy baby. They made a lovely family. And then their lives changed suddenly and drastically. Luke became unwell at around six months old. He was admitted to the local hospital and then was transferred to Bristol for radical emergency brain surgery for an aggressive brain tumour ... But this is a story of triumph in the midst of pain, frustration, bewilderment and uncertainty; of peace and confidence where normally there would be none."

– Rev. Patrick Whitworth

Available now from all good bookshops or direct from the publisher:

www.onwardsandupwards.org/product/my-mighty-son